About the author

Deborah Williams is a former journalist, news editor and local government PR manager. *Seven Daughters of Eve* is her first published work of fiction. Deborah lives on the coast in South West Wales.

Seven Daughters of Eve

Deborah Williams

Seven Daughters of Eve

Vanguard Press

VANGUARD PAPERBACK

© Copyright 2018
Deborah Williams

A CIP catalogue record for this title is
available from the British Library.

ISBN 978 1 784655 03 7

Vanguard Press is an imprint of
Pegasus Elliot MacKenzie Publishers Ltd.
www.pegasuspublishers.com

First Published in 2018

Vanguard Press
Sheraton House Castle Park
Cambridge England
Printed & Bound in Great Britain

Dedicated to the special women in my life – Allison, Angela, Catherine, Diane, Dija, Laura, Lisa, Rhian, Sophie, Una, Ursula, Vicky B & Vicky W.

It is said that every woman in the world is descended from one of the seven daughters of Eve. It is also said that everyone is joined to everyone else by no more than seven connections. The seven women in this book have their own separate stories to tell, but all are connected.

Book One – Annie

Chapter One

A body had been found in the old quarry. The news was spreading like wildfire. Mum told me, Mrs Jackson next door told her, and she said everyone in the post office was talking about it. In a sleepy town like ours, that was big news. My first thought as a trainee journalist for the local paper was that at last we had a really great story. My second was wondering if the body they found was my Uncle Dan who had disappeared over ten years before. Then my third thought, which should have been my first I realised guiltily, was that it could be my best friend Emily's brother Rob.

I rushed over to Em's house and I soon as I went in I could see they were all wondering the same thing. Her dad was sitting with his head in his hands, while Em and her mother were huddled together on the sofa, arms wrapped around each other as if to keep the bad news out. "I'll put the kettle on," I said, as people do when they don't know what else to say.

"Thank you dear," Em's mum said absently. We sat in silence with our mugs of tea, each of us not wanting to be the one to voice our thoughts. A loud knock on the door made us jump. It was two policewomen. Em's mum gave a low moan like an animal in pain as they walked into the room.

Oh, no, dear," one of them said quickly approaching her. "We have no news, we're just visiting families who have reported people missing to keep them informed.

We know you'll be thinking all sorts so we just wanted to let you know that we'll assign you a family liaison officer to support you and keep you informed every step of the way." Em's dad asked if they knew anything at all about the identity of the person who had been found. "Not at this stage," the policewoman answered. "Tests are being carried out now but it'll take some time to get the results." The other policewoman stepped forward.

"Hi, I'm Elsie and I'll be your liaison officer," she said. "Shall I put the kettle on?" As they all nodded I mouthed to Em that I was going and I'd call her later. She smiled back and mouthed thanks.

On my way back home, I wondered if there was a liaison officer in my house about Uncle Dan, and how many other families were getting visits from the police. That's what gave me the idea for the story. Oh, I know I should have been focused on supporting my friend and my family, but being a journalist I just can't help feeling that excitement in the pit of my stomach and the adrenaline flowing as I realise this is going to be big.

There wasn't much in the way of news in our town. We're a pretty little place along the south coast with no more than 80,000 residents in the whole town and surrounding area. We've got no beach to speak of, just a small sandy cove, so we don't attract tourists the way they do in neighbouring towns. Paxtown is just local people going about their business. At the paper we get excited if someone is caught drink driving. One week our front page headline was 'Killer jellyfish washed up on beach'. Actually, we weren't at all sure that they were killers, but our editor said he was sure they killed some things just to eat so technically it was true. The last truly big story was six years ago in 1985 when a truck smashed into the butcher's shop window. So, you can see how big this was that a dead body had been found in our town. And a mystery dead body at that.

Instead of going home I went to the newspaper office. It was no surprise to see the editor James there, or Sue the senior reporter. "What are you doing here on a Saturday?" James asked.

"It's about the body," I said breathlessly, "I've got an idea for a story." Sue laughed.

"Don't worry about that, I've got it covered," she said. "I've had a statement from the police and I've interviewed the boys who found the body. Joe's up at the quarry with them now taking a photograph of them pointing at the police tent. It'll be front page news in Monday's paper."

"No, it's a different angle I'm thinking of," I said. "Of course, I knew you would be doing the main piece but I was thinking of more like a colour piece to go inside."

"Oh, really, Annie, please stick to writing about jumble sales and leave the big stuff to the experts," Sue said condescendingly and walked off.

"So, what's this idea?" James asked grinning at me.

"I want to find the families with people missing who are wondering if the body is their relative."

"Nice idea," James answered. "Do you know where to start?"

"Yes, I know of two already, one is my Uncle Dan and the other is my best friend's brother. I know the police have listed all the people missing so I'll contact their press office and see how many more there are."

"OK, nice idea, I like it," James said. "It puts a human face on a tragedy. Police won't give you names though you'll have to do some digging for that."

"Oh, thank you, thank you, thank you," I said excitedly. "I'll get straight on it."

Chapter Two

It turned out that since the quarry closed twelve years before there had been eleven people in our town and surrounding area reported missing. Of these, six had been traced but five remained a mystery. I knew of two, of course, but the only information the police would give me about the others was their gender and the year they disappeared.

The three others were two male, one female. Uncle Dan had gone missing ten years before, Rob five years ago, the first man six years before, the second six months later, and the woman two years ago. The police wouldn't reveal anything about the body at that point, not even the gender. Tests were being carried out on it, along with the area it had been buried in before removing it to the lab for the coroner to start further testing.

I started by questioning my mother about Uncle Dan. "Please tell me what happened?" I begged. "I really need this for my story to prove I am a decent journalist."

"There's nothing to tell," Mum said, but she wouldn't look me in the eye. "Your Uncle Dan and your dad had a row and he moved away, it broke your gran's heart and she was never the same again."

"Who reported him missing? Have the police been in touch?" I asked.

"His girlfriend reported him missing when he didn't go home, the police checked everywhere but they never found him to my knowledge. No police have been here, as we weren't the ones to report his disappearance they probably won't. Now I really have to get on with things," she said and marched off into the kitchen. I knew Mum was holding something back, but I also knew better than to push her when she was in that kind of mood.

So, I focused on Rob. Gorgeous, funny, lovely Rob who had gone missing just days after his seventeenth birthday. A talented sportsman, Rob was due to have trials with Manchester City the following week. He was the apple of his parent's eyes, they were so proud of him. Em said if it had been anyone but Rob she would have been jealous, but he was just so nice you couldn't help but love him. He went soccer training with the college team one Tuesday evening in November, just over five years ago, and he never came back. They never found a trace of him. Police looked everywhere, questioned all his teammates, no one had noticed anything unusual, he had played well, had a shower and shouted 'I'm off now', as he left. His parents and Emily were distraught. As time went on they became more and more convinced that something terrible had happened to Rob, it was so completely out of character for him to just disappear like that. As his mum said, he wouldn't even go to the shop without telling her and asking if she wanted anything. When the police stopped actively searching, they got in touch with the Salvation Army and other organisations which helped to find missing people, but they never had any news. I thought they had given up hope, but looking at their faces when the police walked in I realised they never had, they still weren't ready to let him go.

I found the woman's identity quite easily, just by going through the newspaper cuttings for that year. Her name was Frances Thompson, she was fifty-two years old at the time, and she just walked out of the house one day never to be seen again. I contacted her daughter Jenna who had reported her missing, and arranged to meet her at her dad's house.

"Thank you for seeing me," I said as Jenna let me in.

"Hi, this is my dad, George Thompson," she said.

Before I could say hello he cut in, "You're too young to be a journalist, tell the paper to send someone with experience."

"Dad!" Jenna admonished.

"It's OK," I said. "Hi, Mr Thompson, I'm Annie Perelli, I've got a degree in media studies and I've worked for the Globe for a year and a half. I realise that at twenty-three I need a lot more experience but this is how I get it, by covering stories such as yours. I can assure you that I know my job and that my reporting is fair and accurate. Please could I just ask a few questions?" He nodded gruffly and Jenna motioned for me to sit down. "Could you tell me what happened the last day any of you saw Mrs Thompson?" I asked.

"It started like a normal day," Jenna said. "Mum made breakfast and waved us off as usual. Dad and my brother Michael went to work and I went to college. When I got home that evening Mum was here and everything was spick and span just like normal. She liked to clean and keep everything tidy. But she shouted at me that there was no tea. When Dad and Michael came in they asked where tea was and she went berserk. Shouting and screaming, even swearing which she never did. Dad said it was the change, the menopause you know, making her go mental. Next thing we knew she walked out and never came back. When she hadn't

19

come back after a few days I reported her missing. The police investigated but never found anything, they told us that due to her emotional state we should consider the possibility that she had taken her own life."

"Oh, I'm so sorry," I said. "Do you think that's what happened? Are you worried that the person they found in the quarry might be your mother?"

"Honestly, I have no idea what happened," Jenna said. "Michael thinks she just walked out on us, he said she could have been having an affair but she never left the house. I don't know what to think. In a way, it would be a relief if the body was her, at least then we wouldn't have to keep wondering where she was or what had happened."

"That's enough now," Mr Thompson said. "You've given her the story, now she can leave." I thanked them for their time and asked Jenna if I could borrow a photograph of her mum, which she gave me. Looking at the picture of Frances Thompson on the way home, I wondered what had happened to her. She was a smart, well-groomed woman but she had such sad eyes. And I wondered why neither Jenna nor her dad had said anything about Frances as a person or even that she was missed.

Chapter Three

I went back to the office and wrote up the stories about the three missing people I had identified. James was looking over my shoulder as I wrote. "I like it," he said. "I like it a lot. It's front page stuff – headlines screaming the body in the quarry, could it be one of these? with pictures of the missing people underneath. It'll only work if we have the identities and photographs of all five, can you get that before we print on Monday morning?"

"Yes, I can," I said more confidently than I felt and headed off to the library to search through back copies of the newspaper.

The librarian was really helpful, she said she remembered a report of a young man going missing, he was a twin and the family had looked everywhere for him. It was in the summer of 1986, so it narrowed my search down to a few months.

I found what I was looking for quite quickly. Ethan Andrews, aged twenty-one when he disappeared. Tall, blonde, surfer type. There was another photograph of him with his identical twin brother Will, you couldn't tell them apart. I wondered if they had that twin bond thing, when one could sense when the other was in pain or trouble, it would make a great angle for the story.

Before I headed off to knock on the door of the Andrews family, I kept looking through back copies to find the fifth missing person but there was absolutely nothing. I called James and he said he'd phone a police contact to see if he could get any off the record information that would help.

In the meantime I set off for the Andrews home. I didn't like to just knock on the door out of the blue but they weren't listed in the phone directory. The only reason I knew where they lived was because Ethan and Will had been photographed outside their home, the big white house on the clifftop overlooking the bay. I'd always wondered who lived in the houses up there, posh people Em said, nobody you're ever likely to meet, my dad said. Normally, I'd call Em to share the moment with her, but in the circumstances it would have been insensitive.

The house looked even grander close up than it did looking down on the rest of us from far away. I had butterflies in my stomach as I rang the bell, expecting a butler or a maid to answer. When the door opened I was surprised to look up and see Will. There was no mistaking it was him, a little older than in the photograph and the blonde surfer locks had gone to be replaced with a neat haircut. His blue eyes were piercing and he smiled warmly as he said, "Can I help you?"

"Hi, I'm Annie and I'm from the Globe," I said breathlessly. His eyes clouded over and he started to shut the door. "Please," I begged. "I just need to ask a few questions, I can't go back to my editor with nothing." He looked at me for what seemed like a long time, then he held the door open.

"You'd better come in then," he said.

Their home was as I imagined it would be, beautiful and very classy. Photographs of Will and Ethan, along with trophies they had won for sports like surfing and tennis, were littered around the room. Will made us a pot of fresh coffee and took me into the conservatory where we had the most breathtaking view of the estuary. Even on a cold February day, with the wind whipping up the waves it was an awesome sight. Imagine waking up to this every morning I thought, as I compared my modest two up two down home to this palace.

Will was charming but very guarded. All he would say is that his brother didn't come home one night after going to visit his girlfriend, and hadn't been seen since. When pushed, he said his family had never stopped looking and had never given up. I thanked him for talking to me and for the coffee, but as I got up to leave he said, "No need to rush off, finish your coffee. I saw you admiring the view, it's even better from the upstairs balcony, I'd be happy to show you if you like?" I know it was risky agreeing to go upstairs in a strange house with someone I'd only known for a few minutes, but I instinctively knew Will was one of the good guys. And he was right, the view was even better, you could see around the cliff to the lighthouse and the next bay where the fishing boats were docked.

We talked for ages, he told me he was an architect and he preferred the big old grand buildings to the modern, glass covered structures which were popping up everywhere. He was designing homes for the new housing development along the clifftop where the local council had sold the land to help bring more people into the area and boost the economy. Our paper covered the protest, locals didn't want fancy houses on their coast, they needed affordable housing in the town. Will said you couldn't stop progress, and that his designs would be tasteful and blend in with the surroundings. Never one to miss out on a story I asked if he would give me an interview about it to help persuade people it would be a good thing. To my surprise he agreed and we arranged to meet for lunch the following Tuesday. I think I would have stayed and talked all day if I hadn't remembered that I had a job to do.

Chapter Four

James said the fifth missing person was a college lecturer. His disappearance had never been publicised because both his family and the police believed he had committed suicide. He was still listed as missing because no body had ever been recovered. Police had asked his family to put out an appeal for information or to ask if anyone had seen him, but they refused. James said they were very private people and didn't want anyone to speculate about the circumstances surrounding his disappearance.

Of course, the journalist in both James and me was curious to find out what circumstances they were referring to. I suppose the nosey parker in most of us would have been aroused by such a mystery. "The family's not likely to talk," James said. "If they didn't then to help find out what happened to him, they're not going to do it now. Police won't even give me his name or age, so we're at a bit of a dead end."

I wrote the main piece about the five local people who had disappeared suddenly and mysteriously, never to be seen again, and about the five families being supported by the police waiting to see if the body found in the quarry was their loved one. I wrote that their agony could go on for weeks as police and the coroner worked on identifying the body. Of course, James and me were hoping it would go on for weeks, it meant we could keep the story running. Then I felt bad for all the families waiting for news, especially Em and her parents, and my parents too.

I said I hoped it was one of them and not some random stranger. James said it didn't matter we would campaign to find out what happened to the others, it was a human interest story that could go on for months.

I wrote Ethan's story last, all the time trying to get his brother Will out of my head. Goodness knows why he'd had such an effect on me, I'd never felt that way just after meeting anyone before. I didn't have much to go on with Ethan so I added in some of the information about him reported at the time of his disappearance, like college tennis star, popular with everyone, stuff like that. James seemed pleased, he was busy phoning around all his contacts to see if he could find out anything about the missing lecturer. Then I had a brainwave. I had stayed in contact with my English lecturer Joanne, she might possibly know something.

"Hi, long time no speak," I said as she answered the phone.

"Well, hello, Annie, it's been too long, how are you?" she asked.

"I'm good, I'm actually working on my first big story and I was hoping you could help." Although Joanne vaguely remembered people talking about a disgraced lecturer who had vanished she didn't know any details.

"I'll make some calls and let you know if I get anything back," she promised.

Back at home, I intended to quiz my mother again about Uncle Dan, but Dad was in the room so I knew better than to bring the subject of his brother up. Mum had told me that they had never got on, even as children. Dad was always serious and hardworking, while Uncle

26

Dan was apparently what they called 'a bit of a lad'. Always getting into scrapes, usually with a different girl on his arm, and generally under the influence of too much alcohol. While Dad went into the family business as expected, Uncle Dan refused. His father kicked him out so he joined the Navy and wasn't seen again for a few years. Mum said no doubt he had a girl in every port and wreaked havoc wherever he went.

When I say family business, I mean the bakery. My grandfather and his brother opened it up years ago before Dad was born. They'd be in there baking from the early hours of the morning, and Mum said there were always queues of people waiting for them to open to buy hot, fresh bread. When I was growing up I remember huddling with my friends against the bakery wall on cold winter nights to feel the warmth of the ovens seeping through.

Dad joined the bakery when he left school and he's worked there ever since. My grandad stayed on as long as he could after Uncle Dan refused to join them, but Dad has run it on his own for the last few years. There's a girl who comes in part time to serve in the shop, but it's not really busy any more. People don't queue for hot, fresh bread these days, they go to the supermarket where everything is under one roof and half the price.

Mum said Dad would never give up the bakery, no matter how slow the trade was. I know he was disappointed he never had sons to take it over. I asked Mum once why they'd never had any more children, and she said that it just didn't happen. I thought that was maybe why my dad was so grumpy, but she said no he'd always been grumpy. I asked her why she married him then and she told me, "He was dark, handsome and brooding, just like whatshisname in Wuthering Heights."

"Heathcliff?" I said, finding it hard to believe she was comparing my dad to him.

"Yes, that's the one," she said. "I thought underneath that dark serious exterior there would burn a fire and a passion. But no, he was just dark and serious right through!" she laughed. "But I loved him and I still do, grumpy ways and all."

I looked at him across the room reading the newspaper while he waited for Mum to dish up our evening meal. He looked old these days, but there was never a chink in his armour. I couldn't ever remember having an intimate conversation with him. Don't get me wrong, we talked, but it was about ordinary everyday things, nothing too deep. He was good to me, never unkind, he provided what I needed and I knew he would kill anyone who hurt me, but I can't say I ever felt close to him, not like with Mum.

After dinner, I went over to Em's to see how they were. Her mum Pauline and dad Brian were watching television just like every Saturday night. Em and me went up to her bedroom. She still slept in the small box room; even though Rob's room was twice the size her parents had never allowed her to move in there. They had kept the room exactly as it was when he had been there, and her mum cleaned it every week, even putting fresh bedding on, so that it would always be ready for him to come back.

"How are you all?" I asked.

"Not sure," Em said. "It's a weird, surreal feeling, we're not quite sure what to do. They wondered if it was OK to watch TV or whether they should be sitting in the dark waiting for news. I wondered whether I should call you to go to the pub but then I thought people would think I didn't care that the body could be my brother. Truth is, even as I say it out loud I still can't quite get my head around it. The police say it could be days or even weeks before we know for sure. Anyway, let's talk about something else, I need my brain to stop whirring and focus on something else."

"Before we move the conversation on, I have to tell you that Rob is one of the missing people who will be in the paper on Monday morning. There's a lot of speculation about who it is, and it turns out that there are four other people missing too. Of course, it may not be any of them, but there are five families wondering if is their relative who has been found."

"Including you," Em said. "I'm so sorry, Annie, I completely forgot about your Uncle Dan."

"That's OK," I said. "I wouldn't expect you to think of it with what you're going through. Besides, I only saw him a couple of times a year, and I really don't think my dad will be heartbroken, although Mum speaks of him fondly."

"There's something different about you," Em said studying my face intently. "What aren't you telling me?" she quizzed.

"I really don't think this is the right time," I answered, but knowing Em as I did I knew I would have to talk anyway. "I met this man," I said and couldn't help smiling.

"Who, when? Tell me everything," Em said. "This is exactly what I need to take my mind off Rob!"

"Well not exactly… " I said. "The thing is he's the brother of one of the other missing people, and we met when I went to interview him. As soon as I saw him I felt my stomach lurch and I got all girly and stupid. Had to keep reminding myself I was a journalist, well, a trainee anyway. But after he told me a little bit about his brother he invited me to see the view from the balcony, I forgot to say he lives in that big white house on the cliff, you know the one we were always curious about, wondering who lived there and what it was like inside?"

Em nodded, "Tell me all about the house, every detail, I can't wait to hear, but first I want to know all about your romantic encounter with this man."

"It wasn't romantic," I said. "But we did really get on, it was like we just hit it off straightaway, we talked for ages. He's an architect designing the new homes on the cliff, he's meeting me for lunch on Tuesday to give me an interview about the plans, try to persuade people it's not a bad thing."

"Good luck with that," Em said. "Can't ever see locals being pleased with that development. But lunch! Excellent, it's about time you got back in the dating game."

"It's not a date, it's an interview. There's no possibility of it going any further. He's a God, like an Adonis, a ten. I'm a six on a good day."

"Don't be ridiculous, Annie," Em said. "You're an eight on a bad day."

"You have to say that, you're my friend," I answered. "But I don't kid myself. My bum is too big, my boobs are too small, my nose is slightly crooked and my eyes are too dark. I'm at least two inches shorter than I'd like to be and my feet are weird, the second toe is so much longer than the big toe. Weird."

"Annie, stop it," Em said crossly. "How many times do we have to do this? You are a nice shape, with a tiny little waist I am insanely jealous of, there's nothing wrong with your nose or eyes and you have the most beautiful hair." OK, I agree about the hair, it's long, luscious and auburn with gold flecks that dance in the sunlight. I looked like my dad but I'd inherited my hair from my mum. I wasn't wrong about the rest of me though, and I admit that I was very much looking forward to seeing Will again, although I had no illusions about it going any further than lunch.

Chapter Five

Sunday morning I went into the office early to find James already there. He had planned the front page with just the headline and five photographs. On pages two and three were Sue's story with the picture of the boys who had found the body, and my stories about the missing people. Of course there was a gap on the front where the fifth photo should be, and a gap on page two where his story should be. "Any luck yet?" James asked.

"No, nothing sorry," I said.

"We're not going to give up until we have to give up," James said. "Try going in the cafe or the pub, ask people if they remember anything, you never know what you might turn up."

I walked out into the High Street pulling my coat around me as the wind started to bite. I looked left and right wondering where to start. It wasn't much of a high street, apart from our newspaper office, the minimart and the post office, there were just a coffee shop, charity shops and a couple of banks. Sad how high streets across the country are losing out to the big out of town shopping developments I thought. Then I thought you hypocrite, you love the out of town complex, you buy everything there.

The café by the station was open on Sundays so I decided to start there. Two hours and three cafés later I was no closer to finding anything out than when I started. It was almost lunchtime so I headed for the pub, that was always busy on a Sunday, lots of locals went there for lunch. The landlord said he did remember something about a lecturer who had been sacked but he didn't know anything else and he couldn't remember who had told him. Head down, more in disappointment than because of the wind hurtling at me, I returned to the office.

"You've had a call," James said. "Said she'd tried to call you at home and your mum said you were here, can you call her back." I looked at the name and number he'd written on the pad and my pulse started to race. It was Joanna, maybe she had found something, maybe all was not lost. She answered on the second ring.

"Hi, Annie, I've got the name of your missing guy but there's something else and I can't tell you until you promise me it's off the record." I didn't hesitate, I just had to get the name to get our story. "His name is Christopher Matthews," Joanna said. "He was a science lecturer at the college. Now this is the off the record bit – he was caught having an affair with a student. He resigned before he could be sacked and then he disappeared. Neither the college nor his family wanted news of the affair to come out, so they kept it quiet and never publicised the fact that he was missing. It's widely believed he killed himself."

"Thank you so much, Joanna," I said gratefully. "I promise to keep the affair out of the story."

Shame really, I thought, an affair would make it juicy and gossipy, just what people like to read. Still, I had the name and that would be a really good start. I told James, who was naturally delighted. "We just need a photograph and someone to say something about him now," he said. Is that all? I thought as I wondered how the hell we were supposed to do that in the little time we had left, then James remembered that the college sent us a prospectus every year for us to publicise some of their courses and they always had photographs of the lecturers in them.

I was sent to the store room to search for a five-year-old college prospectus while James called the police press office to confirm the name. I'd almost given up hope when I came across the pile of booklets. And there he was smiling up at me in the middle of a group of lecturers – Christopher Matthews. He was taller than the others, he was easily six foot two or three, fair haired and a kindly face. Excitedly I ran back into the office to show James. "Good work," he said. "We'll have to cut him out of the crowd and it'll be a bit grainy when it's blown up but it's a photograph. Police confirmed his identity, they were a bit arsey about it, wanted to know how we got the name, I laughed, told them they knew better than to ask me that. Now get me a quote from someone who knew him and we can put this paper to bed."

I mentally ticked off all my friends and classmates at school for anyone who had done science at the local college during the time Christopher Matthews was there. I couldn't think of anyone at first but then I phoned Em to see if she had any ideas and she reminded me that Kieran Connor went to college to do science and maths. I got his number from directory enquiries and thank goodness he answered. "Hi, Kieran, you probably don't remember me it's Annie Perelli I was in the year above you at school."

"Well, hello, Annie," Kieran said. "Of course I remember you, I believe you were one of the many who was after my body. You don't still want it do you? Is this a booty call? Because I'm so sorry to disappoint you but I am now a happily married man."

"Ha, ha, Kieran, ever the joker," I said. "You did science at college, didn't you? Do you remember a lecturer called Christopher Matthews?"

"Mr Matthews, yes, I remember him, young for a lecturer, trendy, good teacher, knew his stuff. He left suddenly to go work somewhere else. We were all a bit pissed off actually, it was just weeks before our exams and the temp they brought in was effing useless."

I told Kieran that his former lecturer was one of the missing people, who could be the body found in the quarry. He couldn't wait to get on the phone to his mates to give them the gossip so I left him to it while I wrote the last piece of our front page jigsaw. James was thrilled, he gave me a front page byline – my first ever. I couldn't wait to see the paper in print the following day. I suddenly realised I hadn't eaten all day and headed home for the Sunday roast I knew Mum would have kept for me.

Chapter Six

Monday morning I couldn't wait to get to work to see the paper with my first ever front page byline. The office was buzzing, everyone was in talking about the brilliant paper we had that day. Of course, we did all sympathise with the families affected (including mine), but we're newspaper people and just couldn't help but be excited by the story. It wasn't a large staff, we're only a small town paper after all. There was James and Sue, then two reporters Iain and Amanda, me the junior and Petra the office manager who kept us all organised. We were located in the newsroom on the first floor, on the ground floor was the front counter where staff took adverts and sold the paper, and one commercial manager who was always on the look out for money making opportunities. I loved working there, loved the buzz of the newsroom, it never got stale.

I had never considered going away to work, although most of the people in my university course went to London looking for fame and fortune with the national papers. But I'm a home bird, I like being close to my family and friends, I love where we live, I like to walk along the clifftop and look down at the bay and the town and know that I know every inch of it.

Monday afternoon the police made an announcement. The body found in the quarry was male and foul play was suspected. Sue was dispatched to see if she could get any more information from them while I was given the job of phoning Jenna Thompson. As I said hello she interrupted, "Hi, Annie, we've heard the news, thank you, the police have been to tell us."

"Yes, of course," I said. "I just wanted to let you know that the Globe will continue to look for your mother."

"Fine," Jenna answered, "But I can't see you having any more luck than the police did."

"We can appeal to our readers, keep the story running, we'll keep trying, you never know something may turn up."

"Whatever," Jenna said absently and put the phone down.

My story actually read 'family doesn't give up hope of finding loving wife and mother'. I know it was a bit of a stretch but who wants to read a story about a daughter that says 'whatever' when I tell her we'll keep looking for her mum? James liked it anyway and gave me the page three lead for the following day. I thought of Em and Will and Uncle Dan and felt sad to my bones, but again the journalist in me kicked in and I wrote a really good piece about the four families waiting, wondering if the body lying on a slab in the morgue was their loved one. Em gave me a really heartfelt quote saying although her family was desperate to find out what had happened to Rob, they still clung to that little sliver of hope that he was alive somewhere. Was it better to have the peace of mind of knowing what happened and having a body to bury, or to keep that hope alive?

James said I had a gift for human interest stories, he said that I cared about the people I wrote about and that came across in the story. "Your piece is a real tearjerker," he said. "If Sue can't get any more info from the police I'll run it on the front tomorrow." I gasped, a second front page in one week was like all my dreams come true! Well, all my professional dreams anyway, my personal ones were wrapped up in Will. Oh, I know I should have been thinking about Em and my parents, all waiting for news, but all my thoughts revolved around Will. It was stupid I know, we'd only met once.

I'd dressed up for lunch with him that day, wearing my navy dress that was nipped in at the waist and hid my big bum. He greeted me warmly as I walked into the coffee shop; for a moment when he leant towards me I thought he was going to kiss me and my heart stopped, but he was only pulling out my chair. I felt like a right plonker and prayed he hadn't seen me pucker my lips.

Lunch was lovely, I can't remember what I ate, some kind of bagel I think. Will showed me the plans and explained why the housing development was important for the town. I tried to be professional and take it all in, but thankfully I was recording it because I just stared at his face and watched those gorgeous lips move. I did have the presence of mind to take a photograph of him with his plans for the story. As we left the coffee shop I thanked him for the interview and said I'd let him know what reaction we had to the article. He said great and how about dinner Friday night and you can tell me all about it then. Wow! I nodded yes, managed to squeeze my address out of my brain and my mouth, then floated back to work.

It was hard trying to focus on work but once I got started on Will's story I really got into it. James was pleased again; much to Sue's disgust I was definitely teacher's pet that week. James said the article was topical, it was what people were talking about, and he loved the new angle coming from the architect. I got a page five lead with it! There was no denying that the body in the quarry had really given me a career boost. I felt bad though for all the people hurting and worrying.

Chapter Seven

On the Wednesday after the body had been discovered the police held a press conference. Our story about the five potential victims had attracted the attention of the national press, and they were clamouring for more news. Both Sue and I were sent to represent the Globe. She wasn't happy of course but it was James' decision. I had no idea why Sue didn't like me, it wasn't just about recent events, although they definitely seemed to make things worse, she had been horrible to me since day one.

We had to share a car to the town hall where the press conference was taking place. The local police station was much too small to cope with the number of reporters and photographers present, so we were all bundled into the council chamber where their main meetings were held. The journey was silent apart from Sue asking me where my own car was. She knew very well I couldn't afford one, bitch. I'd been to the town hall before with Amanda when she was covering the planning meeting about the clifftop housing development. This was very different, my first police press conference and I had no idea what to expect.

The chief constable took centre stage, flanked by two plain clothes CID officers. The police press officer stood on the end, looking very pleased with himself. Probably his first press conference too, I thought nastily as he puffed out his chest ready to tell us all what to do. "OK, folks," he started importantly, "This is how it's going to go. Chief Constable Billings will give a short statement, then you will have the opportunity to ask a limited number of questions of the chief constable, DI Greenwood and DS Jones. Photography is allowed but please stay in the seats allocated to you." Saying photography was allowed was really stupid, all the photographers present had been flashing away since arriving and moving around the chamber to get the best angles. I'd like to see Mr Important Press Officer try to stop them!

The chief constable went over the discovery of the body by the two boys, and preliminary tests. He then said that the coroner had determined the body had been there between five and seven years, and that foul play, as previously stated, was suspected. He said that due to the waste materials in the ground in the quarry it was difficult to narrow the death down any further. He confirmed the coroner believed the person had been killed where he was found, so the death had happened in the quarry, but he wouldn't give any details about how the person was killed as it was part of the ongoing investigation.

He then said that although there was no certainty that the person found in the quarry was one of the four missing local men, all four families were being contacted and asked to provide DNA to help identify the victim. Despite a barrage of questions no further information was forthcoming.

My mind was racing as we headed back to the office. It couldn't be Uncle Dan I kept thinking, I have to tell Mum and Dad. I pleaded a headache when we got back to the office, I think James believed me because he said I looked pale. I rushed home to find Mum in the kitchen preparing a salad. "It's not Uncle Dan!" I shouted as I raced into our tiny kitchen nearly knocking Mum into the sink.

"What do you mean" she asked. "What's happened?"

We went into the living room and I told her about the press conference and the announcement that the body had been there between five and seven years. "So it can't be Uncle Dan, can it, Mum?" I said. "He's been missing ten years." Mum looked crestfallen.

"I'm sorry, Annie, we haven't been altogether truthful with you," she said sadly. My eyes widened as she told me that Uncle Dan had moved away ten years before but that he had kept in touch and visited five years ago. "They had an awful row, your dad and Dan," she said. "Dan walked out and your dad followed him, they went towards the quarry. Sometime later your dad came back with mud and quarry clay on his clothes and his knuckles bruised and bleeding. All he ever said was 'he won't be back'. He hasn't spoken another word about Dan or their fight since." I didn't know what to say, I couldn't understand why they would say he'd been missing for ten years when he hadn't. "Oh, Annie, I'm so afraid your dad killed Dan," Mum said wretchedly.

Before I could answer, a knock on the door made us jump. Mum straightened her dress and wiped her face putting on a smile as she answered. I wondered how many other times she had put on a face to mask something. It was the police. One policewoman, one man. They had come to tell us the latest information. "We're sorry we couldn't speak to you before the information became public in the press conference," the woman PC told us. "But as you weren't the ones who had reported Daniel Perreli missing we have been trying to contact the woman who had. Unfortunately, she moved from the address she gave us some time ago and we haven't been able to track her down. When we checked the file for any other information we found the record of Mr Perelli's brother. Is Mr Frank Perelli home?" she asked. Mum said no, he was at work but that she would pass the information on. The woman PC gave her contact details for dad to call her if he needed anything.

She explained to Mum what she already knew about the length of time the body had been in the quarry. "Unfortunately, all four missing males, including your husband's brother, went missing during that period and we can't narrow it down any further. We're asking all the families to provide DNA so that we can carry out tests and determine whether or not the victim is one of those missing men. As your husband isn't here, could you ask him to call me to arrange a time for me to collect his DNA please? Obviously we want to do it as soon as possible, it takes some time to get the results, and we appreciate how awful this must be for the families involved."

The male PC spoke then for the first time, addressing me. "Can I ask what relation you are to Mr Daniel Perelli, please?" he said.

"I'm his niece," I answered. "My dad is Frank Perelli."

"In that case, would you mind giving us a DNA sample?" he asked. "It would show familial links which would prove whether or not the person found is your uncle." I agreed, still in a bit of a stupor, opened my mouth for him to swab it and signed the label to confirm my identity and that I had given the sample voluntarily.

After they left I started to cry, I was really scared that my dad would go to prison for murdering his brother. I know my mum felt the same, she was crying too. I went to Em's before Dad came home from work, I didn't think I could look at him without crying. I know he was grumpy and had never been affectionate, but he was my dad. He pushed me on the swings when I was little, he taught me to ride a bike and how to swim. When I managed he said 'well done' in that gruff voice of his but I knew he was pleased. He had supported my dream of being a journalist, paid for me to go to university, and never once suggested I go to work in the bakery. I couldn't bear the thought of him being locked away from us. Whatever my Uncle Dan had done must have been really bad, I thought.

Chapter Eight

I told Em what Mum had said. We never had any secrets between us and I trusted her completely. She decided we needed wine so we got very drunk in her tiny little bedroom. We laughed, cried, hugged and then passed out, both of us curled up fully clothed in her single bed.

I woke feeling cold in the middle of the night, wrapped the quilt around Em then went home. It seemed like only seconds later Mum was shouting that I was late for work. "I'm not well," I moaned, "I'm not going in."

"Oh, yes, you are," Mum said pulling the quilt off me. "You get in that shower, you go to work and you get on with this day just as you would any other day. We will deal with whatever comes our way when it comes our way. Now go!" She pointed to the bathroom and dutifully, holding my aching head in my hands, I went.

Work was a struggle, between the hangover and the worry I was good for nothing. Sue noticed of course. "Not so chipper today Annie?" she said cattily. "What's wrong, run out of ideas?" James gave me the local Women's Institute's monthly newsletter and told me to get what I could out of it to plug some gaps in the paper. I was glad to do something boring that required little effort and kept my head down until the end of the day.

I couldn't wait to get to bed that evening. We ate our meal as usual, but as I'm the one with the chit chat, and as I could barely summon up the energy to eat, it was a bit of sombre affair.

The following day I met Em for lunch. "I can't keep my date with Will tonight," I said sadly. Through all the drama that date had never been far from my mind.

"Why ever not?" Em asked.

"I'm too mopey, I'm all doom and gloom. I feel really down. I never stood a chance with Will before when I was happy and breezy, what chance do I stand now that I'm misery itself?" Em laughed.

"Oh, Annie," she said. "You're still cute and funny even when you're miserable! You have to go meet him and if you don't feel breezy as you call it, just ask him questions and listen to him talk, men like that apparently." She finally persuaded me to keep the date which sent me into a panic about what to where, how would I fit in time to wash and dry my hair. And don't even think about waxing and plucking, there was certainly no way to accomplish all that. Ah, well, at least I wouldn't be letting him ravish my body on our first properish date if I hadn't shaved my legs or waxed my bits. Oh, who am I kidding? If Will wanted to ravish my body he could have it, hairy legs and all. Who shaves their legs in winter anyway?

I wore the bottle green dress with the swirly skirt that covers my big bum. The colour looks really good with my auburn hair which had been hurriedly washed and dried. I was cleaned and perfumed, nicely made up with knee high boots covering the hairy legs. When Will arrived I rushed to the door and shouted bye. I'm ashamed to say I didn't want to invite him into the house to meet my parents. I couldn't help but compare my modest home and working class parents with his grand house and lavish lifestyle. His mum was captain of the ladies golf team and was always pictured in the paper for some charity do or another. His dad was a bigwig in the city. Ah, well, I had no illusions about going to meet them anytime soon.

Will drove to a seafood restaurant in the next town along the coast. It seemed very classy and I was glad I'd worn the green dress. Will suggested I should have the special, which was lobster, but I plumped for salmon. Not because I didn't fancy the lobster but because I had no idea how to eat it. Even I couldn't go wrong with salmon. I made a mental note to find out the correct way to eat lobster just in case the opportunity ever arose again. Will had the black pepper crab which looked delicious, I wouldn't have known how to eat that either.

He ordered a bottle of wine which cost more than my dress had, but he only drank one small glass as he was driving. So I was glugging away, mindful of the fact that he'd paid so much for it we couldn't waste it, and I didn't think it was the kind of place you could ask to take the leftovers home. Of course, as the wine went down so I started to relax and soon I found, to my horror, that I was telling Will why I hadn't ordered lobster. He was smiling sweetly at me the whole time. "Annie, you are a breath of fresh air," he said laughing.

After that I thought 'what the hell', I am who I am and if he didn't like that he wouldn't want to spend time with me. It was only at the end of the night as we headed home that I realised I hadn't told him the reaction to the story about his house designs. "Oh, well, we'll have to go out again then," he said smiling. "How about Sunday lunch?" I grinned and nodded and as I moved to get out of the car he pulled me back towards him, ever so gently, and kissed my lips. I felt something like an electric shock go through my body and pulled back in surprise. "Goodnight, Annie," he said. "See you Sunday."

Chapter Nine

Saturday was spent in the pub with Em and some of our other friends, with me alternating between being on a high because of my date and the kiss with Will, and being in the depths of despair because I'd pulled away and he might think I didn't want to kiss him. Which of course I did, very much. I also wondered why he hadn't asked to see me that night, and why our dates so far had been out of town. "Do you think he's ashamed of me, Em?" I asked for the umpteenth time. And for the umpteenth time Em told me to shut up and drink.

He arrived bang on time for our lunch date, and this time I called him in to introduce him to Mum and Dad. He was very polite, shook Dad's hand, said all the right things to Mum and he didn't seem at all uncomfortable or out of place. I thought of his balcony overlooking the bay, then shook the image out of my head. I wasn't going to risk letting that nonsense spoil a minute of the day.

After a long lunch, mostly spent talking and laughing we went for a drive along the coast and parked up in an isolated cove. My stomach was doing cartwheels as Will reached for me. "Annie, I'm falling for you," he said tenderly as he kissed me. I remember thinking I fell for you the first time I saw your face, but then thoughts went as my body took over. It's so hard to explain but I felt like I had no control. I couldn't stop my mouth reaching for him, couldn't stop my hands touching him, couldn't control my legs as they wrapped themselves around him. It was like I was a puppet and some wanton, wild woman inside me was pulling the strings.

We stayed there for hours until it got so cold Will had to turn the engine on and I said we'd better head back. "Annie, come away with me next weekend," Will said. "I know it's a bit sudden but something clicked and it just feels so right. I'd really love for us to spend some time together alone, before all the results come back and our lives are turned upside down again." It was the first time either of us had mentioned the DNA tests or when we could expect the results. They said a week to ten days. I didn't want to think about it until I had to.

"Where would we go?" I asked.

"My parents have a fishing lodge up by Barker Lake, we could go there," he said.

"Ooh, my parents have a fishing lodge," I repeated in a posh voice, making fun.

He laughed, "Shut up, commoner, is it a date?"

"Yep, it's a date," I said.

I couldn't wait to tell Em and I couldn't wait for the following weekend to come. In the meantime, Will and I spent every minute together that we could. "God, I can't wait to shag you in a bed instead of a car," he said. "I have got to get my own place."

"Why haven't you?" I asked. "I mean you have a good job, you could afford it. Although if I lived where you do I wouldn't want to move out either."

"It's just that after Ethan went, Mum and Dad were kind of lost and they liked having me around. I just wanted to be there for them. But I'll let you into a secret – I've put a deposit down on one of the new houses, when it's ready in about eighteen months' time I'll be moving in."

"Wow, I'm impressed," I said. "So you won't be losing your spectacular view after all."

At work we carried on trying to find fresh angles for the body in the quarry story but there was nothing new to report. Until the phone call at mid-morning that Wednesday. Amanda took the call and shouted over to me: "There's a guy on the phone who won't give his name and he insists he'll only talk to you." I picked up and said hello.

"Is this Annie?" a man's voice asked. I confirmed it was.

"This is Chris Matthews," he said.

For a second I didn't realise who it was, then the penny dropped. Christopher Matthews the missing lecturer! "Hi, are you the person reported missing?" I asked.

"That's me," he answered in a friendly voice. "But clearly I'm not missing so I thought I should let you know so that you don't waste any more time looking for me."

"Thanks, Mr Matthews," I said, "and I mean no disrespect but how can I be sure it's you?" He told me a story from his childhood that only he and his parents would know, and the name of his first pet.

"You can check the facts with my family," he said. "I suppose you should let them know I'm not missing."

"I'm sure they'll be really happy and relieved to know that you're OK, can I have your contact details to pass on to them please?"

"Look, I'll be popping in the local police station here so that the police can remove me from their missing person files. I'll give them my details and if my parents want them they can get them off the police. I'm sure they won't though."

"Oh, don't say that, Mr Matthews," I said. "They were afraid you had killed yourself after what happened at the college." I couldn't believe I had blurted that out. "Oh, I'm so sorry," I said quickly, praying he wouldn't put the phone down.

He laughed. "Call me Chris," he said. "And don't worry about offending me. It's true I had an affair with a student, we were caught, I resigned before I could be sacked. I told my parents, they said never darken their door again, so I upped and left which I should have done long before actually. I came to London, lived on my savings for a while, then got a job in a lab, got a flat and here I am talking to you."

"Do you mind if I report that you left after a family disagreement and are living happily in London, with no idea that you had been reported missing?"

"D'you know what, go for it, it'll piss off my family mightily! They really hate a scandal, and even a minor one like a family disagreement would send them into shock." Chris laughed, I liked him, he sounded really nice and genuine.

"Could I have your contact details please in case I need to get in touch for anything?"

"No need," he said. "If there's anything else I'll call you." And off he went.

Chapter Ten

I told James and he rang his police contact to arrange for me to meet with the Matthews' police liaison officer. She interrogated me before allowing me to accompany her to their home. It was exactly what I expected, a middle class semi in a desirable neighbourhood, a new BMW parked out front, and neat borders around a neat front lawn. It would be an understatement to say that Mr and Mrs Matthews did not want me in their home. They could barely look in my direction, let alone speak to me. When I asked them to confirm the information Chris had given me they replied to the liaison officer. When I told them he was in London and working in a science lab, they kept looking at her. They didn't even ask me to sit down. When I'd finished speaking, Mr Matthews told the police officer I could leave. Something in me snapped, they had just found out their missing son was alive and well and they couldn't even acknowledge my presence. After all, if it wasn't for the story in the Globe they never would have known. "So, can I ask if you are pleased to find out if your son is alive and well after thinking he had killed himself all these years? Or should I report that you are not in the least bit interested?" For the first time, they both looked at me.

"Get out of my house!" Mr Matthews shouted. Chris was right, they really didn't give a shit.

I had another front page with Chris' story and I took great pleasure in writing that he had left after a family disagreement and had no intention of coming back to see them. I knew they'd be furious, the shame of it all. James was pleased and said I definitely had a future at the Globe. I was over the moon and couldn't wait to tell Will. But at the same time I was mindful of the fact that there were only three missing people left who might be the body in the quarry – Uncle Dan, Ethan or Rob. It was hard to believe that I was connected so closely to all three. I couldn't bear the thought of my dad going to prison for killing Uncle Dan, but I also couldn't bear to think of the pain Will or Em and their families could go through if their loved one had been killed. Killed. It was the first time I really thought about that. This was no accidental death, this was foul play. Murder. How do you live with knowing someone you love was murdered? What would you imagine their last moments to be – fear, pain, terror? What if the police never found the killer, they would never know why someone so precious had been taken away from them.

The weekend came at last and we took off for the fishing lodge. More like a luxury log cabin actually. Two floors, a master bedroom with en suite and a balcony with views overlooking the lake. Outside was a deck and a hot tub. I was so excited, I'd never even seen a hot tub, let alone been in one. "But I haven't brought my swimming costume," I said to Will dejectedly.

"You won't need one," he said grinning.

We had the most amazing, idyllic weekend, the best time of my life. Neither of us wanted it to end but Sunday came too fast and it was time to get back to reality. The DNA results were due back within days so we would soon know who the poor person who had lost his life in the quarry actually was. I floated into the house on cloud nine, but soon came crashing back to earth as I saw my mother sitting on my bed sobbing.

I rushed to her side. "What's wrong?" I cried.

"Annie, I'm so sorry," she kept saying.

"What's happened? Where's Dad?" I asked.

"Your dad's fine, it's not that. There's something I should have told you before, but the police came and then the moment went, and then I didn't want to hurt you any more and I'm so sorry," she sobbed.

"Mum, you're not making any sense," I said. "What are you talking about?"

"I didn't tell you what your dad and Dan fought about, but you have to know now."

I couldn't breathe. I didn't know what to expect, or how much more I could take. She looked at me and I saw how much she loved me and the sorrow in her eyes as she told me that Dan was my father.

I didn't speak as Mum told me that she and Dan had a fling just after she married my dad. She didn't try to justify it, just said that Dan was fun and exciting, everything my dad was not. When she found out she was pregnant with me she ended the affair and told Dan the baby was definitely my dad's, although there's no way she could have known for sure. When I was five and no more babies had arrived she went for tests. They said she was fine. My dad agreed to go, and they said the chances of him fathering a child was millions to one. Mum wouldn't tell him who my father was, they went through a rough patch but stayed together and got through it. Until my thirteenth birthday when Uncle Dan bought me the designer jacket I had been longing for, but Mum and Dad couldn't afford.

Mum said Dad was pissed off with Dan for buying it, trying to show us up. But Dan didn't care, he put it on me and, as I turned to admire myself in the mirror, he stood behind me with his hands on my shoulders grinning. Dad saw the likeness and suddenly he knew who had fathered me. Mum saw his face, ushered me out and all hell broke loose. They argued, they fought, Dan cried, begged for forgiveness, told my dad he had no idea. Eventually, Dan left promising never to return.

For the next five years, he sent me a Christmas card and a birthday card, always with his address and phone number in case I wanted to see him. Mum handed me the cards from the pocket in her apron. There they were – ten cards from my father. I didn't read them, I don't know why, only that I wanted to do it when I was alone. When I was eighteen, he turned up at our house and said it was time I knew the truth. "Frank and Dan argued," Mum said. "Dan left to find you and tell you. Frank went after him, you know the rest. I had to tell you now, if it is Dan, the body you know, and I'm really scared that it is, then the DNA test will show that you're his daughter, not his niece, and I didn't want you to find out that way." Mum put her head in her hands. "I'm so sorry, Annie," she said. "But please know your dad, Frank, has loved you and treated you as his daughter always, and that we both love you very much."

Chapter Eleven

I opened the cards after Mum had left the room. She didn't want to go, but I couldn't speak, my world had been turned upside down, and I just wanted to be alone. They were nice cards with nice messages but they made me angry. He had tried to upset my cosy little life. I didn't want him to be my father, I wanted everything to be the way it always was. For the first time in my life I didn't want to talk to Em, I didn't want to talk to anyone. All the happy memories of my weekend with Will had vanished. I wanted to run away, bury my head in the sand, pretend like nothing had happened. I heard Dad coming in, well, he was my father, he had been all my life. I heard Mum crying as she told him what had happened. Then I heard footsteps on the stairs and my door opened.

"You know you're my child and nothing changes that right?" Dad said. I ran to him and hugged him and for the first time in my life I was the first to let go.

"I know," I said and I went to bed.

The following day, the police press office issued a statement. The DNA tests had been mixed up and had to be redone. They blamed a lab tech who had apparently not only removed the donor consent forms to file, but also the identity of the donors. So we all had to do it again. They promised to rush it through, but of course our front page story was lab mix-up, families' agony prolonged. I got a quote from Em's father saying how awful and unprofessional it was, and we had loads of people phoning in to sympathise with the families and criticise the police. Dad gave the second sample so if Mum had waited a day longer she wouldn't have had to tell me.

I told Will about my parentage revelation and he was really lovely. "It takes more than a sperm donor to make a dad," he said. He was right, of course. I told Em too. She was shocked but just as supportive. We were all a bit strung out with events to say the least.

And then I had another call from Chris. "Hi, Annie, how's tricks?" he said as though we were best buddies or something.

"Good, thanks," I answered automatically while thinking that they weren't good at all. "How are you?" I asked. "I saw your parents and I wrote the story, I hope it was OK?"

"Yes, it was fine," he said. "I'm not phoning about that, there's something else I need to tell you. It's about the person I had the affair with." As I listened carefully and scribbled notes frantically, I was a kaleidoscope of emotions. When the call ended I looked at James who was watching me carefully and told him I needed an early lunch. He nodded, waiting for an explanation but I just grabbed my coat and rushed out.

I ran to the pharmacy, I had to talk to Em. She was in the middle of serving a customer but I shouted to her boss,"Mr Tanner, I need Em to come with me for an early lunch, it's important."

"It always is," he answered sighing. Em grabbed her coat and followed me outside. I couldn't wait to tell her. "Rob's alive!" I burst out. "And I know where he is!"

Her face was a mixture of shock, delight, doubt and questions. Then she crumpled and started to cry.

"They're happy tears, Annie," she said. "Please tell me everything."

So I did. I told her Chris Matthews had called again and said there was something else he had to tell me about the person he'd had the affair with. It was Rob. Em's eyes widened as she realised I was telling her that her brother was gay, a secret he'd kept well-hidden all this time. "They were in love," I said. "When they got caught Chris had to leave. Rob wanted to go with him, but Chris persuaded him to stay at least until he had a job and somewhere to live. He told Rob to try to make a go of things back home, pursue his career in sports. Rob promised to wait six months, and he did. When the six months was up, he packed a few things in his holdall, went soccer training then caught the bus to London to meet up with Chris. They're still together, Em, and really happy."

"Oh, my God, he's really alive!" Em said as the news finally and truly sunk in. "But why on earth has he never contacted us? Why would he let us suffer and worry like this?"

"You can ask him yourself," I said. "I have the phone number right here."

We went to Em's house where she could make the call in private. Her parents were both at work, she was going to speak to them after talking to Rob. As Em sat in the hallway speaking to her brother I danced around the lounge, so happy for my friend. They spoke for a long time, I knew I should have been back at work, but I didn't want to interrupt. When the call ended, she looked elated but there was a flicker of concern in her eyes. "I can't believe it," she kept saying. "Rob's OK, I've just spoken to my brother!"

Rob told her that he couldn't face telling his parents that he was gay and in a relationship with one of the college lecturers. He said they would never accept it. He was the macho sportsman, they were so proud of him. He truly believed it was better for them to think him dead than know the truth. "Of course, I told him he was being ridiculous," Em said. "But I can understand why he would think that, my parents are very traditional, and they were so proud of their athletic son. He gave up his soccer career too, said he would never be accepted in any team as a gay man. It's so wrong, isn't it, Annie, that people should be judged like that?"

"Very wrong," I agreed, "but, unfortunately, in a small town like ours there are far too many people who think that way. I understand now why Chris knew his family wouldn't want to know him, they would have preferred to think he had killed himself over the shame of the gay affair, rather than be alive and well and living openly as a gay man. But I can't believe your parents would think that Em, they loved Rob so much, they'll just be glad to know he's OK, and to have him back in their lives."

"Yes, of course," Em said. "I don't know what I'm worrying about. I'll call them now and ask them to come home."

"I'll get back to work and leave you to it," I said and we hugged tightly.

"Thanks, Annie, thanks so much," Em said.

Chapter Twelve

Back at work, I suddenly realised that we were down to two – just two missing people who could be the body in the quarry. Dan or Ethan. For the first time since the discovery I was really hoping it would be a random stranger. I didn't want my life to be turned upside down and I didn't want it to happen to Will either. Our relationship was going so well, I couldn't bear it if the strain of events tore us apart. No, I determined, if it was Dan I knew Will would stick by me and support me, and if it was Ethan I would be there for him.

James asked me what the call had been about, but I just said Chris wanted to ask what his family had said when I told them about him. I don't know why, but I wasn't ready to share their story in work. Oh, I knew it would make headlines again – two missing men, believed dead who had run away to be together. But I needed to speak to Em and her family first, they had to be prepared. James didn't believe me, I could tell, but he didn't press it any further.

Later that afternoon, Em phoned me in floods of tears. "Rob was right," she said between sobs. "They would rather he was dead. Dad said he's going to kill Chris for corrupting his perfect son, Mum is just stony faced, she won't accept it. They're really angry and I'm scared about what they're going to do."

"Give it time, Em," I said. "It's a shock for them, but I'm sure once they calm down they'll accept what's happened and be happy to welcome Rob back into the family."

Two days later, Em persuaded her mother to talk to Rob. She told him to come home, forget everything that had happened, put it all behind him and get back to his normal life. It took a while for Rob to finally convince his mother that there was no turning back. He told her he had known he was gay since he was very young, that he'd tried really hard to fight it and suppress his feelings, but he couldn't. Chris hadn't been his first relationship but when they met it was instant attraction which quickly turned into love. They were still devoted to each other and were really happy. Em said her mother put the phone down, then, without another word, went into Rob's bedroom and started clearing it out. That evening, she told Em she could move into the larger bedroom as her brother would never be coming back.

Em walked out and stayed with me for a few days until she could find a flat. She had savings and could afford to live her on her own. I'd move in once I got a properly paid job as a journalist. We were both stunned by their reaction. I had known Em's parents since I met her at nursery school when we were just three years old. They were the nicest, kindest people you could ever wish to meet. "They're bigots," Em said. "And they've lost their daughter now as well as their son."

James called me into his office the following day. Sue was standing there looking very pleased with herself. "The phone call from Chris the other day, do you want to tell me what it was about?" James asked.

"I told you already," I answered quietly, instinctively knowing that something was wrong.

"Annie, I'm disappointed in you," James said. "You have been doing so well, but we know you're suppressing a really good story, and I'd like to know why." Sue produced my notepad which had been in my desk drawer, and there it was – Chris and Rob, affair, ran off to be together. Why, oh, why didn't I practice shorthand more, I thought to myself, they wouldn't have been able to read it then.

"I'm waiting for the family to consent," I said lamely.

"You don't need their consent," James said sternly. "You've got the story and you've got the agreement of the people concerned to publicise it. Chris knows you're a reporter, he knew he was speaking on the record, read your own notes, Annie – it says quite clearly it's time their story was told. I know Rob is your best friend's brother and that you're close to the family, but as a journalist your first loyalty should be to the paper, your first instinct to write the story. If that's not how you feel then maybe journalism isn't for you. Take the rest of the day to think about that," he said and waved me out of his office. As I was leaving he said, "Annie, if you don't write it someone else will,", and Sue grinned at me over his shoulder waving my notebook.

Chapter Thirteen

My stomach was churning and I felt sick as I walked home. Being a journalist was all I had ever wanted. The job at the Globe meant the world to me. And I had been doing so well, getting front page stories, being praised by the editor. The same editor who was now threatening to sack me if I didn't write the article. Oh, I knew exactly what he meant when he questioned my loyalty and intentions. There would be no place for me at the Globe unless I went crawling back and delivered the goods.

I sobbed in Mum's arms as I told her what had happened. "The bastard!" she said. I was shocked, I'd never heard her swear before. "And that bitch must have gone through your desk to take your notes. Disgusting way to behave. Serves them right if you don't go back, you're better than that."

"Mum, it's all I ever wanted," I cried. "And James is right, Chris and Rob have given their consent for the story to be published so Em's parents don't have the right to stop me. It's just that I know what it'll do to them, they would be devastated if their son's gay affair was front page news in the local paper, they probably wouldn't leave the house again. I have to at least tell them I've been told to write it."

I met Em for lunch and told her that I had to write the story, I asked if she would let her parents know. I wasn't at all prepared for her reaction. "I can't believe what you're saying!" she shouted. "Do you have any idea what that would do to my parents? How could you be so disloyal to them? To me?" I tried to explain that Chris and Rob were happy about it, that it was my job, that my editor had told me to do it, but she was having none of it. "I can't believe you would even consider it," she said. "You're my best friend, some things are more important than a story. Today's headline is tomorrow's chip paper, my gran used to say. Are you really willing to risk our friendship for tomorrow's chip paper?" I didn't answer, I didn't know what to say. "Oh, Annie, your silence speaks volumes," Em said sadly as she walked away.

I told Mum what had happened, she asked me what I was going to do. I had no idea. Em and me had been joined at the hip since we met, life without her would be unbearable. But I was sure she'd understand once I could explain properly. "Would you understand?" Mum asked.

"What do you mean?" I said.

"If it was the other way around and Emily was the journalist writing the story about you, the fact that you've found out your missing uncle is actually your biological father, and that the man you think of as your dad could have killed him? That's another juicy front page isn't it? Have you thought of writing that? Do you think Emily would in your place?"

"Oh, God, I've made such a mess of things," I said, as I realised I had almost sacrificed a lifelong friendship for a job.

I went to the pharmacy where I apologised to Em and told her I wouldn't write the story. I said I was so sorry for hesitating and asked her to forgive me. She was pretty cool, but she did say OK talk later. I had to warn her though that even though I wouldn't write it, Sue certainly would.

On my way back to the office, my mind raced as I tried to find a way of keeping my job without writing the story, but I couldn't think of a thing. I went straight into James's office and told him that I was really sorry but that I couldn't write the story. "I understand if you want me to leave," I said, "but I'm hoping that the work I've done so far will be enough to convince you that I really would be a good journalist. It's just that some things are more important than a front page story."

"You understand that the story will be written anyway?" James said.

"Well, actually that's the thing, I spoke to Chris again and they've withdrawn consent. He said some of the things he told me weren't true, he just wanted to upset his family. So, we don't actually have a story anymore."

"I don't believe that for one second, but I suppose I'll have to take your word for it," James replied. "But if you'd said that in the first place I wouldn't have to decide whether or not to sack you, as you did refuse to write a story. Go back to your desk. I'll talk to you later."

I left his office thinking 'idiot' why didn't you just say the story was a no go any more. But it just popped into my head as we were speaking, and besides there's no point in letting James think I would always do the story no matter what, because I knew then that I wouldn't.

Chapter Fourteen

The DNA results were due the following Monday. On Sunday, Will called around and asked me to go for a walk. "We have to talk," he said. He looked so serious I was a little scared, praying that he wasn't going to dump me. When someone says 'we have to talk' it's never good is it? He walked towards the quarry, which was strange considering the circumstances. The police cordon was still at the place they found the body, it was the first time I had seen it, it made it even more real.

"Annie, the body's not Dan, it's Ethan," he said. Well, that took my breath away, I was expecting the break up speech and he comes out with that.

"What do you mean?" I asked. "Is it the twin bond thing? Do you sense it?" He smiled wryly.

"We never had that twin bond," he said. "We were identical in looks but nothing alike otherwise. We were really competitive, everything he did I tried to do better and vice versa. We used to drive our parents mad! We used to drive each other mad, but now I miss him so much it's like he was a part of me that I've lost." It was the only time Will had spoken about his brother and I could see the pain it caused him.

"It might not be Ethan," I said. "It might not be Dan either, we'll just have to wait and see."

"It is Ethan," Will said with certainty. "And I know because I killed him."

I couldn't breathe, I couldn't speak, I felt like a boulder was crushing my chest. I stood looking at this man I had grown to love so much in such a short time, and thought that I really didn't know him at all. Will kept talking, I think he was relieved to finally say it all aloud. "We went for a run," he said. "Like usual, we were trying to go faster than each other. All the way Ethan was taunting me about a girl we had both fancied who had chosen him. When we got here, to this part of the quarry, I slipped in the mud and fell. Ethan was laughing, saying it suited me to be covered in shit. I picked up a rock and threw it at him, fully expecting him to dodge it or catch it and throw it back at me, but it was dark and raining, and he didn't see it come. He turned to run off and the rock caught him on the back of the head. I heard a dull thud then he fell. I ran to him but as soon as I rolled him over I knew he was dead. I tried mouth to mouth, I tried CPR, I shook him, I prayed, and then finally I gave up and sat there rocking him in my arms and crying. I don't know how long I was there for, hours I suppose, I couldn't face leaving him and I couldn't face going home and telling my parents what had happened.

"In the end I was frozen with cold and I knew if I stayed much longer they'd find two bodies instead of one. So I went home, showered and got into bed. The next morning when my parents asked where Ethan was I said I thought he'd gone to see his girlfriend. If I'd only had the courage to tell them then it would have saved years of searching and wondering. But they clung to me so tightly when they realised Ethan was missing that I just couldn't do it to them. They'd lost one son, if I spoke out they would lose another. As time went on, it became harder and harder to tell the truth, I couldn't bear to think of the pain it would cause them to find out. But, of course, the not knowing can be just as bad. Never having a body to bury, never knowing what happened, whether they are dead or alive, whether they had suffered, or were still suffering.

"It's because of you, Annie, that I am speaking out now," Will continued. "I know we haven't been together for long, but it feels so right and I think I'm in love with you. I want us to have a future together but it couldn't happen with such a big secret between us. I know you're shocked, and hurt that I have kept this from you, but I had to be sure that we were the real thing before I could burden you with this. I am so sorry, Annie, for everything. I hope you can understand and forgive me."

We walked home in silence. My head was reeling and I really didn't know what to say. The past few weeks had been one shock after another, my ordinary little world had been turned upside down. But to find out that my boyfriend, my lover, was a killer who had been hiding it for five years was almost unbearable. I felt lost, betrayed, angry and a myriad of other emotions, all swirling around in my head making me feel dizzy and sick. Will didn't try to kiss me as we reached my house. "Bye, Annie," he said sadly.

The weeks that followed went by in a blur. So much had happened in such a short space of time, my head was still reeling. Will confessed to his parents. I don't know how they reacted at first, but they stood by him. He was arrested and remanded in custody. His parents had hired a fancy barrister and wanted to apply for bail but Will refused, he said he needed to pay for what he had done. The coroner confirmed that Ethan had died of a single blow to the back of the head, just as Will had said. He also confirmed there was evidence of CPR being carried out in an attempt to revive him, although it had no chance of succeeding, death had been instant and final. The CPS wanted to charge him for disposal of a body, but Will hadn't tried to bury Ethan, it hadn't been found due to the weather conditions and mud shifting across the quarry. He pleaded guilty to manslaughter and was given three years in prison. His parents spoke up for him in court. A lot of people did, actually, he was well respected and well thought of. I didn't of course. I was a bit of a mess.

I resigned from my job at the Globe before I could be sacked. They wanted me to do a piece on being the girlfriend of a killer and that was the last straw. "Annie, a good journalist would sell their soul, or their granny, for a story," James said. "But you just don't have it in you."

"No, I don't" I said, "and I'm glad." I got a job in the marketing suite of the new housing development. It reminded me of Will, but it paid well enough. I wrote a couple of features and short stories for a national women's magazine. It didn't pay much but it was a start.

I could have afforded to share a flat with Em but she'd started seeing Ben who lived in the flat next door and they were talking about buying a house together. "One of the affordable ones on the clifftop," she said.

"Hypocrite!" I said. "You were one of the loudest protestors against it!"

"As were you," she reminded me, "and where is it you work again?"

Em made up with her parents but things weren't the same. She visited Chris and Rob, but her mum and dad still refused to acknowledge them. As for Uncle Dan, turns out he was alive and well and living in Italy. He'd visited the home town of our great grandfather and liked it so much he stayed. He married a local girl and I have two half brothers, aged two and three. He phoned my mum after he was contacted by a mate telling him about the story in the papers. He invited us over, we said we'd think about it, maybe one day. My dad said it was typical of him to just shoot off somewhere on another adventure without any thought for anyone else, but he was smiling when he said it.

Will wrote to me from prison, mostly apologising again for deceiving me. He asked me to go visit but I wasn't sure that I could face it. Maybe one day.

Book Two – Frances

Chapter One

I screamed. "Biddy come here! Quick Biddy come here!" She came running in from the kitchen.

"What's wrong, Frances? What's happened?" she asked.

"It's me!" I shrieked jabbing my finger into the paper. "It's me on the front page!"

"What, why? Let me see," Biddy said taking the newspaper from me.

"They think I'm in the quarry!" I said hysterically. Biddy humphed.

"Don't be so dramatic, Frances," she said. "It says you're one of five missing people who might be the body found in the quarry. Well, we both know it's not you, so what are you getting so antsy about?"

"They reported me missing," I said in surprise. "I didn't think they'd bother. Maybe George has a life insurance policy on me and they needed to report me missing to claim it."

"Really?" Biddy said. "Even George wouldn't be that callous, I must say I was surprised they never looked for you. Maybe they did after all," and she returned to the kitchen to prepare our meal.

I'll never forget the day I walked out, just over two years before. It had started just like any other day, me making breakfast, running around after all of them, making sure they had everything they needed. I had wondered, not for the first time, when I had stopped being a wife and mother and turned into a slave. When Michael was born I stopped work to take care of him, it was the done thing in those days. I had a promising career as an artist and had dreams of opening my own little gallery one day. George never took my art seriously, he thought of it as a hobby, and got quite cross if I neglected the housework to paint.

When Jenna came along three years later I had no time to think about painting, let alone doing it. With a busy three year old and a baby, plus a husband working long hours, I had no time to myself at all. Life was a merry-go-round of feeding, changing, cleaning and grabbing a few minutes' sleep whenever I could. George always said I should be better organised, he was one of five children but when his father got home from work the house was spotless, they were all bathed and fed and his tea was on the table. Try living up to a mother-in-law like that!

Well, I did try. I tried hard, but it was never quite good enough. As the years went by the children started criticising me the way George did. It would be 'Mum why haven't you washed my sports kit? I need it today!' And instead of answering 'Maybe because you left it under your bed instead of putting it in the washing basket,' I would say, 'Sorry dear, I'll do it now and bring it to school in time for your sports lesson.' Life was just easier that way.

I never went anywhere or did anything apart from visiting Biddy once a month. It was an unlikely friendship, we were chalk and cheese. I was staid and serious, very proper with good manners, and generally dressed in a neat skirt and twin set, with flat, practical shoes. Biddy was bohemian, yes, that's the word, bohemian. She wore brightly coloured clothes which never matched, she had pink streaks in her hair and she either wore knee high boots or high heels. She would totter about attracting looks wherever she went, either of ridicule or admiration for her confidence. We met at art school before I married George, hit it off straightaway, goodness knows why. I mean I know why I liked her, I wished I was her, flamboyant, confident, unique. I was never sure why she liked me. But she does. When I met George a few years later, he didn't approve of our friendship, of course, he thought she would be a bad influence on me, so, all those years I never told him we kept in touch. My monthly visits were my little secret.

I hadn't planned to leave that day. I did the breakfast dishes, cleaned the house, changed the bedding, did the washing, then sat down for half an hour to rest my eyes as I'd got in the habit of doing. I hadn't been sleeping very well for the past year. I was on the change, you see, going through the menopause. No wonder they call it the change, it changes everything. The flushes during the night, every night, were just torture. They call them flushes, but it should be floods. I had rivers of sweat running down my chest, my back, my legs. You could have wrung my nightie out and filled a bucket. Biddy told me not to wear a nightie but that wouldn't be proper, and, besides, George really would think I'd lost the plot. It had been a long time since we had sex but that was fine with me. It had become a chore instead of a pleasure. It's strange how things can change so much without you even noticing, I thought.

And then I thought about the children and how much they had changed towards me. When they were young I was the centre of their world, they came to me for everything, we had some wonderful times together. Then gradually as they grew up they turned into mini Georges – telling me what to do and expecting me to wait on them hand and foot. Oh, I know it was my fault, I let it happen. I'm not the kind of person who looks for a fight, I'm all for a quiet life. George is such a strong character he just took over and kind of swallowed me up. I realised that neither my husband nor my children had any respect for me, and I started to cry.

That was another thing about the change – the constant crying. Most of the time I didn't know what I was crying for; if you'd asked I couldn't have told you. Then there was the anger. So many times I had wanted to shout and scream, so unlike me. I had managed to bottle it up so far but sometimes I came really close to telling George to bugger off. I laughed to myself, imagining the look on his face if I had.

I decided that was the day I was going to rebel. Make them see me as a person, not as a drudge or a doormat. I decided not to make dinner. Yes, my big rebellion was not to make dinner. I know how pathetic that sounds but for me, on that day, it was a pretty big deal.

Chapter Two

Biddy interrupted my thoughts. "Grub's up," she shouted.

"Oh, joy," I said to myself as I walked into the kitchen to see what delights were on offer. Biddy had insisted we take turns to cook, I really wish she hadn't. She would throw all sorts of ingredients into a pan, add some spices and hope for the best. Some of her creations were barely edible but I tucked in just the same.

"Have you decided what you're going to do?" she asked.

"What about?" I asked as I tried to swallow a mouthful of the green soupy stuff she had dished up. "Is there bread?" I asked. Bread could mop anything up.

"I keep telling you bread takes away the flavour of the dish," she said pulling a face, but handing me a roll at the same time. "Are you going to tell them where you are?" she asked.

"Tell who what?" I said, then I realised what she meant, "Good God, no!" I said. "Go back to that house, face them after all this time? Are you mad?"

"OK, calm down," Biddy said. "I was only asking, seeing as they reported you missing and all. Will you tell the police?"

"If I talk to the police, they'll tell George. I need to think about it," I said and concentrated on mopping up the green mush.

We settled down to watch television after dinner and my mind wandered again, back to that day. I spent the afternoon stuck to my chair, face glued to the TV screen even though I had no idea what I was watching. I dug my nails into the palm of my hands every time I felt my resolve waiver. I almost ran to the kitchen to start dinner so many times but something stopped me. Enough was enough. I was determined to make my protest.

I was still sitting there when Jenna arrived home from college. "Mum, you'll have to keep my food for later, I'm going out for a run with Judith."

"There's no food," I said, quietly but firmly.

"Thanks," she shouted as she raced upstairs to change. She hadn't heard me, of course she hadn't. When was the last time she actually listened to me or we had a real conversation? Instead of shrinking into my chair something in me just snapped. I marched to the foot of the stairs and shouted up to her.

"Jenna, you are not listening to me." She ignored me, so I shouted louder until she finally leaned over the bannisters looking cross.

"What is it, Mum?" she said. "I told you I'm going for a run, I've got to change and you're holding me up."

"Oh, I'm so sorry," I started sarcastically, when she interrupted saying 'OK, now I've got to go'.

"You are going nowhere young lady until you listen to me," I shouted. Her head popped back over the landing bannister, she looked surprised.

"What's the matter? Are you ill? You look flushed. Are you having those flushes things again?" she said.

"No, I am not having flushes. I am having a meltdown," I shouted. "I am fed up of being ignored in this house, treated like a skivvy, no one ever listens to me. When you came in, I told you there was no food," There. I had told her. My big rebellion – I was not cooking tea.

"What d'you mean, no food?" Jenna asked looking puzzled.

"No food," I repeated. And I went back to my chair.

Jenna had just come back from her run when George and Michael arrived home. She had looked into the kitchen, probably thinking food was after all being cooked, and seeing that it wasn't disappeared upstairs. She came running down as she heard the door open. "Dad," she called breathlessly. "There's something wrong with Mum. She's just sitting in the chair and there's no tea."

"No tea?" Michael said, disbelieving, "Is she ill?"

"I'm not ill, and neither am I deaf," I said from my chair. "I am just not making you all food."

"All right, Frances what's this all about?" George asked frowning as he walked into the room. "I know you've been having women's problems but there's no need to punish us."

"Women's problems!" I shrieked, and then I really did lose the plot. "It's called the bloody menopause, the change, and it's really shitty, actually. Not that any of you would either know or care because I don't exist for any of you. I'm just the cook, the cleaner, the person who runs around making your life more comfortable. You take me for granted, you show me no respect, when did any of you do anything for me? Has any of you ever even made me a cup of tea? Do you not think I might like a meal cooked for me for once?"

"Hang on now, Frances," George interrupted. "Cooking and cleaning is your job. You've never complained before. Now, just calm yourself down, we'll have fish and chips for tonight, and we can just get back to normal tomorrow."

"I don't want to get back to normal!" I shouted. "Don't you see – my normal life is miserable, nothing but drudgery. I don't go anywhere, I don't see anyone, you go to the pub every Friday night and every Sunday lunchtime but you have not invited me once! I am not just a cook and a cleaner, I am a person, and I have bloody well had enough."

George sighed, I could tell he was already weary with the conversation. Michael and Jenna stood in the doorway, open-mouthed and looking at me as though some monster had taken place of their mother.

"OK, what do you want?" George asked. "Please don't tell me this is about you going to work again, or back to that painting class. You know they just wouldn't fit into our lifestyle. Look, Frances, you've got it pretty good here, you have a lovely home, everything you need, no money worries, a lovely family. What more do you want?"

"What do I want? What do I want?!" I shrieked into his face as he coiled back. "I want a life. A real one. Where people are interested in me, talk to me, listen to me, where I feel I matter and make a difference. As for my lovely family – seriously? Have you looked at yourselves lately? You, George, just sit with your paper or watching television and don't interact with any of us. None of us have a fucking clue, yes, I said fuck, you can close your mouths now, what you do all day, what you like, what you think, what you feel, because you never fucking tell us. You act like the world owes you a living and we are just the little people sent along to please you.

And as for you two," I said pointing at Michael and Jenna. "You can't be in the same room for more than five minutes without arguing with each other. You are both spoilt, selfish and downright rude. When you were children, you were both so sweet natured and so loving. You have turned into monsters. Yes, that's right, I said monsters," I repeated as they both stared at me clearly thinking that I was in fact the monster. "Well, I have had enough!" I shouted. "You don't care for me, you don't care about me, you never show me any kind of affection or respect, or any thanks for everything I do for you. Well, let's see how you all manage without me, shall we?" I said, grabbing my coat and bag and running out of the house, slamming the door behind me.

Chapter Three

The following morning, Biddy woke me with a cup of tea in bed. "To what do I owe this honour?" I asked.

"Heard you tossing and turning all night," Biddy said. "Thought you might appreciate a bit of a lie in. You're not in work until this afternoon are you? And don't forget we're out tonight so you'll need all your energy." Ah, yes, tonight. Tonight we go line dancing. We go every Tuesday, have done for the past year. It's one of the many experiences I have enjoyed, (well, mostly enjoyed!) since moving in with Biddy. I remember when I bought my first pair of jeans to go the class. I was adamant I couldn't wear jeans and boots, I mean it's ridiculous at my age right? Wrong, said Biddy. You are as old as you feel and it's time you felt a lot younger. I didn't even own a pair of trousers, let alone jeans, I felt like a scarlet woman trying them on. But since moving in with Biddy, minus any clothes, I must admit it had been really liberating wearing hers. Long floaty skirts, brightly coloured tops, and sparkly shoes with heels.

I had let my hair grow, only because I couldn't afford the hairdresser any longer. Within weeks it was past my shoulders, longer than it had been since I first got married. I grew it before the wedding so that it could be put up in a chignon for the big day, but I cut it soon afterwards as I just didn't have time to do it anymore. It was easier having a short, neat cut every six weeks, then I never had to do anything other than wash and comb it.

Biddy said longer hair suited me. "You would look so much younger if only you didn't have all that grey hair," she said. Over the past few years, my hair had been increasingly flecked with grey, but, although it depressed me to look in the mirror, it really didn't matter. After all, who looked at me? Next thing I knew Biddy rushed off to the shops and came back with rich brown hair dye and I was head down over the sink having my grey obliterated. Biddy was right, I looked years younger. And that was the start of the new me. I decided I wanted to look as good as I could, for me, no one else, but because it made me feel good. And I wanted to do things I hadn't done, see things I hadn't seen and experience things I had only ever dared dream about.

Biddy and me drew up a bucket list. She didn't have a lot on hers, Biddy had lived a pretty full life. Mine, on the other hand, stretched to two pages. Most of them were simple little things, like spending a whole day in my pyjamas or eating an entire chocolate cake without sharing it. Others were a little more ambitious…

The day I walked out I got to the end of the road before stopping and taking a breath. I was suddenly overcome with panic, couldn't believe what I'd done. I sat on the bench near the bus stop and wondered what on earth to do. It was all very well making the dramatic exit but what came next? Go home with my tail between my legs like they no doubt expected? No, that would mean going back to my dull, dreary life and I just couldn't do it. Not any more. So, I thought I'd go away for a few days for them to see what life was like without me, maybe then they would at least appreciate all I did. But where could I go? Then it struck me, I could go to Biddy. I knew she'd let me stay for a while. So, I got on the next bus and turned up on Biddy's doorstep later that evening. That was two years ago, and I haven't left since.

I went to work that afternoon still wondering whether or not to contact the police.

Part of me wanted to reassure them I wasn't dead in the quarry, part of me thought good, hope they are suffering, serves them right, but mostly I was scared. Scared that any kind of contact with any of them would drag me right back into my old life.

I work in Biddy's shop. She has a small place in the High Street where she sells her pottery, other people's arts and crafts, and some antiques. The shop doesn't make much money but it's enough for us to live on. And I'm painting again, and actually selling some of them! I started about a year ago after months of Biddy nagging me to pick up a paintbrush, and once I started I couldn't stop. I realised then that George or the children or time hadn't stopped me painting. After all, the children had long since grown up, there was no reason to stop me. But I was scared. Scared that the years of drudgery and misery had taken away all my creative instincts. What if I couldn't paint any more? What if my talent, the one thing that made me stand out from the crowd, had left? I missed painting so much it was like a permanent ache in my stomach, but the fear was stronger. Biddy was stronger still. In the end I couldn't stand her nagging any longer.

"Fine," I said. "I will go and paint. But I warn you if I can't do it, if it doesn't feel the way it did, I will never forgive you for making me do it."

"Bog off and paint," Biddy said. So I did and the second I mixed the paints on the palette the blood started rushing through my veins and I couldn't wait to see the colours take shape on the canvas. I paint most days now, either in the room at the back of the shop, in the conservatory or the garden at home, or on fine days I go to the coast and paint the clifftops.

We display my paintings in the shop along with Biddy's pottery, her brightly coloured cushions and handmade necklaces. Other artists come in with their products and we sell them for a small commission. The antiques are things that Biddy has picked up over the years, she has an eye for anything unusual. Recently I started buying vintage jewellery and that's proving very popular with customers. We've had quite a few young people come in for them. So we're doing OK, making enough to live and we put a little by every week to fund our adventures.

Chapter Four

I really did mean to go home after a few days but I kept putting it off. Biddy said there was no rush, she was enjoying the company. I said nonsense, she liked her own space. She said that was true once, but since her niece Caitlin had turned up on her doorstep she had got used to having someone around. Caitlin was Biddy's brother's youngest daughter, she had never got on with her family and the age of eighteen walked out and turned up at Biddy's door. Caitlin is a lovely girl, she calls at least once a week to see us. She moved out about eight years ago to live with her boyfriend Jack. Fiddy and me are still waiting for the invite to the wedding, but Caitlin said Jack wasn't the marrying kind. Neither was Biddy. Oh, she had her offers over the years, but had never loved anyone enough to give up her independent lifestyle. "Why would I want to shag one man my whole life?" she asked me.

"I'm the wrong person to ask," I said. "I can't think of anything worse than having multiple bed partners, one was more than enough." Biddy did want children once, but she never found the right man to father one. For all her hippy chick ways, Biddy was quite traditional when it came to bringing up a child, she believed that it was important for two parents to be involved. I suppose that's why she's so close to Caitlin, she's the closest thing Biddy has to a child of her own.

I found I didn't miss my children for the first few weeks. I was surprised, I thought I would have. Biddy said, although I loved my children, I didn't really like them. I think she was right. I know it was my fault they turned out the way they did and I would always regret not having the strength to do it differently. I didn't miss George at all. Still don't. After nearly thirty years of marriage he still feels like a stranger to me. I know I am to him.

The shop was quiet that day and I found myself wondering what George would say if he knew I was alive and well and living with Biddy just half an hour's drive down the coast. I wonder what Michael and Jenna would think if they knew. I didn't mean to hurt them, didn't want them to worry. All this time I had truly believed they didn't care. I never saw an appeal in the paper, no one ever came looking for me. Well, maybe they wouldn't have looked in Biddy's, no one knew I was still friendly with her. I suppose it was possible they had reported me missing and that they were concerned.

I mustered up as much courage as I could, locked up the shop and went to the police station. The desk sergeant looked bored. I don't suppose there's much to excite him here. "It's about the dead body in the quarry," I said, and suddenly he looked interested.

"Have you got any information about it?" he said.

"It's not me," I replied. The bored look came over his face again.

"I can see it's not you, dear, now run along, please, I'm busy here." Busy my arse I thought.

"No, I was in the paper, my picture, one of the missing people." Now he looked interested again. After we had finally established my identity and that I was telling the truth he went into the back room to phone the officer in charge of the case.

He returned with that same bored look. "They know it's not you, it's a man."

"Oh," I said relieved. "So my family know it's not me do they?"

"No idea, love," the sergeant said.

"Well, could you check please?" I asked. "Could you let them know I'm fine but I don't want them to know where I am, can we keep that confidential?"

He sighed. "I'll get an officer to take a statement from you, just wait over there." Forty minutes later a young PC finally emerges and calls me into a side room. Five minutes later I am back out in the street.

I told Biddy over tea that evening. "I didn't want them to worry I was dead or anything," I said. "The PC told me he would let them know I was fine but he wouldn't disclose my whereabouts. So that's that, drama over." Biddy humphed as she did when she clearly disagreed with me.

"It's not over by a long way," she said.

We set off for line dancing, held in the village hall. Me in straight cut jeans, check shirt and ankle boots, Biddy in skin-tight white jeans with an orange shirt. Biddy has a moped we travel about on. I must admit we look a sight riding around town. Two middle aged women on a moped, with fluorescent helmets and sparkly shoes. Biddy's helmet was shocking pink with purple and red flowers, mine was bright green with yellow stars. We really didn't care what anyone thought.

Along with line dancing we go bowling. We joined a team that plays every Sunday, it's good fun. We have a few drinks and our bowling gets better by the glass. At least it does to us! We know that lots of ladies of a certain age join the WI or go to bingo, but Biddy would never fit into that stereotype, and, surprise, surprise, neither did I. The change had certainly brought about a major change in me, and in my life. I hadn't been so happy, alive and confident since I was a teenager. The article in the newspaper had stirred up lots of long forgotten emotions.

It had also brought my feelings about my children back to the surface. After the first few weeks, which actually passed in a bit of a blur, I started missing them. Really missing them, so much that I was tempted to go back just to be a part of their lives. Biddy encouraged me to contact them but I was scared that it would either drag me back or that they wouldn't want any contact with me. I didn't know which was worse. They certainly didn't seem to be missing me, I believed they didn't care. After all, I was sure they'd never looked for me. Knowing that they had, it changed everything. Biddy was right, it wasn't over yet.

Chapter Five

The decision to contact them was actually taken out of my hands. The nice young PC came knocking on the door the following day with a message for me. "Your daughter Jenna would like to speak to you," he said. "She asked me to pass a message on, asking you to phone the house between 4 p.m. and 5 p.m. any week day." Ah, that meant she would be alone. George and Michael never got back before five. What did that mean? She didn't want them to know? She was defying orders? What?

"How did my family take the news?" I asked the PC.

"Oh, um, relieved of course that you're OK," he said but he didn't look me in the eye.

"My husband was angry, was he?" I asked, knowing he would have been. Typical George reaction, not thank God she's alive, but how dare she do this to us.

The PC nodded. "Your son too," he said. "I'm afraid your daughter was the only one who showed an interest in contacting you. I'm sorry."

Long after he'd left I was still going over our short conversation in my mind. I knew George would be angry, knew he would react that way. Maybe when he calmed down he would want to talk to me. Maybe not. But Michael – that hurt. My son, my firstborn, my baby, he wasn't happy to hear I'm OK and he doesn't want any contact with me. I cried myself to sleep that night, for the first time in a long time.

I alternated between being really excited to talk to Jenna, and being really worried that she just wanted to give me a dressing down for the trouble I'd caused. I just hoped she didn't say anything too hurtful that I'd never be able to get over. My hand shook as I dialled the number, I could barely breathe. She answered after two rings. "Hi," I said, "It's me, Mum."

"Hi," she answered, "It's me, Jenna. Remember me? I'm the daughter you abandoned." Oh, God, I thought, I can't do this, can't bear to hear her talk to me this way. Better not to have any contact than this. "Have you nothing to say?" she asked.

"I'm sorry," I said. "I didn't mean to abandon you. I didn't know you'd reported me missing, I didn't think any of you would care."

"What?!" she shouted. "Seriously, Mum, you walk out of the house in a hissy fit and just never come back. What kind of person does that? We're your family, of course we cared, what did you think – that we would just carry on as normal?"

"I don't know," I said. "It's so hard to explain. I was in a bad place I just had to get away. And then it got harder and harder to come back. I didn't think you'd want me back."

"OK, Mum, I get it, you were going through a bad time, blah blah blah. For two years? Are you still going through a bad time? Were you ever going to contact us?"

"Jenna, this is really hard to explain but you do deserve an explanation," I said. "But not like this, not over the phone. Please can we meet and I'll tell you everything?" She reluctantly agreed, I think she just wanted to keep ranting at me but I couldn't take any more. We arranged to meet the following Saturday at a café in the town which lies between her home and mine.

Needless to say I was a wreck in the days that passed in between the phone call and the meeting. Biddy tried her best to take my mind off things but it was useless. On Friday night she made a jug of margaritas and got our holiday snaps out. She knows I love to reminisce about the good times we've enjoyed since I turned up on her doorstep.

Our adventures we call them. Biddy didn't like the idea of it being a bucket list, she said that sounded as though we were about to die. So we called it our adventure list, we had a target of five a year. I worked out we would have to live into our eighties to do it all. Biddy said we would then. Some of them were expensive, like scuba diving in the Red Sea. We used up a lot of our adventure fund for that but it was worth every penny. That was on Biddy's list of course, not something I had ever imagined myself doing. When she wrote it down I said I couldn't do that one, couldn't even swim. "Time you learnt then," she said. Next thing you know I am signed up for swimming classes in the local leisure centre. It was ridiculous I had argued, a fifty-two year old woman learning to swim. Biddy didn't agree so off we went. To my surprise I wasn't the oldest one there, in fact most were over forty. Who knew so many middle aged people had suddenly decided they wanted to swim? Anyway, by the end of the course I could swim a length without stopping, do front crawl and breaststroke, tread water and dive in off the side. I couldn't have been more pleased with myself if I'd won an Olympic medal.

So, off we went scuba diving after getting lessons in that too. They didn't let us go down too far, of course, as novices, but it was absolutely breath-taking, one of the most wonderful experiences of my life. Hill walking in Scotland was on my list. Not as exciting as scuba diving I know, but something I'd always wanted to do. So, off we went backpacking around Inverness, stopped for a visit to Loch Ness of course. It's difficult to describe the scenery up there, I could paint it better than I could tell you. It's rugged and wild and beautiful. It's like time has stood still in places. Biddy agreed it was well worth doing and seeing, and we both lost a few pounds through the walking so that was a bonus.

We had matching tattoos done in Venice. Believe it or not, Venice was Biddy's idea, the tattoos were mine. I'd always wanted one but never dared mention it to George. I knew what he'd say – a woman with a tattoo is nothing but a cheap tart. Well, George, I am now that cheap tart, I laughed to myself as the tattooist began. We opted for very tasteful tattoos on the back of our necks, nothing too obvious. We both had a friendship symbol, which looks like a swirly plus sign, then I had the Celtic symbol for new beginnings underneath and Biddy had the symbol for adventure. We both thought our tattoos were amazing. As was Venice, probably the most beautiful city I've ever visited. We went on a canal boat, we drank cocktails in Saint Mark's Square and visited the Peggy Guggenheim museum. Looking at the art and sculptures by so many famous and talented people was an inspiration.

We went to a nudist beach in the South of France (Biddy's idea) followed by a visit to a vineyard (mine). I said we should have done it the other way around to give me Dutch courage for baring all. Biddy didn't agree. Can't say I enjoyed the nudist thing, while Biddy was dancing around in the dunes arms spread open, all her bits bobbing, I was curled up in a ball on the towel. I lasted for fifteen minutes before getting my bikini back on and spent the next two hours sunbathing while Biddy danced her way along the beach.

We are saving for our next big adventure which, actually, is the only thing we both had on our lists. A visit to Las Vegas! We want to do the whole Vegas thing, we want to stay in Caesar's Palace, see the Bellagio fountains dance, take a helicopter ride to the Grand Canyon. We have a whole ten-day itinerary planned, but it's going to cost a whole lot more than the adventure fund holds at the moment. Biddy says don't worry, something will turn up and we'll do Vegas baby!

Aside from our adventures we live a pretty good life. We both love our work, and the shop. Biddy has a two-bedroomed bungalow with a large conservatory which we spend a lot of evenings in, usually drinking our gin and tonics. We make wine and we drink that sometimes, but oh, my, it's killer stuff, we are good for nothing the following day. Apart from line dancing and bowling, we go to water aerobics and visit the local pub most Saturday nights where Biddy likes to sing in the karaoke session. The more she drinks, the more wonderful she thinks she sounds. Believe me, it's not wonderful, but it is fun to watch her dancing around and kicking her legs up to the strain of 'New York, New York'.

She occasionally went out on dates, said she still enjoyed sex now and again. They never lasted more than a few weeks, she got bored easily. She tried to get me to date but I have no interest. I mean, I wasn't even that interested in my husband. I told Biddy she was probably the greatest love of my life and I was fine with that. She said OK, but don't be expecting any sex with me.

It was worrying to think that the life I had learned to love with Biddy could be over. I was so afraid that getting back in touch with my family would turn me back into the mouse I had used to be. But George and Michael didn't want to see me so I just had to stay strong when I spoke to Jenna.

I longed to see her but I dreaded it too. She had been so angry on the phone, I wasn't expecting it to be a joyful reunion. Saturday lunchtime I sat at a table in the window of the coffee shop, nursing my mug of tea with shaking hands. I was there half an hour early, I wanted to see her walk along the street before she saw me. I wanted to enjoy a moment of my daughter before the angry look appeared on her face.

When I saw her coming, I couldn't catch my breath, I started panicking, I wanted to run to her and hug her, and I wanted to run away. Instead, I just sat there waiting. She looked around as she entered the coffee shop and I waved. Her first reaction was surprise. "Hello," she said as she sat down. "I didn't recognise you, you look so different."

"Different good, or different bad?" I asked smiling at her.

"Just different, not like my mum used to look," she said scowling.

"Oh, well, I feel different too," I said. "I really want to try and explain how I felt, why I left and why I didn't get in touch." The waitress came and took our order. Jenna nodded at me.

"I'm listening," she said.

I talked for what seemed like hours but was in fact only twenty minutes. Two years of my life wrapped up in twenty minutes. Jenna didn't interrupt. When I stopped talking she said, "OK, I can understand that you were miserable and didn't feel valued, but to just walk out like that was a bit dramatic. And then not to let us know where you were, how you were. Nothing for two years! You say you thought about us all the time, well, you clearly didn't think enough of us to want to be in our lives or even to give us the peace of mind of knowing you were OK. It's a lot to forgive and I'm not sure I can."

"I'm not asking you to forgive me," I said. "I just want you to understand why I had to go and why I couldn't come back. I very much regret not contacting you and Michael, but I have no regrets about everything else. Do you know this is the first real conversation we have had in years?" I asked her. Her eyes widened.

"Yes, I suppose it is," she said. "But you surely can't blame me for that? You're the parent, I was just a teenager."

"Oh, Jenna, this is not about blame, don't you see that? My life in that house was miserable, my relationships with you and Michael non-existent. If I'd stayed and tried to talk to you, you never would have listened, none of you, you know that. I very much want you and Michael in my life, but it can't be the way it was."

"I'm not sure that I can forget what's happened, and I know Michael can't," Jenna said.

"How is Michael? How are things at home?" I asked. Jenna pulled a face.

"Michael moved in with Daisy a few weeks after you left, when it became clear you weren't coming back," she answered. "Dad expected us to do the cooking and cleaning and all the stuff you used to do. It was really unfair, we didn't have a clue how to make beans on toast, let alone a roast dinner. So, Michael, typically selfish brat that he is, packed his bag and left us to it. Him and Daisy moved into a flat together, but he had a shock! Daisy is no pushover, Michael has to do his share of housework and making meals. He's still not very good apparently, but Daisy won't let him off. It amuses me no end!" she said smiling wickedly. "When Dad finally gave up on you coming home he hired a cleaning lady, she's still with us," Jenna continued. "But I have to cook, which believe it or not I am actually quite good at. When I first started I was rubbish, so I got some recipe books and started watching cookery shows on TV. Within a few months I was experimenting with my own dishes, which of course Dad didn't like, if it wasn't meat and two veg or fish and chips he wouldn't touch it. So I changed my course in college and now I'm training to be a chef. It means I won't qualify for another year but I really love it."

"Well done, you," I said. "That's really good to hear. You could come and give Biddy a few lessons in cooking, that's for sure!" At the mention of Biddy's name Jenna's face clouded over.

"Look, I'd better get going," she said. "I'm meeting friends in town."

"Oh, OK," I said trying to hide my disappointment. "Can we meet again?" I asked. Jenna shrugged her shoulders.

"OK, same place, same time next week," she said and she was off, gone through the door in a flash.

Chapter Six

We met every week, same time, same place, for four weeks until I think Jenna had eventually stopped venting her anger on me. We actually started to talk properly and have pleasant conversations. Then she dropped the bombshell. George wanted to talk to me. I felt my insides drop to my feet, I went cold all over. "Jenna, I don't know," I said. "I really don't think it would be a good idea."

"You owe him a conversation," Jenna said sharply. So, not wanting to piss her off again, as Biddy would say, I agreed. Next bombshell was that he wanted me to go to the house. Now, that was a step too far. I said I wasn't ready for that, I stalled and said I needed more time. I asked about Michael and was told again that he didn't want any contact.

I started telling Jenna more about my life with Biddy. She had already told me George blamed Biddy for leading me astray. Jenna refused to come and meet her, but gradually I was bringing her into the conversation as I described our life. When I showed Jenna my tattoo she couldn't believe her eyes. "Who are you?" she said, "and what have you done with my mother? I hardly recognise you, with your long hair and your jeans, polished nails and jewellery. I mean scuba diving for goodness sake! You wouldn't even paddle in the sea before. You and Biddy are like a geriatric Thelma and

Louise, and you'll probably end up going over a cliff too."

"Who are Thelma and Louise?" I asked.

"A new film that's just come out," Jenna answered impatiently. "But that's not the point, I mean have you lost your mind? What are you doing? Women your age should be knitting or something not line dancing for heaven's sake!"

I was quiet for a moment, the last thing I wanted was to push Jenna away just as we were building a relationship but she had to know me as I am, and not as I was. So I took a deep breath. "Jenna, this is me, this is the happiest I have ever been, except for when you and Michael were small. This is who I am. I love scuba diving, line dancing, bowling, drinking margaritas in the afternoon, all of it. I love my life. And I know I look ten years younger. I wish you would come and meet Biddy, see the shop, look at my paintings."

"Are you and Biddy… " she started with a shocked look on her face.

"No, no, nothing like that," I laughed. "Biddy likes men far too much and I don't like sex at all."

"Oh, Mother, too much information," Jenna said holding her head in her hands. Then she laughed, and so did I. And we laughed until we cried. And then she said: "Actually, you do look ten years younger and so much happier. I'll make a deal with you, I'll come meet Biddy, see the shop and everything if you come to the house to talk to Dad. It's only fair!" she said as she saw my face clouding over.

Well, what could I do? I really wanted my daughter to have a place in my life, I wanted her to see my life. If going back to the house and talking to George was the price I had to pay, then so be it. Biddy offered to come with me, but that would have been like a red rag to a bull. No, this was something I had to do alone.

The day came. I deliberately wore my gaudiest top and jewellery. I straightened my glossy, rich brown hair so that it came halfway down my back, I took care with my make-up, and then for the final flourish I put a pair of Biddy's sparkly red high heels on. I could barely walk in them but I didn't care. I wanted to make a statement, and I felt like I could draw courage from Biddy through them. I was sure I was going to need it.

I caught the bus, and Jenna met me at the bus stop, the same one I had left from over two years before. The short walk to the house was agony, not only because I was sick to my stomach at the thought of going back in there and facing George, but because the heels really had been a mistake, my feet were killing me.

Jenna was quiet, she asked how I was, I said fine, that was the only conversation until we got to the house. It looked smaller than I remembered. I noted that the flower beds in the front garden were starting to bloom. Jenna saw me look. "He got a gardener, too," she said. Dear Lord, could the man not do anything for himself?

He was standing in the living room. Typical George. At 5'11" he's six inches taller than me so he looks down on me, mentally and literally. His hair was flecked with grey, he looked a few pounds heavier, but otherwise the same old George. "How are you?" I asked politely.

"I'm fine," he said. "But you don't need to do small talk, that's not what you came for, is it?" I nodded, no. "Put the kettle on, we'll have a cup of tea and a chat," he said. Automatically I walked into the kitchen and reached for the kettle before realising what I was doing.

I hadn't been in the house two minutes and here he was ordering me about again! And worst of all, here I was doing it.

It was too late to go back in and say do it yourself, so I took some time while the kettle boiled to compose myself and take a look around. The kitchen was exactly as it had been, apart from the cookery books filling the top shelf, which were obviously Jenna's. It was clean and tidy, George's cleaning woman was clearly doing a good job. Shame. I had hoped to see it all rundown and falling apart without me.

I carried the teas into the lounge and set them down on the table. On coasters of course. We didn't have any coasters in Biddy's, there were rings all over the coffee table, but neither of us cared enough to do anything about it. "Right Frances, you've made your point," George said. "We should have appreciated you more, we understand that now. But this life you are living with your friend is not you. You didn't suddenly turn into a different person overnight. You walked out on your home, your marriage and your children. Most men would have nothing to do with you but I'm willing to give you a second chance, for the sake of our family."

Well, that was unexpected. I just sat there gaping at him, then I felt the shoes pinch. "George, I am not here asking or expecting you to take me back," I said. "I am here because Jenna wanted me to do this and for no other reason. The life I lead now is me, it always was me, but you, my life, everything, just stifled it. I couldn't ever go back to that." To say he was surprised would be an understatement. He had clearly been expecting me to be grateful to return.

"Frances, you're still not well, you're not thinking clearly," he began when I interrupted.

"If you mention women's problems I am walking out," I said sternly. And I realised that was the first time I had ever spoken sternly to George. He didn't see that coming either. After an awkward silence he asked if I would like to take any of my things. Now, that took me by surprise again. But there were photographs, a couple of ornaments that had belonged to my mother, personal stuff that I would like to have. So, I thanked him and asked if he had a bag I could use. My old suitcase was still on top of the wardrobe, he said.

I really didn't want to go in our old bedroom but I was close to getting out of there in a pretty civilised fashion. I looked into Michael's old room, exactly as it was. Jenna's bedroom door was shut. I passed it and went into the room I had shared with George all those years. It hadn't been all bad, we did have some good times. We even had some good sex in the beginning until it got so same old, same old, it was no fun anymore. I reached up for the suitcase and laid it on the neatly made bed. Cleaner must have been there early that day, I noted.

I looked around the room and was surprised to see all my things where I had left them. In the drawers there were my little piles of jumpers, neatly folded, my underwear arranged according to colour, nightwear divided into four parts – one for each season. When I had become so obsessive about stupid things like that? I wondered. I knew I hadn't been before I married, and I certainly wasn't now. I opened my jewellery box to get my mother's brooch and the silver earrings Michael had bought me the Christmas before I left. George walked into the room and gave me a start. "Sorry, didn't mean to startle you," he said. "You can take whatever you want, of course, but I'd rather you didn't."

"What do you mean?" I asked puzzled.

"Frances, I don't want you to go," he said. "We can put all this behind us and move on. I mean exactly that – move forward, not back to how it used to be. You can keep working if you want to, I'll keep the cleaner and the gardener on. You can even keep going on your adventures with Biddy if that's what you need. But we need you here. Jenna needs you. Michael wouldn't admit it but he needs you too. If you came back you could mend fences with him, I know it. And I need you," he ended quietly.

,"Oh George, I was desperately unhappy here, you know that," I answered. "And I can't go back to that. I really appreciate what you're saying about moving forward but I'm scared it wouldn't happen and that in time everything would be back to just how it used to be."

"If you're so sure you don't want to come back why do you still wear your wedding ring?" he asked. I looked down at my hand. Good question, and one I had asked myself many a time. I just couldn't bring myself to take it off, it would be symbolic of cutting all ties to the past. Something I think I want but I have children and I am torn. "Look, take some time to think," George said. "There's no need to rush into anything."

Chapter Seven

I went back and told Biddy what had happened. She said she wouldn't try to persuade me to stay, it was my choice and I had to live with it. I know it should have been simple – stay with Biddy, continue to enjoy the life we had made. But George had looked wretched when he entered the bedroom, I'd never seen him like that. If only he'd been so kind and shown those feelings while I was still there, maybe everything would have been different. I felt guilty for walking out on my marriage. I had been brought up to believe that marriage was for life, no matter what. "You made your bed, you lie in it," my mother always said. Mostly though my thoughts were about Michael. I missed him desperately. Yes, Biddy was right, I hadn't liked my children much, but I still loved them with all my being. If I went back I would see Michael again, and eventually he would accept what had happened, just as Jenna had. We could build a real relationship, the way I was with Jenna. It was so hard to think.

I made a jug of margaritas that evening. "It won't help," Biddy said disapprovingly, but it didn't stop her filling her glass. Halfway through the jug, I suddenly remembered what Jenna had said.

"Have you heard of Thelma and Louise?" I asked Biddy. "Jenna said it's a new film out and that we are like the geriatric version, and that we're going to go over a cliff." Biddy nearly choked on her drink.

"What on earth are you talking about?" she laughed. We got the local paper and turned to the entertainment section. There it was – Thelma and Louise starring Susan Sarandon and Geena Davies – showing in the local cinema. "If we hurry we'll get there before it starts," Biddy said pulling her coat on and grabbing the bike helmets.

Riding the bike was not a great idea after drinking margaritas, we nearly fell off a few times, now that would have been a sight. Biddy in her flowing gold skirt and green flowery coat, me in my shirtdress with knee high boots, in a heap at the side of the road. We got to the cinema in time for the trailers. Then we had to decide whether to keep drinking and leave the bike until the morning, or sober up and ride home. Well, it was no contest. Biddy went to fetch us two beers.

We loved the film of course. We laughed and cried and talked about it all the way home. "Am I Thelma or Louise?" I asked Biddy.

"You're Thelma, of course," Biddy said giggling. "The more staid, sensible one. I, of course, am the beautiful Louise."

"But Thelma drives the car," I said, wanting to be Geena Davies. Well, who wouldn't?

"Then you'll have to learn before you take us over the cliff," Biddy said.

I met Jenna for coffee the following day and she agreed, as per our deal, to come and see Biddy who was working in the shop at the time. Jenna was pleasant and polite, Biddy was Biddy. She admired my paintings, she was obviously surprised that they were quite good, even though I say so myself. She liked Biddy's pottery and she loved the vintage jewellery. "It's really popular," I told her. "We've made more money on that this month than on anything else."

"I love this ring," Jenna said holding the ruby and diamond dress ring and admiring it under the light.

"Have it," I said. I would pay for it later, of course, the fact that it was the most expensive piece we had was just unfortunate.

"Have you thought about what Dad said?" Jenna asked me, back at the bungalow.

"I've thought about little else," I said. "I'm torn. I so much want to see Michael, I feel so guilty about your father, but I'm so happy with the person I am here I don't want to go back to who I was."

"You don't have to, Mum," Jenna said. "You just have to have the strength to be yourself wherever you are."

She was right, of course, but I doubted myself. I'd never been confident or self-assured like Biddy, I would run a mile rather than have an argument, I never even complained if I had the wrong change in a shop, or returned faulty goods. I could rarely bring myself to swear in case it sounded aggressive, and I couldn't even answer Biddy back even though she told me to. "If I'm being bossy or getting on your tits, tell me," she had said. Course I never did.

George wanted an answer, Jenna told me two weeks later. Naturally I had not made my mind up. "Do you think I could just talk to Michael first?" I asked. Jenna sighed.

"Mum, I told you he won't consider it," she answered. "There's no point asking any more, he just gets angry, then puts that stubborn face on and there's no talking to him. Don't know how Daisy puts up with him. They're talking about getting married, you know," she said looking at me intently.

"Married?" I squeaked. My son was thinking of marriage and he didn't want me involved. How could I bear it if I wasn't invited to his wedding? I couldn't, I would just curl up and die.

I tossed and turned all night, still not coming to any decision. The only thing I knew for sure is that I had to talk to Michael. So, as dawn was breaking I decided if the mountain wouldn't go to Mohammed then Mohammed (that's me, by the way) would go to the mountain. And finally I fell asleep.

Chapter Eight

Michael saw me at the entrance to his flat and stopped in his tracks. I had been there for what seemed like weeks waiting for him. He hesitated then carried on walking towards the doorway and went to go straight past me. "Michael, please," I begged. He walked into the building, I followed. He ran up two flights of stairs and into his flat slamming the door shut. I went up the stairs and knocked on his door. No answer. I knocked again. No answer. I banged. One of the neighbours came out to see what the noise was about. I apologised but then I banged again, and I shouted, "I will do this all night if I have to, I'm not leaving until I speak to you." It had taken so much courage to go that far, I knew if I gave in then I would never do it again.

The door opened. It was Daisy. "For heaven's sakes come in," she said. "Talk to your mother before we get noise complaints off the neighbours," she said to Michael. I stood in the entrance hall, it was surprisingly long with four doors leading off it. The door to the left was open, it was the kitchen and Michael was standing at the sink with his back to me.

"Tea would be nice," I said and took a seat at the table. He turned and glared at me, I swear there was hatred in his eyes, mine filled with tears to see it, but I brushed them away. This was not the time to fall apart.

"Fine, let's be civilised and have tea, shall we?" he said nastily. "Then when you've drunk it you can respect my wishes and leave, never to return." I gulped.

"You look well," I said. "Your flat is nice." He scowled.

"Seriously? Small talk? You got nothing else to say?"

"Of course I have," I said. "There's so much I have to say. I know how angry you are with me, I don't blame you. I'm not here to ask for forgiveness, I'm not even here to explain everything to you, you're not ready to hear it."

"Then why the hell are you here?" he snapped at me.

"I have a decision to make," I said far more calmly than I felt. "And you are a very big part of it. I expect you know your father has asked me to go back. He understands how unhappy I was and promises it would be different. He also said you would be back in my life if I moved back there. I need to know if that's true. I need to know if you will ever be ready to talk to me if I don't."

"Well, it would be a start!" Michael shouted at me. "At least make up a little for what you've done to Dad and Jenna. I've got my own life here, I'm not making any promises."

"Please think about it Michael. I miss you, I love you so much. I'm still your mother and no matter what has happened over the past two years, you at least owe me that – just to consider letting me back in your life."

"Like I said, I'm making no promises," he said. "Now, I think it's time you left."

So I did. And cried all the way to the bus stop. It was clear that my only chance with Michael was to go back to George. Do I give up my life to have my child back in it or do I accept that Michael may never again be a part of it?

"He's a stubborn twat," Jenna said. Biddy laughed.

"I like you more every time I see you," she said.

"Ditto," Jenna smiled. She'd come over to help us taste test our latest batch of elderberry wine, poor girl had no idea what she had let herself in for.

"Try this, Thelma" Biddy said passing me a full glass.

"Thelma?" Jenna said questioningly.

"You started it," Biddy said pointing a finger at Jenna. "Saying we were a geriatric Thelma and Louise, so we went to watch the film and sometimes now we call each other by those names."

"So how did you decide you were Thelma, Mum?" Jenna asked smiling.

"I am more staid and sensible, apparently," I answered. "I have pointed out that I don't drive and should therefore be Louise, but no, Madame Butterfly here wanted to be her, so I got stuck with Thelma."

"You can't be Louise, she is more colourful and feisty than Thelma," Biddy said. "Besides, the fact that you don't drive means we won't be going over a cliff any time soon. Now, why is your brother a stubborn twat?" she asked Jenna.

"He just won't consider changing his mind about talking to Mum," Jenna said. "I've spoken to him, so has Daisy, but he won't budge. For goodness sake, he's a grown man, he was a grown man when you left, he should have moved out before. But he was such a spoilt brat he expected everything on a plate. It was the best thing you could have done for Michael, moving out forced him to grow up. He'll come round, Mum, he will. You can't make this decision be about him. He's

110

stubborn, spoilt and selfish but he's got a good heart. He will come round one day, you have to believe that."

"I want to, I truly want to," I said. "But I'm afraid he never will and I'll miss his wedding and he'll have children one day and I won't be a part of their lives. I couldn't live with that Jenna, I really couldn't."

"Actually, you leaving was the best thing you could have done for me, too." Jenna looked at me sheepishly. "The more time I spend with you the more I understand how miserable you must have been. And I was spoilt too. I was nineteen when you left, I hadn't washed a dish, cooked a meal or even made a bed in my life. Worst of all, I didn't expect to. Now I'm training to be a chef and I'm perfectly capable of looking after myself. And you are so different from the dreary person I remember. I look at you now, and I marvel at the change in you. I just wish you hadn't had to leave for me to know this."

"Oh, Jenna," I said and hugged her tightly, tears running down both our cheeks. It was so wonderful to hear. "It means so much to me to hear you say that." Biddy was crying too and came to hug us both. That's how Caitlin found us when she walked in, the three of us huddled in a heap sobbing.

"What the hell is going on here?" she asked. We all turned, laughed, told her it was happy tears.

"Well, OK, I was just stopping by on my way to Angie's but now I see you have a new batch of wine I might stay a while," Caitlin said smiling. Biddy was thrilled, we settled down to a nice girly night with lots of very strong elderberry wine. "Have you tried their wine before?" Caitlin asked Jenna. "No! Oh, my gosh, you are in for an experience. Have you got drunk with these two before?" Jenna said no again, smiling. "Oh, God help you!" Caitlin said.

Chapter Nine

D-Day had arrived. I had set a deadline to make my decision and that day was today. I had arranged to go to the house to meet George at 11 a.m. Jenna was out with friends all day, I knew she was keeping out of the way. Up until that very morning I didn't know what I would do. Biddy told me to follow my heart, Caitlin said do what feels right, and Jenna said, again, don't make this decision about Michael. But how could I not? I still felt guilty over leaving George. He hadn't been a bad husband and I had never spoken up to tell him how I felt. He was willing to make an effort and be different. I know that for George the compromises he had offered me were really hard for him to do, and I appreciated that. I had loved him once, trouble was I don't think I was ever in love with him. When I see people who are in love I know it was never like that for us. I've never felt that. It was probably why I married so late in life, well, late for those days anyway. I never met anyone who swept me off my feet, no one I wanted to kiss and touch, let alone kiss and touch me. But George and I had clicked, we got on well from the start. He was sensible, reliable, he had a good job, and I knew he would be a good provider and father. So, for a woman of a certain age, I suppose I was running out of options. My parents had passed away when I was a teenager and I'm an only child. I wanted a family, I had never doubted that, and I suppose George was my best way of getting one. Not the right reason to marry I know, but I had been good, loyal and faithful. I had cooked, cleaned and waited on him hand and foot. I had sex with him every Friday night and never nagged. I turned myself into someone I wasn't just to have a family, I suppose. I don't regret it, I wouldn't have Michael and Jenna if I hadn't married him. But it wasn't fair on him, he thought he was marrying one person only to find out many years later that I was someone else entirely.

When I got to the house I knocked the door. I still had my old key but it just seemed wrong to use it. He answered and smiled. "You don't need to knock Frances," he said. "This is your home." We went inside and I made tea. He was first to break the silence. "I understand you weren't happy before," he said, "but it will be different now I promise. Soon we'll all be back together, but this time we'll be a happy family. Wouldn't that be nice?" I nodded at him with tears in my eyes.

"Yes, that would be nice," I said.

"You don't need to go back to your friend's house," he said. "You have everything you need right here. If there's anything you want I can fetch it, or Jenna could. Later on, I'll phone Michael to confirm that he and Daisy are coming to dinner tonight. I have made him promise to be here. It will be a new start, put the past behind us, never to be spoken of again. You know Michael and Daisy are planning to get married in the autumn? You'll have to have a new hat and outfit, not from those cheap shops, something really nice. It'll give us something to look forward to, won't it?" he asked. I nodded again. "Good," he said. "That's settled then. Now Jenna usually cooks but she's gone for the day.

You could rustle something up, couldn't you?" I tried to smile but failed miserably.

"Yes, I could," I said.

I got up and walked toward the kitchen. Then I stopped and turned around. "But I won't" I said.

"Won't what?" George said absently. He had already turned the television on and was looking for the horse racing.

"I could cook, but I won't," I said.

"Why ever not?" George asked in disbelief. "You know I can't. We can't have Michael and Daisy over for dinner if there's no dinner!" I was crying as I walked up to him.

"I'm sorry," I said and I handed him my wedding ring before leaving the house for the last time.

Biddy was thrilled, so was Caitlin, even Jenna said I had made the right decision. I know I had, I just have to have faith that one day Michael will find it in his heart to let me back into his life.

I needn't have worried about George. Once he knew I was never coming back he asked his cleaner to marry him and divorce papers landed on my doorstep weeks later. I signed them, of course, my solicitor said I was entitled to half the value of the house, the mortgage had long since been paid. I didn't want anything but Biddy said why should the cleaning lady have it, Jenna said I had worked for it, so in the end I agreed and walked away with £75,000. Me and Biddy are now looking forward to the Vegas trip, and we've already booked flying lessons, too. Jenna moved in with us, we turned the conservatory into a bedroom and I'm closer to her than I've ever been. I know I owe it all to the love of my life – my dear, dear friend Biddy. "Hey, Thelma," she shouted, "put the kettle on."

"Bog off, Louise, and do it yourself!" I shouted back. We both laughed until we cried. And then I put the kettle on. Well, some things never change.

Book Three – Caitlin

Day One

Being naked in public is not such a big deal. To think I haven't slept in four weeks worrying over this. Of course, Jack hasn't slept much either – but that was excitement, not fear. Can't think what my greatest fear was, although the thing I worried about most was my less than perfect body. I'm not terrible with clothes on, but it's a completely different picture when they're off. Everything goes south and my podgy stomach flops down like a lump of goo. The rest of me's not so bad for someone who's the wrong side of thirty. Jack says I have great legs, he loves my long red wavy hair and he says I've got a very pretty face with the biggest, darkest, deepest blue eyes.

Anyway, diary, I digress. This is day one of our first ever naturist holiday. The suggestion, of course, came at the end of a drunken night out. As they do. Jack said he'd like our lives to have more excitement, try new things before we settled down into middle age. I was so thrilled he'd actually mentioned settling down with me after ten years of waiting for him to pop the question that I just agreed. The following day he was in the travel agents and booked us on a plane to a naturist resort in the Canaries.

I remember the following morning thinking, 'Bloody hell, what have I signed up for?' Second thought was, 'Ah, my yukky body – it'll be on public view.' Over the last four weeks, those thoughts have been at the forefront of my mind. At times, I wondered what our friends would think if they knew what we were planning. I know Aunt Biddy would be tickled pink, not sure that Frances would approve though.

I have to remember we're naturists – not nudists. Apparently, they don't like to be called that. Been reading up on the subject since we booked. It's all about being at one with nature, shedding your inhibitions.

My stomach was churning in the car all the way from the airport, I just wanted to go home. It's the first holiday ever I haven't looked forward to. I mean, for goodness sake, it's March, it's raining again at home, we're jetting off to the sunshine for two weeks and all I've been doing is whingeing and worrying. Last weekend, I threw a right wobbly. Made Jack promise we'd find a normal hotel if I couldn't go through with it. Of course, he did promise, and, of course, he didn't mean it for one second.

When we entered the complex there was a sign saying nudists only past this point. It was like Colditz. Big locked gates, high fencing with barbed wire on top. Nobody's going to sneak a peek at these guests. Passing the sign I thought' "Caitlin, this is it. You've entered the nudist zone there's no going back.' My stomach was in bits.

Anyway, the wines on the plane must have helped because when it finally came down to it I wasn't as nervous as I thought I'd be. We stood in our chalet, naked apart from sandals and sunglasses. I took a huge deep breath to suck my tummy in and off we went. We'd already read the guide book left discreetly on the coffee table with the welcome basket of fruit. Naturists must take towels with them wherever they go and sit on them when at the poolside bar. Nudity at the bar is optional, at the poolside it is compulsory.

Anyway, out we walked. I actually went first, Jack close behind me. Holding my towel over one arm, my bag on the other. Lost my nerve slightly as we approached, thank goodness our chalet was close to the bar and patio area, I couldn't wait to sit down. Plonked myself in the first available chair and told Jack to order me a large pint of lager. Dutch courage and all that. He strolled to the bar as if he'd always done it, I was quite impressed. Looked around after a while, about a dozen couples lying on sunbeds.

They just look like ordinary people. I don't know what I expected, maybe model girl types with perfect figures, and hunky men. But they're just ordinary, less than perfect, just like me. Mostly middle-aged, some older people, few in their thirties like us and two couples who look younger. It's a bit hard to tell without actually staring. One couple was lying right next to the poolside, I could study them without being too obvious. They were married, she was wearing a wedding ring glistening gold in the sun and looked much younger than him. She had a nice figure, slim with everything in the right place. Her husband must be in his fifties. He has greying hair and a big beer belly, he looks friendly. He catches me looking and waves. Damn. Must be more discreet.

There's another couple in the corner we can see quite clearly. They look very small, I think I will call them Mr and Mrs Small. She looks like a dormouse. Mr Small is very thin, puny body, long shoulder length, sandy hair. Weirdly though, his manhood is huge, looks all out of proportion with the rest of him.

Next to the Smalls are Little and Large. Mr Little is in his forties, balding, even skinnier than Mr Small and probably not much taller. Unlike Mr Small, he has no redeeming features. Miss Large has the most enormous boobs which you just can't help looking at, and hips which could spread across two sunbeds. She's got curly ginger hair and pale white skin which is turning a very sore looking shade of pink in places. She is sitting up reading a book, cross legged. I admired her confidence.

Squinting over to the far corner of the pool, I see a short red-haired woman who is obviously tearing a strip off the big blonde bloke lying next to her. Next to them are another couple just gathering their towels up. Mr and Mrs Average. That just about sums them up actually. Average everything, height, weight and age. On the far side of the pool are Mr and Mrs Haughty. They are the kind of people who don't even have to move or open their mouths for you to know they think they're a cut above. They're just standing up to go, both very tall, she must be about 5'10" and he's at least 6'2". Both dark haired, reasonably slim bodies in pretty good shape, the perfect couple. They walk off hand in hand.

It suddenly hit me that my biggest fear about this holiday was that Jack's getting bored with me. Maybe he thought going to a nudist camp, sorry, naturist resort, would add some spice to our life. I admit I'm bored with him sometimes, and sometimes he gets on my nerves, and he moans a lot, and he goes on about budgeting and he keeps everything in neat files, but God, I don't want a life without him. Problem is I've been a bit moody the last few months. I want Jack to commit to a future with me, but he won't.

This is getting depressing. Jack's calling, we're going out tonight to the nearest town. A boozy night out, that's exactly what I need in this maudlin mood. Just wish I could switch my brain off and enjoy myself. Anyway, glad I brought some clothes. Can't go on a pub crawl in the nude.

Day Two

Did I say Jack wasn't romantic or loving? Last night was amazing. The kissing, the attention, the romance, the sweet nothings. When was the last time he said I was the best thing that had ever happened to him? If this is what getting naked in public does to him, I'm all for it.

Just got back from breakfast. Or no breakfast, I should say. What a disaster. Turned up in our sandals and sunglasses, towels draped appropriately over arms and everyone else was dressed! Damn it and blast it, why didn't the guide book say everyone dressed for breakfast? Felt like a prize idiot. Sat on nearest chair again and wanted to curl up and die.

Jack was really brave. Went up to the bar to collect his orange juice, in front of all these people who suddenly looked like something out of Debenham's shop window. Or Dolce and Gabbana, if you include Mr and Mrs Haughty. I just muttered I wasn't hungry and tried to sink into my towel. Bless him, Jack sensed my discomfort and sank his orange juice in one. We did a quick march back to the chalet. Hope they didn't hear my screams. Oh, well, lesson learned. Naturists dress for breakfast. Had some tea and biscuits, grabbed towels and headed off for first shift on sunbeds.

Long walk around the pool. The only free sunbeds without towels on them are next to the loud red-haired woman with the blonde bloke. Just wanted to lie down and be inconspicuous. Jack looks good. He's got a fair body, bit of a gut but nothing awful. Lovely bum, rugby player's legs, nice shoulders, looks good naked, unlike me.

Mr and Mrs Small are talking about going down the beach after lunch. Apparently, there's a nudist beach just down the road. Quite famous it would seem. Mr and Mrs Haughty walk in, saw them go out earlier, obviously been shopping judging by the number of bags he is carrying. She just carries her Chanel handbag. There's something about her I instantly dislike, don't know why, it's not just the fact that her figure's better than mine. Mr and Mrs Average arrive, smile and wave at everyone. They are obviously the couple who are friends with everyone. They seem to know the staff and all the people around the pool.

Checked out Mr and Mrs Haughty as they walked towards their chalet – they're wearing designer sunglasses and her sandals are definitely Prada. Don't even start me on the jewellery – the chain around his neck is worth more than the entire contents of my giant suitcase. I can see one ring on her finger which you could use to remortgage your house, never mind the earrings, chain, bracelet, and so on and so on. Yes, I'm jealous, but mostly of the wedding ring.

Jack is being polite and wants to mix with the natives. Mr Average says they always have drinks at the bar in the evening and would we like to join them? I am thinking I would rather go die in boiling oil and Jack is saying we would be delighted. Oh, bliss and joy. We were meant to have a romantic holiday, not play happy campers.

Red-haired woman is mad and Irish. She hasn't stopped nagging the big blonde bloke. 'Fetch me water, rub cream on me, test the temperature of the pool, I'd like a sandwich' and on and on and on. Beefy blonde is up and down off his sunbed like an umbrella back home. Every time he moves he gets himself a pint at the bar. Don't blame him if you have to listen to that all day. Mad Irish woman is now complaining the sun is too hot. Don't know what she expects Beefy to do about that. He gets up again and stretches. Not a bad body apart from the beer belly and thighs are a bit too chunky. Beefy strolls to the bar, downs another quick pint then fetches Mad Irish woman a parasol. That should shut her up for all of five minutes if we're lucky.

The Haughtys take up their positions on the sunbeds the other side of us. He winks at me and says good morning. She gives a half smile but I can tell it doesn't reach her eyes even through the designer glasses.

Big guy 'Call me Mal' is standing up and parading around the pool stopping to talk to everyone on the way. He is definitely preening, goodness knows why, he's not in particularly good shape. He reaches us and he leers at me. I swear it was leering. Ugh!

Mr and Mrs Average take up position at the bar stools. In the sunshine but close to the shade, talking to the staff, who are all fully dressed. They're really nice, very polite, never avert their eyes from your face. The gardener boy is so sweet, he goes around face forward the whole time. Wonder what they think of us?

Got very hot, sweat running everywhere, little rivers going down my boobs. Decided to be brave and take a dip in the pool. Haven't walked around naked without my towel before. Took a deep breath, stomach in, seemed like miles to the pool ladder. Lowered myself in, it was bloody freezing! How the hell can water be so cold when the temperature is like thirty degrees outside? Did a quick length and got out as soon as I could. No wonder the pool is usually empty.

Went for an afternoon snack at the bar. Sat there naked with my juice and toastie, felt good actually. Could get used to this. Very civilised. Think this naturist thing is growing on me. Must admit it feels very liberating.

Back at the sunbeds, Mr Haughty definitely gave me another look and a wink. He's OK actually, something about him I like. Did a six hour shift by the pool. Enough. There's only so much sun and Mad Irish Woman rants you can take. Beefy was pissed by the end of the afternoon, Mad Irish was just pissed off. Permanently. Does nothing please that woman?

Mr and Mrs Average come to check on our evening drinks date before heading back to their chalet. Apparently, most people have dinner and drinks at the bar every evening. No one usually ventures outside. How weird.

We took tea on the terrace at the chalet, naked, of course. Two new men are in the chalet down the path from us. The fair guy is obviously the boss, he leads the way and barks things back at the dark one. Don't know what he said, he was speaking German. The dark guy didn't say a word. Mad Irish and Beefy have gone inside the chalet, hope they keep the windows shut, I've heard enough from that woman today. Mr and Mrs Average are also on their terrace, drinking a bottle of wine. Their eyes are everywhere, they know exactly who's who and what's what.

Complex is lovely. Chalets dotted around the pool and bar area. From our terrace we can still see what's going on. Next door comes out onto their terrace. Turns out our neighbours are Little and Large. He's got a paper, she's got her book, every once in a while they have a quiet conversation, they seem so content with each other.

Day Three

Dinner and drinks was nice. There's a camaraderie among naturists, a common bond. Us free spirits against the uptight clothed people. Everyone sits together and talk about such normal stuff. Mr Average is a second-hand car dealer, Mrs Average a secretary. They live in the heart of middle England and have no children. They go on about four holidays a year and talked about this amazing naturist place in Mexico. Everyone joins in with their stories. Yes, they are all practiced naturists, we are the only new recruits. Wonder if they know?

Call me Mal and Miss Brazilian (no prizes for guessing why I call her that) are a couple. They sat on the table with us and the Averages. The Haughtys sat at their own table nearby but he joined in the conversation occasionally, she spoke only when spoken to. Mad Irish and Beefy turned up at the end of the evening.

Call me Mal was absolutely coming on to me. Every time Jack went to the toilet or the bar, he made a point of speaking to me. Jack has stopped paying me attention, he is engrossed in being sociable and getting to know everyone else. Getting a bit pissed off at him actually. Mr Haughty brushed my shoulder lightly as he passed. Wondered if it was deliberate.

Discovered over sausage and eggs this morning that Jack has booked us on a nudist cruise this weekend. Apparently 'the gang' are going. Now, there's public nudity and then there's really public nudity. Would have been nice to have been asked.

Mr Haughty rubbed my shoulder again this morning on his way to the poolside. Must be deliberate surely? Find myself sneaking a look at him frequently.

We had an incident after breakfast this morning – the peace and serenity of the poolside was shattered by a row over music. The fair German guy, who we will call Mr Music Man from now on, has complained about the radio blasting out songs in the bar and patio area. He says we are at one with nature and do not want artificial noise being piped into our space. Jack says he'd like to stick something artificial up his ass. Mal says he was enjoying the music actually. Complex manager Maria has to come out of the office to calm everything down. Radio is turned down slightly as a compromise. Not good enough for Mr Music Man – he marches off pouting, barking at the dark guy to follow.

Half an hour later, Mr Music Man struts back out and nicks a sunbed to take back to his chalet. The cheek! Everyone tuts, of course. Mrs Average tells tales. Off goes Maria to give him a row and tell him sunbeds must not be taken from the pool area. Everyone is pleased, we have all decided Mr Music Man is the enemy.

Mr and Mrs Haughty settle down next to us again, he positions himself on the sunbed next to mine and winks again. Shit, I felt my heart aflutter. Little and Large go to their usual spot, she opens her book, sitting up cross legged again. It occurs to me that naturists are very comfortable with their bodies. Must be nice. I'm getting more and more relaxed, but no way have I forgotten about my podgy tummy and less than perfect figure.

Delighted to see that Mrs Haughty has a little cellulite around her bum and her thighs. Surprised she hasn't had plastic surgery or something. Someone else who definitely needs surgery is Mrs Two Bums. Only noticed her today. First time in my life I've ever seen anyone with two bums. It's not that big, but she's got the shape of an ass with curvy lines halfway down her bum, then a bigger shape further down where it should be. One of the weirdest things I've ever seen in my life! Poor thing really should get it sorted. She should get it done on the National Health – it's a disfigurement.

Jack whispers to me there's a guy a few sunbeds down with a piercing. He's wincing as he tells me, like he's feeling the pain. I try to sneak a look without being obvious but can't see properly. Will watch out for him moving about. Take another dip in the freezing pool, it's the only way to cool off, so bloody hot here. Jack refuses to join me again, he could at least keep me company on the walk to the ladder. Water's a little bit warmer today. Did three laps, might help slim the belly and offset the effects of too much food and wine.

Jack very kindly points out, after I come out of the pool, that I should have gone under the shower first. Apparently, everyone else does and there's a sign on the wall saying you should. Well, thanks for that, Jack, made a plonker of myself again.

The menus have been handed out for dinner tonight. Jack had promised me a steak and a walk to the nearest town. Suddenly he wants coq au vin. I bet he does. I pout, he sweet talks me. About time too, I'm starting to feel neglected.

Agree to have dinner in the complex if we can go for a walk afterwards. Go for our afternoon juice and toastie.

Mad Irish and Beefy are there with two large pints of lager in front of them. She is yak, yak, yak, he's smiling and nodding. Turns out she's very pleasant when you get past the constant demands. Had a lovely chat with them. She's from Kerry, he met her while he was working over there building a new road (it's what he does) and she moved back to England with him when the job was over. That was five years ago. They're thinking about getting married at a naturist resort in Mexico. Apparently you can do that, with a nude vicar and all. Stood on the beach with nude witnesses and just a garland in your hair. Well, would save all the hassle over the wedding dress and all that. Don't quite know who you could show the pictures to though – could hardly send one in to the local paper. Don't think a nude wedding would do for me. I've waited so long I want the dress, the church, the limo and all the trimmings. Beginning to think it'll never happen, feel quite envious of Mad Irish. Jack changes the subject. Typical.

Back on the beds, Mr Haughty positions himself to look directly at me. There is no doubt it's intentional. Mrs Haughty dozes off with her earphones in listening to music from the top-of-the-range radio she's got. He starts a conversation with me about the pool temperature. Says he'll join me the next time I'm brave enough to take a dip. Sounds perfectly innocent but feels almost like a date. Wonder how long I can leave it before going for a swim again? Don't want him to think I'm keen, or up for it or anything like that. But don't want him to think I'm unfriendly either. Can't figure out why he's having this effect on me, I'm never like this. Ten years with Jack and I've never seriously considered cheating on him. Not that I'm doing that now, it's just a swim. Besides Jack is busy getting to know a Belgian couple.

Wait an hour, then get up to take a dip. Dutifully, go under the shower. Bloody hell, it's colder than the pool! Won't be doing that again in a hurry, rules or no rules. Mr Haughty casually gets up and follows me after an appropriate couple of minutes has passed. He must have been lying there watching and waiting. Mrs H still has her eyes shut and earphones in.

Swim to the shallow end where I am quickly joined by Mr H. Am very aware of the nipples standing to attention. He talks to me about the weather and the complex, stuff like that. His eyes move from my face to my chest and back again. First time I've been chatted up by a man while I'm naked. Bit like the cart going before the horse really. Got out of the pool, with Mr H climbing up the ladder behind me, his face an inch from my bum. God, hope it didn't wobble like a big pink jelly.

Am very careful to apply factor twenty to the parts of my body which have not been exposed in my thirty-three years. Apart from going topless for half an hour in the South of France once, my tits and bits have never seen sunshine. Last thing I want to do is burn and peel.

Get twenty questions from Jack about Mr H. Could he actually be jealous? He's never shown signs of that before. I quite like it. Got bored after a while. Jack offers to go buy me a magazine, I tell him I'll go too for a walk. Starting to get a bit stir crazy, haven't been outside the walls for so long.

We had a lovely walk, hand in hand, don't usually do that. He was sweet and nice and everything, whatever the reason (and I don't want to think about that) this holiday is bringing out the best in him. Actually felt weird wearing clothes. Stopped for a milkshake, bought some trinkets in a souvenir shop, normal holiday stuff.

Mr H must have missed me, he was looking out for us coming back and smiled as soon as he saw us. Clothes off, back on sunbeds, read magazine while still discreetly staring at what's going on over top of sunglasses. Mr Piercing got up to go in pool and walked right in front of us. My God, that must have hurt! He's got a huge bar, but not much to hook it onto, I'm surprised he wants to draw attention to it.

Back at the chalet we shower and shave, him his face, me under my arms. Quick it grows out here, must be the sweat and sunshine. Make mental note – next time wax bits, legs <u>and</u> underarms.

Oh, my God – disaster! Jack's bum and bits are bright red, he looks like he's wearing a pair of Speedos. My bum is lily white. The rest of us is turning a lovely shade of brown. It is so obvious we are new to this and our naked bodies have never seen the sun before. Everyone must have noticed! I was so careful not to burn I used too high a factor on my bum. But the rest of me is OK. The boobs are browning nicely as is the lower half of my belly. Jack was so keen to tan he didn't use cream at all on his nether regions. He's paying for it now – the skin looks like raw meat.

Decide we will give the pool a miss tomorrow and go to the beach. Try to repair some of the damage. I will wear factor five on my bum and the usual ten on the rest of me to help it catch up. Jack will factor twenty his bits to give them a chance to cool down. If all else fails, we will visit supermarket and get fake tan.

Day Four

Headed for the beach after breakfast. There was no missing the nudist area, huge signs pointing to it wherever you looked. Hell of a walk though, thought we were never going to get there.

And what a disappointment when we did. The nudist zone is right in the middle of two normal beaches and people just walk up and down right through it. Bit of a tourist attraction, definitely. Don't tell me all these people are just out for a stroll, it's like Oxford Street at Christmas.

One woman, who must be in her fifties with a far from perfect figure is really brave. She walks through the hordes of marching people in her birthday suit to take a dip in the sea, then comes out and goes through them all again. It is so busy they have to step aside to let her through the crowds.

This might have been a bad idea. While I am getting quite used to the naked bit while surrounded by other like-minded people, this is like being on display. Bit like the meat in the butcher's shop. Takes a while but we finally find somewhere behind the main body of sunbeds which is sheltered from the passing hordes. Strip off, first thing I notice is strap marks from the bikini top I wore to walk along the beach. Great, two parts of me have to catch up with the rest now.

There are people playing naked volleyball just down the beach. Now there's a sight. Jack says he'd go check it out.

Nude people are all over the place, apart from the beach and the volleyball, in the sea, they are walking all over the dunes. Stark naked just strolling through the sand dunes. Amazing. A row is breaking out by the camels. A woman wants a camel ride but is refusing to put her bathing suit on. The camel guy won't let her ride in the nude. Is he serious? Does he think the camel's going to catch something off her naked bum? The animals are full of fleas, you can smell them from way down the beach, it's far more likely she'd catch something from them. Besides which, I'm sure she's got her towel, us naturists never travel anywhere without them. Camel guy sticks to his guns, naked woman says she'll take him to the European Court of Human Rights. He has obviously never heard of it and doesn't give a shit anyway. She goes off in a huff, towel over her arm.

Entertainment over, I try to relax but when people say sand goes everywhere, they really mean it goes everywhere. Grains in my mouth, in my ears, up my bum. Not a particularly comfortable feeling. And what are you meant to do about it? Could hardly scratch away in front of hundreds of people. And most certainly would not be venturing down to the sea to wash it out. Tried to wriggle and shiggle on the towel, but of course that was full of sand too, just made it worse. This was not a good idea. Jack agrees. He says stuff it, let's go to the pub. Best thing I've heard all day.

Four pints of Strongbow later and I really don't care about my white bum. Jack's Speedos become funnier and funnier with each pint, he is not amused.

We discuss the various shapes and sizes at the complex and agree I have the best female figure and he has the best male. Four pints of 'Bow and all is well with the world. Stagger back to the complex, use the double keys to get in through the giant gates. Walk past the people at the poolside.

Mr Music Man is back, he must have stopped sulking. All the usuals are there. Mr and Mrs Average are in position at the bar, she will fill me in later on anything we've missed.

We decide we like being naked and strip off to join them all. However, the taste for more alcohol is strong, we adjourn to the bar area where much more is consumed. It is during this conversation we agree to come back again in a few months' time. We are officially naturists now. Of course, next time we will make sure the red and white bits match the brown.

Mrs Average says Mr Music Man and partner are joining us on the cruise. Great. Maybe someone will push him overboard.

Tomorrow is the welcome barbecue, Maria is handing out leaflets. For fifteen euros per person we get food, punch and party games. Oh, joy. Happy campers that we are, Jack buys two tickets. It is, of course, a naked barbecue. Now there's something to write home about, if there was anyone apart from Aunt Biddy I would want to tell.

Course the good thing is you don't have to worry about what to wear although I find myself thinking the silver diamond-encrusted cross with matching earrings and bracelet would look nice. And should I wear my hair up or down? Naturally, the face will be fully made-up and there will be varnish on the hand and toe nails. The silver sandals will match the jewellery, nothing else for them to co-ordinate with. Weird how things like that still matter when you're naked. Instead of agonising over the outfit, you worry more about jewellery, make-up and stuff. If Jack thought no clothes would mean I'd get ready quicker, he's going to be in for a shock.

Getting a bit nervous about this boat trip. Wonder what it's all about? It's a private charter trip, so we won't be with any strangers. Maybe it just goes way out to sea and no one gets a look at you. Don't like the idea of being on public view. We'll see. Jack has paid now and it wasn't cheap so we're going.

Bloody hell, who'd have thought it? Naked barbecues, boat trips and beaches? My friends would never believe me. Or maybe they would. Considered telling Angie and Maggie, I had no secrets from them.

We stagger back to our chalet around six, and pass out in bed for two hours. Afternoon drinking in hot sunshine really takes it out of you. When we wake up the sun is not so strong, it is lovely sitting on the terrace with an orange juice, watching the world go by. Almost forget sometimes that I spend most of my time naked. The belly looks much better with a tan. Stuff the white bum, the stomach is much improved.

Mr and Mrs Haughty are all dressed up. They're going out to some posh restaurant for dinner. He stops to tell us they will be back later – why would I care? Jack laughs, he knows Mr H is coming on to me, he thinks it's funny. I am offended.

After getting bored with sulking, I ask Jack if we can go shopping, he is pleased I am talking to him again so agrees. Found a gorgeous Dolce and Gabbana watch in the jewellers. All the jewellers have designer goods but none have got prices in the windows. You ask how much and they take you inside and give you a chair. Talk about pressure. Discovered you can haggle, this is not like the shops back home. Walk away and they reduce the price. Got the D&G watch knocked down from one hundred and fifty euros to ninety-five, what a bargain! Pay by credit card and they ask which hotel I'm staying in, apparently this is standard procedure for the bank. Felt like a right idiot giving them the name of the complex. Saw the eyes widening and the look on the salesman's face – he knew straight away it was a nudist camp. Actually looked me up and down as if he was trying to guess what I'd look like with my kit off. Cheek!

Had a lovely Chinese meal with a bottle of wine, bought some perfume, really cheap. Headed back to the complex with my packages. My new sandals are giving me blisters. Jack hails a taxi. Same look on the driver's face as the salesman's when he tells him where to go. Oh, who cares, these people don't know us and will never see us again.

Put packages away and join the others by the bar, Jack has gone straight there and has taken his place in the middle of them. Mr H manages to manoeuvre himself into a position close enough to play footsie with me again. Once is an accident, three times is not. I am mad at Jack who has abandoned me so let him. Tell myself it's harmless.

Had quite a nice evening actually. These people are so friendly. We have never been on holiday before and actually made friends with people there. We don't usually like to mix at all, what is it about being naked that makes you act like a totally different person?

Somehow, you want to be nicer and friendlier and calmer.

Finish off a bottle of wine back at the chalet, Jack says really sweet things, he knows he was wrong to abandon me. I pout for as long as I can but give in after he repeats that he loves me and I am the most beautiful woman in the world.

Day Five

Mad Irish has the period from hell. Beefy was spotted en route to the supermarket to stock up on port, brandy, tampons and paracetamols. He was also asking where he could get a hot water bottle from. Is he for real? We're in the bloody Canaries for goodness sake! They've probably never even heard of them. Anyway, we won't be seeing much of Mad Irish over the next few days, bit more peace at the poolside.

The Smalls were out on the sunbeds early. She's reading Woman's Own and he's got the Daily Mirror. Mr and Mrs Haughty stroll out of their chalet hand in hand and occupy the same sunbeds. Funny how everyone has their spot, and returns to the same place day after day. Jack and I have decided we would like Mr and Mrs Average's positions in the corner where you have a great view of everything going on. They're going home on Monday so we will have to be out early to get them before anyone else does. Wonder if Mr H will mind me moving away from him? Bet he does.

It's really, really hot today. There is sweat running off me everywhere, I can feel rivers running down my back, between my boobs and down my legs. Difficult to describe the feeling of being hot, sweaty and naked in the fresh air. Surrounded by lots of other hot, sweaty naked people. Jack never gets as hot as me. He hasn't even ventured into the pool yet. Think I'll be taking a few dips today.

Hear shouting coming from Mad Irish and Beefy's chalet. Oh, dear, he got something wrong obviously. Must be awkward when you have a period at a nudist camp. I mean, what would you do? Nudity is compulsory at the poolside and you'd stand out like a sore thumb anyway if you wore bikini bottoms. You'd look like a right plonker if anyone spotted the little tampon string dangling. Thank goodness mine isn't due while we're here. Poor Mad Irish. And poor Beefy. Something tells me he is really going to suffer over the next few days.

Mrs Two Bums is leaning over talking to an elderly couple. No matter which way she sits or stands, her bum never looks better. She doesn't seem to care. Mr Two Bums (he hasn't got two bums too, he's just her husband and there's nothing special about him to give him his own name) lies around the pool all day never talking to anyone. Mrs Two Bums on the other hand is very sociable. She flits around yakking to anyone with their eyes open. Must be one of those relationships where he never talks to her and she's desperate for some conversation. Mind you, with two bums like that, you'd think she'd lie on it all day instead of showing it off in public. Poor Mrs Two Bums.

Occurs to me I am feeling very soft and sorry for everyone today. Even Mrs Haughty doesn't seem so bad. My theory is that Mr H is unfaithful and she puts up with it for the lifestyle and appearances and all that. She's probably very sad. Poor Mrs H.

Don't feel sorry for Call me Mal at all. He's always bright, breezy and bouncy. Must admit I think he's a perv but he's got a really friendly personality. His companion, Miss Brazilian, is very upper class, ever so. Unlike Mrs H, Miss B was born to it. You can just tell.

Mr Music Man and his dark companion are on the other side of the pool as far away from the radio as they can get. He was naked for breakfast again, the dark companion turned up in a vest and nothing else. That is so strange. You either dress or you don't. What's the point of putting a vest on when all your dangles are hanging out over the cornflakes?

Go for my morning dip, closely followed by Mr H who chats me up again in the shallow end. He actually touches toes with me this time, playing footsie in the water. I didn't move away. Don't know why. Stupid, mad and dangerous but there's something exciting about it all.

Everyone's talking about the barbecue. The people who were here last week said they had a fantastic time. Lots of free flowing booze and games. What the hell games are they? As long as it's not musical girlfriends or pass the partner I don't care. Barbecue starts at four, I am planning to get ready at 2.30 p.m. Jack says I'm mad and doesn't understand why it will take an hour and a half to get ready for a nude barbecue. Men, they know nothing.

Mr H continues to wink and stare at every opportunity. Jack has noticed but still thinks it's funny. I am not amused. Why doesn't he give a damn? He won't commit to me, he's not jealous of Mr H or anyone else. Doesn't care that Call me Mal is definitely leching after me. He takes me for granted, that's what it is. Men have always found me attractive but since Jack I haven't been interested. Can't think why I'm getting my knickers (hypothetically speaking, of course) in a twist over Mr H.

Mad Irish appears on the terrace wearing a huge pair of granny knickers. Beefy is attentively at her side bringing a hot toddy for the invalid. She looks like shit, actually. Maybe she really is having the period from hell.

Mr Piercing is walking towards us, the big gold bar gleaming. He has spotted someone with binoculars on the tower up the hill. We all look. It's true – there is someone spying on us. He's at the information building which looks out across the whole area. It's a good vantage point to get a view for miles around. Obviously the complex owners didn't think of that when they were safeguarding the privacy of their guests. We all agree it's disgusting, Mr Piercing says he's got a good mind to go up there and tear him off a strip. Jack and me decide to go up there for a walk some time to suss out exactly how much you can see.

Mr H joins us all at the bar and manages to rub my back with his hand. Mrs H is cooking nicely on the sunbed, earphones in, eyes shut as usual. The Smalls scuttle off to their chalet. Little and Large come out. She says they had a lazy morning watching television. She doesn't want to be in the sun too long today – her shoulders and boobs are really sore. They look sore. We all give tips on the best creams to use.

Had a lovely Caesar salad for lunch, the food here is really good and the staff are so attentive. Far better service than any other holiday complex we've been too. They really want to please you. Hunky waiter could please me any time. Stop it Caitlin! What is wrong with you?

Head off for my 2.30 p.m. shower. Jack stays on the sunbed. Mrs Two Bums has spotted him alone and makes a beeline. That'll teach him.

Took great care with my hair and make-up. Used straighteners to tame the curls, looks really good if I say so myself. Comes down to my waist when it's straight. Decide on gold jewellery, shows off the tan better. Wear my new sandals from Next, not as good as Mrs H's Pradas I know, but I think they look lovely. Rub gold shimmer over my skin, hope I don't get too sweaty or it'll all slide off. First time I've dressed my bum up to go out. Jack finally gets back to the chalet with twenty minutes to spare before the barbecue. He is ready in ten. Men.

Killer punch at the barbecue. Being naked and pissed in public, now that's a new feeling. Just about everyone turned out, except Mr Music Man and dark companion of course.

Mr Haughty can't take his eyes off me. Think Mrs H has noticed, feel a bit uncomfortable. Jack is talking to Mr Average and Mr Little about football, yet again. For goodness sake, even at a naked barbecue men still gather in packs to talk sports. Food and punch is plentiful, first couple of hours fly by.

And then the games begin. I haven't laughed so much in ages! Rules were that there were five games and everyone had to take part in at least one. First there was naked table tennis. Jack opted for that one, he thinks he's a bit of a dab hand at it because he used to play for the school once. Call me Mal was the opposition, so Jack won fairly easily and preened for ages after. Weird watching them play in the nude, ended up watching the wrong kind of ball most of the time. Second game was pass the balloon. That looked a bit obscene actually, glad I didn't choose to take part in that. Call me Mal took part yet again with Miss Brazilian, Little and Large, but lost to a Dutch foursome who we have concluded are definitely a foursome, and not two twosomes.

Next game was, predictably, musical chairs. I figured there'd be minimal physical contact so opted to play that one. A bunch of people thought the same thing, unfortunately, and it was a pretty small space. Got used to bumping my naked flesh into people after the first few rounds. Got to the last three and I swear I was pushed by Miss Large off the chair. Well, she's a big girl, one shove from her and you go flying. Should have waited for round four, it was fairly timid compared to the others and looked more fun. First one to down three cups of punch. Jack entered that one too, along with Mr H, Call me Mal again, and a few others. Last game was tug of war, it was quite a sight to see naked men grunting and groaning, their bits shaking away, bums wobbling.

Party games over, the real fun began. Everyone was getting hammered, don't know what they put in that punch, but it was bloody strong. Call me Mal got more and more frisky, Mr H touched me up at every available opportunity and I started looking forward to it. Feel bad about that, don't know what it is about him that's making me act like this. Jack finally decided to pay me some attention and I made a catty remark about him tearing himself away from his new friends, so off he went again. Watched him for a while. I do love him so much. He's got the most gorgeous smile, a beautiful mouth, lovely white teeth, dark hair curling slightly around his ears. He kisses like a dream. He's so laid back, and kind and generous. And, deep down, I know he loves me very much. Silly really, needing proof and reassurance all the time. Resolve to stop being such a stupid pouty cow and be nice to him. Beefy came out of the chalet to replenish supplies of alcohol and tells us Mad Irish is not a happy bunny. She is now complaining that there are not enough English channels on the television. It's either BBC or CNN News. Well, you wouldn't expect to watch much telly at a naturist resort in the Canary Islands, would you?

Day Six

Turns out there are fourteen of us going on the boat trip. Jack and me, Call me Mal, Miss Brazilian, Little and Large, the Smalls, Mr Music Man and dark companion, and the swinging Dutch people. Mrs Average will keep an eye on life at the poolside and fill me in later. Jack has promised to devote the day to me. He agrees he has been so busy making new friends he has neglected me somewhat. This morning at breakfast he actually pulled out the chair for me and put an arm around my shoulders. Public displays of affection, whatever next? Mr H said he'd miss me. Don't quite know what to think about that.

Was nice to leave the complex, like a 'school's out for summer' feeling. Have been getting a bit stir crazy. Bus took us to the port where we were introduced to our captain and crew. Felt nervous, kind of shy, wanted to change my mind and go back to the safety of the poolside. Jack is all excited, I try to smile, can't quite make it. He holds my hand tight and leads the way onto the boat. The captain is Spanish and gorgeous, makes me feel even worse. He probably thinks we're idiots. Why would he though? Why is there such a stigma about naturism? Why are we so afraid to tell people? Why do I suddenly feel so embarrassed about it all?

Boat is more like a small yacht, has huge bright yellow cushions spread across the deck, we are meant to take up positions to soak up the sun and the sea and the view. I take the first one I come to, sit down then instantly regret it because it's within six feet of the captain who I have just realised steers from the back of the boat. I now have to strip off within spitting distance of the handsome captain. Talking of stripping off, keep watchful eye to see what happens. Within a few minutes we are out at sea and Mr Music Man gets straight back to nature closely followed by Call me Mal. Just think bugger it, get it over with and take my clothes off. Jack is shocked and impressed – I am third to get naked.

Minutes later, my stomach is churning. Can't believe this, I am sea sick. This is ridiculous, I am never sea sick. It is like a mill pond out here, for goodness sake, what the hell is wrong with me? Feel like a right plonker now. Keep taking deep breaths, vomit coming up in my throat. No good, I have to tell Jack who is tackling his first can of lager (free booze and food supplied) and is gobsmacked. Gets so bad, he has to tell the handsome captain. Now I feel really stupid. Captain brings me water and seasickness tablets, is incredibly sweet and concerned. Also brings me a plastic carrier bag as he doesn't want a mess on his boat. Try to lie down, it's worse, the humming of the engine is making me wretch. Am too ill to suck stomach in even though Captain Handsome keeps looking over. The others are enjoying the alcohol, sandwiches and snacks are passed around.

Jack takes a tuna, the smell makes me worse. We pass a huge sailing boat, there are dozens of teenagers on deck, shouting and waving. Great. Call me Mal asks if I'm OK, can only nod at this point. Wouldn't call it the best day of my life so far.

Tablets start to work after a while, thank goodness. Sit up and try to enjoy the view. It is ocean, ocean and more ocean with a rocky coastline in the distance. Jack is enjoying himself, he is getting quite merry. So is Call me Mal and Miss Brazilian. Tablets have worn off. Pick up the carrier bag and take deep breaths. Captain Handsome notices, Jack doesn't.

Crew member, who looks like a large version of whatshisname – deplane, deplane, you know the little guy on Fantasy Island – puts on some nice soothing music. Also brings me more tablets and water by order of Captain Handsome. Then it all kicks off with Mr Music Man. "Ve are at vun vis nature!" he shouts. "Ve do not vant zis intrusive noise. It is noise, noise! Ve vant it off now. Off, off!" Strange, a nude man shouting off, off to Captain Handsome, a line I might have used myself had I been feeling well. Jack lifts his eyebrows and shrugs as if to tell the captain Mr Music Man was a miserable bugger, Call me Mal glares, Miss Brazilian loudly complains, no one else says a word. I am still too ill to care much. Crew member asks who is the boss, nobody says a word, the music goes off. Jack spends the next half hour telling me he should have said something, he should have told Mr Grumpy Music Man exactly what everyone thought about him, he should have bloody well chucked him overboard. In the end, was hoping Jack would go overboard and leave me to the mercies of Captain Handsome.

We go inshore to dock for lunch. Terrific, there is a passenger ferry about to pass close by. Turn onto my stomach, show them my lily white bum. Call me Mal stands up and waves. Typical. Miss Large remains cross legged reading her book. The woman has guts. Can clearly hear the PA system on the ferry, "To our right is a yacht chartered by nudists. If anyone is offended please turn to your left where you will see the sweeping coastline." Yeah, right, everyone's going to suddenly look the other way. Well, no shit, they don't. We are a bloody tourist attraction. People are taking photographs, waving and getting out their binoculars for a close-up. Wonderful.

Lunch in the cove is more of the same. A number of other boats had the same idea. Or they probably rendezvous there every week for the view. Captain Handsome tells us we are welcome to take a dip in the sea while lunch is prepared. Mr Music Man immediately dives in from the top rail, show off. Hope there are sharks. Call me Mal is inebriated enough to follow. Whatever Mr Music Man can do, he can do better. Or he thinks he can. Call me Mal is soon out of breath, obviously thinking it wasn't such a good idea, while Mr M&M is swimming like an Olympian. Nobody shows they are impressed, heads turn the other way out to sea.

Lunch looked gorgeous, pasta, chicken, garlic bread and salad laid out neatly on white trays. Am afraid to eat or drink anything, would rather die than chuck up in front of everyone. Sip my water and try to avoid stares and whoops from neighbouring boats.

Jack is having a ball. He is walking around the boat like an old pro, helping himself to cans from the cool box, exchanging pleasantries with our fellow sailors. Does dutifully come back to my side occasionally, remembering his promise. Shame I'm not much company on the day he says he'll be devoted to me, he won't want to do it again.

Cast off after lunch, another bloody ferry on the way. Hear the PA system, here we go again. Back out at sea, Jack gets out his camera. Apparently, he has been using it most of the day. There are numerous shots of my naked bum. No prizes for guessing which bit of me he likes the best. Am not best pleased, while I was sick he was taking pix of my bum. Jack reassures me, apparently there are some full frontal shots of me too. Oh, well, that's all right then.

Captain Handsome continues to check on me and smile. Think the last tablets worked, feel much better. Am sucking in stomach whenever I notice him looking now. Also manage a few lusty looks, he really is gorgeous. Bet he has no trouble getting people naked, even without the boat. Wonder how much he's paid for doing this? Jack says captaining a boatful of naked people in the Canary Islands is his dream job, he would do it for nothing.

Head back towards shore, people start putting their clothes on. Call me Mal and Mr Music Man are last, they are glaring at each other, seeing who will draw the shorts up first. Bit like a bunfight at the OK Corral. Call me Mal holds his nerve and hangs on until we are right in the harbour. Say my goodbyes and thank yous to Captain Handsome, he asks if I will be joining the trip next week. I tell him stock up on the tablets, you never know…

Back at the complex, safely behind the barbed wire and big fences most of us adjourn to the bar. Everyone except me is drunk as a skunk, they all want to carry on drinking. Am afraid to consume wine on empty stomach, order juice. Jack brings back wine. Hello, am I here? Predictably, wine goes straight to head. What the hell, if you can't beat them, join them.

Mrs Average comes to tell us day's activities. Two new people have arrived. Mad Irish and Beefy are out on a pub crawl. The couple from Jersey flew home, the family with children are at the beach and Mrs Two Bums hasn't stopped talking all day. Nothing new there then. Mr H waits a suitable length of time before joining us and pulling up a chair next to me.

Stay at bar for far too long. Too much wine, too little food. Sitting naked next to Mr H in this condition is not a good idea. Mrs H has gone back to chalet, Jack is engrossed in conversation with other men on how they will not put up with Mr Music Man's nonsense one more time. Mr H says the place wasn't the same without me, he had been looking forward to me returning. Was very sweet, sincere and flattering. Am usually very good judge of character, have great instincts, he seems genuine. That can't be right surely? Maybe being naked has thrown my radar off balance. He wants to know everything about me, my life, my career, family, friends. He asks about everything, except Jack. Touches my hand at every opportunity, rubs his foot on my leg, doesn't feel sleazy, not like he's hitting on me, seems romantic. Wine is obviously affecting my judgement. Mrs Average is watching. Busted.

Jack eventually remembers he has devoted his day to me and comes to my side. Funny, I am disappointed. What is wrong with me? Hunky waiter, Captain Handsome, Mr Haughty, the list goes on. I am a bloody hypocrite calling Call me Mal a lech. At least he's honest about it. Feel guilty. Start paying Jack lots of attention. Mr H looks sad.

Finally head back for chalet to dress for dinner. Am now so hammered have no appetite. Pick at dinner, consume lots more wine. Jack is no longer ordering by the glass, it is by the bottle. Mad Irish and Beefy return, she is feeling much better. Her PMT is over, she is a normal person. Beefy says he is used to it, she is a grumpy cow. She calls him a piece of shit, they laugh.

Getting increasingly drunker and start making eyes at Mr H again, despite the fact that Mrs Average is in close proximity and doesn't miss a trick. Alcohol makes you brave. Or incredibly stupid. Think Mrs H has noticed looks passing between us and demands they retire. Mr H goes off like a good boy. Wimp. Mrs Average makes a beeline for me and I know I can't have the Mr H conversation with her after a gallon of wine. Alcohol might make you stupid, but not that stupid. Stuck to Jack's side like glue until bedtime eventually beckoned.

Day Seven

When I said hangovers were never so bad on holidays I was obviously asking for trouble. Am not a well person. Jack has been a darling, fetching mugs of tea and tablets. Feel like a right moron today. Memories of last night flooding back. First thought this morning was 'Oh, my head', quickly followed by 'Damn, Mrs Average saw me with Mr H'. It was not just a friendly conversation, it couldn't even be called heavy flirting, it was obviously something far more intimate, which an expert people watcher like Mrs A was never going to miss. Will be all around the poolside by now. Can imagine Mrs Two Bums' eyes widening as the juicy gossip is passed on. Will have to do some damage limitation. Concentrate all efforts on Jack so people will think Mrs Average is making something out of nothing.

Jack fancies Sunday lunch so we decide to miss breakfast (don't think I could have kept anything down anyway) and go for walk. Will clear my head, he says. Think it'll take more than a walk to get rid of the little men with hammers in my head, but make the effort. We go up the hill towards the information tower to check out the view. Jack has his camera, we are taking the tourist shots today.

Bloody hell, very good view of the complex! Even with the naked eye can see lots of naked flesh. Guy with binoculars must have very intimate knowledge of us all. Hope he didn't take photographs. Well, you never know they could just pop up somewhere couldn't they? How d'you explain that? Can clearly see Mrs Two Bums on her morning stroll around the poolside, Call me Mal's big stomach, Miss Large's boobs and other bodies lounging around. Other people join us at the lookout point, complex is clearly another tourist attraction, we are all looking in same direction. Just great.

Point out wonderful view of turquoise sea and sandy coastline, sweeping hills behind us. Hope to take attention away from camp. Nobody looks, even Jack says, "Yeah, lovely, look you can see the Averages sitting near the bar and Mr Piercing having a swim." Jack takes lots of pictures, I ask would he like one of me with the sea and the view in the background, he says no, it's fine, he is busy getting shots of our fellow guests. Don't mind me, then.

Eventually tear him away to walk into town for shopping and lunch. He is sweet and nice again but mostly talks about the view from the tower. Feel like a spare part. Don't know if he'd notice if I wasn't here.

Shops were OK, didn't buy much except a new white dress which will show off my tan. Jack buys new sunglasses which are meant to be Ray-Bans but break after half an hour. He goes on and on about it, apparently they weren't that cheap and he's been robbed. Lunch was lovely, found a nice Irish pub which served the real thing, roast Beef, Yorkshire pud and all the trimmings. Must tell Mad Irish, she would love it.

Strolled back to the complex after lunch for afternoon siesta by the pool. Very civilised. Feel much better now, but still a bit peeved at Jack. He was in an almighty hurry to return, being alone with me is obviously not in his top ten things to do. Wonder what they'd be? Number one – ogle Miss Large's boobs. Number two – stare at Miss Brazilian's Brazilian. Number three – look at Mrs Two Bums' bum (because your eyes just can't help but be drawn to it). Number four – talk sports with Mr Average. Number Five – sneak a peek at Mr Piercing's piercing. Number six – admire young mother's ass. Number seven – compare cock size with others. Number eight – check out bodies of any new arrivals. Number nine – have a few drinks with Beefy at the bar. Number ten – Discuss Mr Music Man's faults with Call me Mal.

Maybe number eleven – be nice to Caitlin?

Ask Jack if I'm in his top ten?. He says yes, behind Jennifer Anniston, Penelope Cruz, Catherine Zeta Jones, Nicole Kidman, Sandra Bullock, Demi Moore, Sharon Stone, Jessica Rabbit (what!) and Michelle Pfeiffer.

No competition there then.

Then he laughs and cuddles me and tells me I am all his top ten. Now and forever. Ahhhh… feel all warm inside now. See – how hard was that for him? Why can't he do it more often. Like once a day – say something nice to Caitlin who is so insecure and stupid, she needs to be told over and over why you're with her.

Mrs Average tracks me down. Not difficult really in Colditz. She is determined to have the Mr H conversation. Decide to get it over with. She has noticed we are very friendly, she says he looks at me all the time and seems to be longing for me. Resist temptation to ask more, would show interest. Say 'Really?' very nonchalantly, and tell her we have just flirted a bit, as you do. And that's it. I am very much with Jack. Mrs Average is not best pleased, she tries her top tactics to get more information or some admission of guilt but I am having none of it. In return for my lack of co-operation she refuses to tell me morning's goings-on at poolside. Says nothing happened. Yeah, right.

It's Mr and Mrs Average's last night tonight so we are joining them for dinner in the complex. Food was lovely yet again, as was the wine of course. Must have gained at least five pounds, probably all gone to my belly. Does feel rather large. OK, larger. Wore the white dress, looks nice if I say so myself. Jack said his usual 'you look fine'.

No sign of the Haughtys. Can't help wondering where they are, haven't seem much of him today at all. Just as well, probably. Jack has suddenly remembered I promised to pose for naked photos. When did I say that? Have no memory of it but was apparently said while drunk yesterday. More good news then.

Decide if naked posing is on the agenda, will need more wine. Order another bottle for the table. Turns out posing for naked photos was fine, am obviously not as shy as I thought I was, although the gallon of wine no doubt helped. Take lots of photos of him too. He is a natural model, loves to pose for the camera. We manage to get some pictures of both of us by holding the camera out in front. One thing leads to another… and yet another good night was had by all.

Day Eight

Mad Irish's period from hell is officially over. Beefy makes the mistake of saying this one wasn't so bad and is soon put in his place. When she's out of earshot, he whispers he meant it wasn't so bad for him.

Mr and Mrs Average are packed, ready to leave after breakfast. There are already towels on their sunbeds. Do people have no respect? They could at least wait until they've gone. Jack and me have obviously missed out on taking the prime positions then.

We all say goodbye to the Averages, they really will be missed. But life at the poolside goes on. Jack and me have decided to do a full shift on the sunbeds today. He goes off to the supermarket to get newspapers, I head for chalet to strip off. Occupy our usual spots and do a quick check around the pool to see who's where. A new couple bagged the Averages' sunbeds. Bloody cheek!

Mr Two Bums is in his usual comatose condition, while the missus is at the start of her morning flit, bending over to talk to the elderly couple. Mad Irish and Beefy resume positions next to us, granny knickers now off they are free to leave the terrace. Beefy seems very happy about it. Until she starts the nagging again. Fetch me water, rub suntan oil on my back, get my book. He is up and down like a yo-yo again, via the bar of course. The Smalls are out, him reading the usual morning paper and her the women's mag. Little and Large are in position. She is a glutton for punishment, her skin looks incredibly sore. Why doesn't she at least go under a parasol? Call me Mal and Miss Brazilian are lying peacefully at the moment. Mr Music Man and dark companion are at one with nature on the far side of the pool. The young couple head off to the beach with the children. Good. No shrieking today to disturb the peace. Except for Mad Irish, of course. Dutch foursome are in a row, beds turned around to make the most of the morning sun. The Haughtys come out and settle down next to us. He smiles shyly at me, she turns her nose up in the air. Is clear I am threat to her. Whatever.

Another new couple arrive during the morning. They're Italian, in their fifties, quite ordinary looking. She has short dark hair, little bit tubby, not very tall. He's balding, wearing specs, dumpy little guy. They head off to occupy the Averages' vacant chalet.

Mr Piercing is first in the pool this morning. Very brave. I like to wait at least until midday to give the sun a chance to take the chill off it. Bizarre, having a freezing cold pool when it's so hot here. My only complaint about the complex, actually, will have to point it out on the leaving questionnaire. With a bit of luck pool will be heated when we come next time. Jack is still keen to come back later in the year. Don't really know how I feel about it. Has certainly been an experience.

Gets so hot after lunch, Jack has to fetch parasol for shade. Cheeky Mad Irish positions herself to take advantage of it, too. When the sun moves a bit and I need the parasol moved, he is too polite to do it because Mad Irish would be exposed. Charming. It's OK for me to burn then?

Mr H joins me again for afternoon swim. Says Mrs H has noticed how friendly we are and the way he looks at me. Says he doesn't care. Theirs is a marriage of keeping up appearances. Says he is very attracted to me and has never felt this way before. Don't really know what to say, ask if he makes a habit of talking to strange women like that. He admits to having had a few 'romantic dalliances' but denies he is a serial adulterer and swears it is something special with me. Like love at first sight or something cheesy like that. Must admit I am pleased and flattered but don't know how to react. He wants my phone number to keep in touch. Tell him I will give it to him before he leaves. Well, it wouldn't be polite to refuse would it?

Back on the sunbed, lie face down, the bum still needs to catch up with the rest of me. Very pleasant lazy day. Even Mad Irish dozes off in the afternoon. Peaceful and quiet, just the occasional splash in the pool as someone takes a cooling dip, the radio playing in the background, the odd clink of a glass. Mrs Two Bums has sensed the mood and has given up trying to engage people in conversation. We are sleepy, happy, laying naked in the sunshine. Decide it doesn't get much better than this. Look at Jack, sleeping like a baby. Love him so much. What the hell am I doing with Mr H?

Slept too long, neck is stiff and dribble sticking to my chin. What a sight. Also, bum is now burnt. From one bloody extreme to the other. Jack laughs at my red ass. His Speedos are now merging nicely with the rest of his body. Show off.

After usual nude tea on the terrace Jack went to collect the photographs from the shop in town. Still can't believe he took the film to be developed at a normal shop – what if they thought it was pornography and called the police? OMG – the scandal of being arrested in a foreign country for a sex crime! What if the government got involved to help us get out of gaol? We would be on the national news, I could never show my face, let alone any other part of me, in public again.

Turns out I needn't have worried, shop does not care about pornography and just handed over pix like normal. Jack said, told you so. Hmph, not happy at his attitude towards my worries. Less happy about the pix. Stomach looks awful, I am seriously depressed. Was just feeling quite relaxed about my figure and this has really knocked me backwards. Tell Jack it is back to the one-piece bather, the stomach will never be seen in public again. Rest of the figure is also not so hot, I decide. Cannot ever show off naked body again. Jack laughs, first of all, before he realises I am deadly serious and this will mean a premature end to his naturist holiday. I tell him not to worry, I will pretend to have a period and stay on the terrace fully clothed. He can still enjoy himself sunning at the poolside. He tries to reassure me, says I am beautiful, have the best figure in the place, have nothing to worry about. He was doing quite well until he said the stomach was nothing more than a cute little pot. Really big mistake.

I exploded. Accused Jack of trivialising my very real concern about my ugly, fat stomach. Said why should he care, he was too busy looking at other women to take any notice of how I looked anyway. Told him I was going home, he could stick his naturist holiday, he obviously wanted to be with other people more than with me anyway. He said I was being stupid, that really helped, as you can imagine. When he realised was another big mistake said I really shouldn't worry, everyone said the camera added ten pounds. I reminded him that was film cameras, not small ones, and if that was the case why did everyone else, including him, look exactly the same size? So, he was admitting that I looked fat then. Jack didn't know what else to say and went off to sit on the terrace. Typical. Every time we argue, or at least when I am upset about something, he always runs away. Can never resolve anything. Just like last New Year's Eve when I got really drunk and demanded to know whether he was ever going to ask me to marry him. He soon left my side at that party and didn't come back until much later.

I thought about marching out onto the terrace after him but he knew I wouldn't carry on the row in public, he was pretty safe there until I calmed down. And, of course, I always did. In the end, my temper or tears subsided and I saw the good in us again and made up with him. Don't know if I should this time though. I feel fat, ugly and horrible and all he does is laugh or make trite remarks. Find myself thinking bet Mr H wouldn't react like that. He'd care and do everything he could to make me feel better, I'm sure. Maybe it was time up for me and Jack. Let's face it, it's going nowhere. I definitely want marriage and a baby or two, he won't even buy a house together. We are still living in the flat he had when we met. Even though I moved in with him eight years ago, my name still isn't on the lease. When I leave the property pages open in the local paper he closes it and turns straight to the back page sport. When I mention houses are a good investment, he agrees but never mentions buying one. When I ask if he'd like to own his own home, he just says one day and changes the subject. As he does. Maybe I just have to wake up to the fact that Jack is never going to give me what I need. I have to decide what I want the most – a ring on my finger, a family, a home – or Jack, the love of my life. The man who has been the centre of my world for a decade, who, despite his lack of commitment, has made me feel more cared for than I have ever been in my life. My friend, my lover, my soulmate. Problem is, I don't know how he feels about me. Of course, I know he loves me, but how much and how long for? Let's face facts, I'm thirty-three and my biological clock is ticking. I could stay with Jack for another ten years and then one day it could be over. And it could be too late for me to have the family I long for. This is too hard. Open a bottle of wine and curl up on the sofa, wrapped in a blanket. Don't care if it's hot, will no longer be naked and can't be asked to get dressed.

Almost finished the bottle before Jack came back inside. I heard him earlier chatting with Little and Large on the adjoining terrace. Charming. He's laughing and talking while my heart is breaking.

His eyes widen as he looks at the almost empty bottle and at me wrapped in my blanket. Then he sits down and puts an arm around me and in his gentlest voice says, "Come on, my baby, you really are beautiful and I love you very much and you honestly have nothing to worry about. For God's sake, you have a gorgeous figure! Do you think I haven't noticed all the other men staring at you? There's not one of them who wouldn't jump at the chance of having you on their arm if they could. Now, come on, get yourself dressed and I'll take you for that steak I've been promising for days." Well, the speech was so unexpected, I just blubbered. Couldn't stop crying. Jack said a few there, theres and kept his arms around me until I finally stopped, got dressed and got out.

Am conscious of the puffy eyes and keep my sunglasses on even when it's dusk. Meal was lovely but still feel very wobbly. Jack is being very attentive, I keep holding onto him. Either for reassurance or because I'm afraid to let him go. Or maybe it's the wine affecting the legs...

It's late when we return to the complex. Only Mad Irish, Beefy, and the new couple at the bar. Hunky waiter looks tired, he just wants to pack up and go home. Bit like I feel actually. Still a bit down. Mad Irish senses my mood and tries to cheer me up with funny stories about Beefy. Must admit I feel a bit better after talking to them. Still don't know whether I can face getting my clothes off in the morning though. Still don't know what decision to make about Jack.

Day Nine

Peer out of chalet window and spot new lady and Mrs Two Bums having a chat. Decide I was overreacting last night, figure is nowhere near as bad as theirs and they don't care. Come to think of it, all the women here, whatever their shape or size, are really comfortable with their bodies. All these stick thin models, beautiful actresses with pert breasts and flat stomachs, no wonder we're all neurotic about our figures. How do you compete with society's image of the perfect woman? Men don't seem to worry about how they look. Jack certainly doesn't go around comparing himself with other men here. Apart from cock size, of course, that's the only thing that seems to matter to the male species. Maybe that's where the word cocky comes from? Someone who's King Cock – bigger than all the rest strutting his stuff. That would be Mr Small here, strangely enough his manhood is way out of proportion with the rest of him. Think I overreacted with the Jack thing too. That's what comes of looking at naked photos of me, vow not to do it again. If Jack wants his own private collection, fine. I will stick to the ordinary tourist photos when I want to be reminded of this holiday. Also vow to be nice to Jack today and not think about the future, will just enjoy this holiday then think after we get home.

Decide to get kit off and sunbathe. I mean for God's sake, it's not like they haven't seen it all before, is it?

Suck in hated belly and call Jack to join me on sunbeds. Fastest he's moved all week! Shorts were off in two seconds flat. Clever boy, he knew not to say a word.

The Smalls are going home later today. Their chalet has been emptied and cases stored. Mrs S is fully dressed on the sunbed reading her mag, Mr S is starkers with a little pile of clothes on the floor next to him. Making the most of every last naked minute. Look around to see who will be King Cock now. Dismiss new people immediately. Then cross off Call me Mal, Mr Piercing, Joe and Mr H. It's not Jack, although he would like it to be, I know. Dark companion is a contender, but Beefy might give him a run for his money. (Done from memory of course, Beefy is not here to study.) Two Dutch men are average size, Mr Music Man's may be long but is too thin to count. Cross off Mr Two Bums and the elderly man. No, is definitely a two-dick race. Will study both later before declaring winner.

Mr H arrives and winks at me. No sign of the missus. Jack wanders off to get his daily dose of sports talk with whoever's around. Mr H wastes no time. I am all he thinks about, apparently. Can't get me out of his head. Dreamt about me last night, thinks about me all day. Has argued with Mrs H because she has noticed the way he looks at me. Left her in the chalet threatening to divorce him and take half of everything. Says he doesn't care, she can have half, it still leaves him with plenty. Asks again for my phone number, really wants to keep in touch, he thinks we have something special. Then says he wants just one kiss before the holiday ends. Something to remember me by. Admit I'm very flattered. Mr H is quite a catch. Tall, dark and handsome, he is also rich, kind, romantic and thoughtful. And obviously wants and adores me. Keeps saying the nicest things. Says if Mrs H left him and he found someone else, he would quite like to have more children. Had always wanted more, but Mrs H would not take the chance of ruining her figure any more than the first one already had. I think it was talking about a future and babies that made me say it more than anything. Before I even thought about it, it was out of my mouth. Told him I'd sneak away for half an hour after dinner. He was very pleased, on reflection it was probably much easier than he'd thought. Said he'd meet me at the end of the road. He'd leave first, I'd go ten minutes later. Could tell Jack I wanted something in the shop, he'd be so busy talking to the others he probably wouldn't even notice I'd gone.

After I said it, wondered why. Mr H is lovely and all that, but he's not Jack. Don't want to see him after this holiday. Tell myself it's just a flirtation, bit of fun, something to massage my ego bruised by the enormous belly. Will tell him later it was a mistake. Catch Jack looking at us. Shit. Immediately turn over, look other way. Must look guilty. Shit. On second thoughts, he probably thinks it's amusing anyway. No shit.

We join the new Italian couple at the bar for a mid-morning juice. Mrs Italy is a devout Catholic and goes to confession in the local church every day to ask forgiveness for being naked in public. Says it can't be right because even though God made us that way, Eve covered up in the Garden of Eden and people have through the ages ever since. So Mrs Italy feels the most terrible guilt. Every holiday, first thing she does is find a church and go to confession. Says all the priests have been very understanding, most don't think it's a sin at all. But she can't help the way she feels and can't take her clothes off until she's said the appropriate number of Hail Marys.

I do another hour by the pool and then have a quick dip to cool off. Mr H joins me in the water of course. Reminds me about our date later. Don't think it's the right time to say I've changed my mind and anyway he looks so pleased hate to burst his bubble.

Call me Mal asks why I am scribbling in a book all day. He has noticed, as has everyone else apparently, that I am always writing. When I tell him it's just my diary, which I have kept since I was fourteen, his eyes light up. He wants to know what's in it, particularly is he in it, are any of the others mentioned. I tell him no one reads it, except me, even Jack has never disrespected my privacy by nosing in it. When we first lived together, Jack asked once if he could read my diary. Apparently Elizabeth Taylor let Richard Burton read hers and he even added footnotes. Well, we're no Liz and Dick and I said a definite no. Hid it for a while after that until he promised he would never read my diary without my permission. I said he could when I was an old lady. And if he's still with me when I am, he can.

Oh, forgot about King Cock contest! In the end, after much discreet studying, couldn't decide so mentally awarded both dark companion and Beefy the title. We have a joint King Cock at the camp.

Mrs H has finally emerged from the chalet. The afternoon is turning into yet another party. Beefy has started drinking games now. Just noticed Jack is quiet. Realise I haven't spoken to him since this morning. What the hell. Somebody thinks it would be a good idea to have a buffet meal tonight and keep the party going until we all collapse or whatever. Maria promises to sort something out. Now that's what you call service, wouldn't get that in an ordinary resort.

By eight o'clock we are all fed and very watered. Maria and hunky waiter are looking a little nervous, we're a bit of a raucous crowd and they don't know what to expect. Naughty nudists.

Mr H is never far from my side, in direct contrast to Jack who has been nowhere near me all day. I am feeling reckless, pissed and pissed off. When Mr H reminds me of our date, instead of telling him I have changed my mind, I tell him give me half an hour. Will give Jack half an hour to take some notice of me, give me some attention.

It doesn't happen. I know he is watching me. He has been looking at me funny all day. But he doesn't come near. I even move really close and look directly at him. He is deep in conversation with Mr Italy. What am I to him – a stupid moody woman with irrational demands and a mind that changes every five minutes? It's like he's just tolerating me, there's no real feeling there. Well, stuff you Jack. Thirty minutes is up. I break into his conversation to say I am craving chocolate, need a walk and am going to the supermarket. Jack gives me that same funny look and says fine. Fine.

Meet Mr H at the end of the road. Feels surreal. Don't know what the hell I'm doing or why. Am I so desperate for attention? Obviously I am.

I reach him and he says he can't control his feelings, he is falling for me big time. His words. I would never say that. He reaches for me and I kind of feel obliged to act pleased. He leans forward and kisses me, just a peck on the lips. It's fine, no problem. Then he starts to put his tongue in my mouth and his hands are around my waist. That is a problem. I don't like it much. I kiss him back because it would be rude not to. After all, I'm here and I've led him on all week. But I don't like it. He's not Jack. I like kissing Jack. Depending on my mood, it's either like coming home or stomach doing flip-flops. Mr H is really nice, I like him and my instincts are telling me now he actually is genuine. Damn and blast it. I can't be horrible and walk away. His tongue is now down my throat, I am going through the motions. What a mess. His hands are starting to move all over me. Oh, shit. Only want Jack's hands on me. What the hell am I doing? He keeps kissing me, touching me, is obviously excited, doing nothing for me. I am just letting it happen. After an acceptable time, say we mustn't do this, he is married, I am with Jack, this is crazy. Tell him he is a very lovely person and in other circumstances would jump at the chance, but the time isn't right for us. Feel very conscious that it is my fault, I led him on, can't just say sorry changed my mind now. He finally lets me go, keeps saying this is something special, best moment of his life. What am I supposed to do? He says he wants a future with me, can imagine children and everything. I just want future and children with Jack. Everything is clear as day. If I can't have it with Jack, then I don't want it with anyone. Suddenly, clear as day. Take a deep breath. Say very sorry nothing is going to happen, tell him it's very hard, he's a wonderful person etc, to make him feel better but just wanted to get away. Leave him with the ego intact, but leave him. ASAP.

Practically ran back to the camp. Fumbled with the double keys, couldn't wait to get back to Jack's side. Walked in breathless, realised I had nothing to show from the shop, didn't care. Went right next to him, held onto his hand, got the funny look again but he held it back. I know now it's him I want, not babies, not marriage, just him. Well, to be honest, I do want the babies, I do want the marriage, but more than anything I want him.

I lean towards him in the middle of the conversation of who is the best all-time Lions coach and kiss him. And he kisses me back. And the lips are the best in the world, this is where I belong. Like coming home.

Day Ten

Feel really guilty this morning. Made beautiful love with Jack last night. It was love, not just sex. Want to hold him and kiss him all day. Make up to him for being such a stupid bitch. Also feel bad about Mr H. I really shouldn't have led him on like that. Can't think what I was playing at. At least it's taught me one important thing – Jack is the only one I want and I mean to stay with him for as long as he'll have me, ring or no ring.

Breakfast was a pretty muted affair. Most of us are sporting hangovers from the previous day's festivities. I asked Mrs Italy if I could accompany her to church today. She is surprised but pleased to have the company and assures me that it doesn't matter that I'm not Catholic, I will be welcome. I feel the need to atone for my sin.

Church is actually lovely. It is a small, whitewashed building, very traditional Spanish place of worship. Almost exactly like the ones you see in spaghetti westerns. Cool and peaceful inside, just a handful of people kneeling, praying. Mostly older Spanish women wearing headscarves. Mrs Italy assures me we don't need to cover our heads. The priest can't hear confession from me because I'm not a Catholic but I can still confess to God and pray for forgiveness. I settle into the nearest pew and Mrs Italy goes off to the confession booth. Think it must be nice to be able to tell all your sins to a person you can trust implicitly to never tell another living soul. It always makes you feel better when you confess, doesn't it? Gets rid of the heavy weight hanging around your heart which I assume is guilt.

Tell God how sorry I am for what I've done. Would like to tell Jack but can't without telling him what I'm sorry for. Tell God I know I've been a stupid bitch. Shit, is it OK to swear when I'm talking to God? Shit, mustn't say shit. Ask forgiveness for swearing too. Tell God I will be good and faithful from now on, will count my blessings, appreciate what I've got which, when you think about it, is a lot more than some other people have. Think how I would feel if Jack had done this to me. I would be devastated, it would rip the bottom out of my world. I know it was just one kiss but the intimacy, the secret chats, all of it. Terrible, I couldn't bear it. Also say I'm sorry for what I've done to Mr H who does seem to genuinely like me. Pray that him and Mrs H will find happiness again. Well, they must have had it at some point surely? Ask God if please, please could Jack stay with me forever even though I know I don't deserve it.

Am much better leaving the church. Me and Mrs Italy have a spring in our step. Feel quite saintly. Well, maybe not saintly but certainly cleansed.

On the way back to the complex I spot a street market. Ooh, I love them! Will grab my purse from the chalet and head off to spend, spend, spend.

Jack asks how was church, I say fine. Realise I didn't ask forgiveness for studying other people's body parts, nosing into their lives or being scathing about their less-than-perfect figures. Oh, well, maybe another time.

Surprisingly, Jack agrees to come to market. Unusual for him, he hates things like that and knows I will want to go up and down every aisle and stop at every stall. Glad he's coming with me though.

Come back laden with blue plastic bags. Really enjoyed my morning. Haggled and got really good deals on silver jewellery for Angie and Maggie, and fake designer scarves for Aunt Biddy and Frances. Bought Jack new sunglasses, obviously they're copies although the guy swore they weren't, but Jack likes them anyway. Got another handbag of course. Also some new strappy sandals. Some fruit, a hairband and make-up which I know I don't need but was such a bargain. Jack says it's not a bargain if it makes my skin come out in a rash but I take no notice. I am very pleased with my purchases.

All is quiet at the poolside. Have a light lunch and take up positions on sunbed. Was kind of dreading being next to Mr H again. He has this very sad, puppy dog look on his face. My fault. As usual, Mrs H has the earphones in, eyes shut. She has a lovely tan and is really quite attractive if I'm honest. Mad Irish is sleeping, Beefy is at the bar. Mr Piercing is doing lengths of the pool. Spot the binoculars guy on the tower again. Sad bastard.

Jack stays next to me even though I know he must want the daily sports talk and would probably like to join Beefy at the bar. He always needs a pint after going to market. I tell him I don't mind if he joins Beefy and he says I bet you don't, in quite a nasty way. Stomach's churning, what does he mean? Can't be Mr H surely? He's never taken notice before. Would be weird if it bothered him now that there's nothing to be bothered about.

Doze off for an hour and wake up feeling really sticky. Sweat running everywhere again. Go in the pool for a cooling dip. Mr H seizes his chance. Damn. He tries to persuade me we have something special and we shouldn't deny our feelings. Haven't got the heart to tell him I don't have the same feelings. Try to let him down gently by repeating that he is married and I am with Jack, other people would be hurt. Then he says they needn't know, we could easily keep it a secret as we live so far apart. There are lots of places in between where we could meet up and no one would recognise us. I tell him I couldn't live with the guilt but really like him and wish things were different. Of course I don't. The only thing I wish was different is that I ever started this thing in the first place. Feel very awkward, just want to get out of the pool and away from this conversation. But I hate to be mean and eventually say I will think about it just to get him to let me go.

Know I shouldn't have said that, it's just leading him on again. Don't know what to do, just keep stalling I guess until he leaves which is tomorrow.

Afternoon passes pleasantly with lots of laughing and chatting, bit of sunbathing and swimming. Jack's still quiet though. Something is definitely bothering him and I don't know what it is. Wish he would just tell me, my stomach is churning all the time, getting worried now. He can't know about Mr H surely? No, if he did I would have heard about it by now. What the hell is it then?

Ask him over tea on the terrace if anything's bothering him, he says what should be bothering him? Shit, I don't know do I? Am I supposed to? Try to think what I've done wrong. Apart from snogging Mr H and all that of course. Can't think of anything else.

We were going to go out tonight but he doesn't want to now. Had a nice romantic meal planned and everything. I was really looking forward to it. Won't tell me why he's changed his mind, just that he had and he wanted to stay in the complex with the others. Is he going off me? Is that it? He doesn't want to be alone with me because he doesn't want me any more. Is this my punishment for what I've done, retribution from God? Oh, please God, no, don't do this to me, I couldn't stand it.

Take great care with my hair, clothes and make-up. Try to look as good as I can, be as nice as I can. Nerves are in bits. Join the others for dinner. Mr H keeps hovering, really not in the mood for this now. He wants my phone number, I don't want to give it. Wants me to promise to keep in touch, I don't want to. Wants one more kiss before he leaves, I really don't want to. I wish he would just go away and leave me alone now, can't think about this at the moment, am too worried about what's up with Jack. In the end tell Mr H, look, this is never going to work, I am really sorry but it is not a good idea to give my number, can't see each other again, no more kisses, sorry, sorry, sorry, I love Jack and that's that. Mr H looks devastated, like he's been kicked in the guts. Oh, for God's sake I'm sorry, I'm really, very sorry.

Jack is looking funny again. I can't stand this. What the hell is the matter with him? However bad it is decide I have to know. Will ask him the minute we get in the chalet.

Really jumpy the rest of the night. Can't enjoy myself at all even though Call me Mal and Mad Irish are really on form. Everyone is having a great time except for me and Mr H. Oh, Mrs H doesn't look too happy either but then she never does. Jack seems fine now that he's with all the others. Maybe I am just imagining things?

No, I'm not. He has gone all silent and moody on me the minute we get back in the chalet. The Mr Sociable of five minutes ago has completely disappeared. Had enough of this. What the hell is wrong I ask him. He says I should know. If I bloody knew, I wouldn't be bloody asking, would I? Then out it comes. Mrs H asked him to keep me away from her husband. Bloody bitch! Jack said he had seen how friendly we were and the way Mr H looked at me but hadn't worried too much because he trusted me completely. Mrs H on the other hand had very real concerns. She thought her husband had such strong feelings for me, it was risking her marriage. And she intended to keep her marriage and everything that went with it. Jack asked me straight out – is there anything going on with you and Mr H? I said no – of course I did – and anyway there isn't now so I'm not lying. I told him we flirted a bit and I think Mr H does fancy me but not to be so stupid. Jack looked at me really intensely and said, "Caitlin, the truth, is there anything I should know?" Oh, my God, I feel sick. I can't tell him, he'll leave me, can't do it. Swear there's nothing going on, there's nothing for him to worry about. And he says again, "OK, but Caitlin is there anything I need to know?" And I shake my head, no, nothing Jack, there is nothing I promise you. He gives me that strange look again but says OK, I believe you. We won't talk about it again. We go to bed and we have sex but it's strange, something missing. It's hard not to cry, have to keep taking deep breaths and biting my lip. He tosses and turns all night then gets up very early. I hear the door slamming shut not much later. Get out of bed and see him through the window marching towards the complex gates. Wonder where he's going, what the hell is happening now? Then I look at the coffee table and see my diary. Wide open. And written in big letters on the last page is LYING BITCH.

Day Eleven

Am physically sick. Shaking, sobbing, head down the toilet retching. Sit on the floor holding my knees rocking, screaming. Can't bear to lose him, can't stand it, couldn't cope. Why the hell did I ever bother with Mr H? What the hell was I playing at? Why did I risk everything I have for something that meant nothing? Oh, my God, where is he? What's he doing, what's he thinking? Sit at the window drinking coffee. Would really like a cigarette, even though I gave up six years ago. Praying and crying. Please, Jack, come back, please forgive me.

Can see Mr and Mrs H with their cases waiting to leave. He is looking towards the chalet, trying to spot me, one last look. He probably thinks I'm a right bitch not even waving goodbye. Well, I am a right bitch, no argument with that.

No one else is out, it's still early. Except the boy who cleans the pool and sweeps the patio area. He's busy, whistling, happy in his work. It's another beautiful day. And my life is falling apart.

Sit at the window for what seems like hours. Am numb now, can't cry any more. Coffee has been thrown up again, feel empty and sick to my stomach. I should have just taken my chances with Jack and told him everything when he gave me the opportunity. It would have been better than lying, adding insult to injury. Still surprised he read my diary, he promised he never would.

It didn't even occur to me to hide it away. I had complete trust in him just like he had in me. Kind of ironic really.

People start to turn out for breakfast, laying towels on the sunbeds along the way. Except for me and Jack. Wonder if we'll be missed? Don't know, don't care. Just want Jack back. Our two sunbeds are bare. Like they're taunting me. See what you've done – if you'd behaved yourself you'd be lying on us now, Jack at your side. Instead you're on your own crying in the chalet and he's gone. Where the hell is he gone? Panic, run to check if his passport is still in the drawer. Thank God it is. Heart is beating like a drum. Go back to the window but stay back out of sight. Don't want anyone to see me, someone would only come to find out why we aren't out. Glad no one saw Jack leaving this morning, at least they'll think we're out somewhere together. Don't think we'll ever be together again. Feel sobs in my throat, too exhausted to cry, just let the tears roll down my face.

Must have dozed off, there is a commotion coming from the poolside. What now? Shitty as I feel, have to look. They are having a limbo competition. Call me Mal has just fallen flat on his backside. Naked limbo. Now there's a sight you don't see every day. Everyone is falling about laughing except Mr Music Man and dark companion who have their sunbeds as far away from the poolside as they can without getting a row off Maria. Mad Irish tells Beefy to fuck off when he says it's her turn. Miss Brazilian gamely has a go and does rather well. Eventual winner is Mr Piercing who, despite his height, is surprisingly bendy. His prize is a bottle of fake champagne donated by hunky waiter. He pops it open and sprays everyone. Another good day at the poolside is had by all. Except for me, sitting at the window crying. And for Jack. Where is Jack? Consider going to look for him, at a guess he will be in one of the pubs near the beach. Can't walk through the crowd outside though. Not in the state I'm in. And no guarantee I would find him. Or maybe he would come back and I wouldn't be here. He wouldn't be happy then. Or maybe he would.

The afternoon is long. Spent either watching out of the window or lying on the bed curled up in a ball sobbing.

The sun starts to go down and, two by two, they retire to their chalets and the poolside empties. Scrub my face, clean my teeth and put a sports dress on. Nothing else, make-up, nothing. Stuff it all. Pull a brush through my hair and tie it up in a pony tail. Look like shit. Feel like shit. Grab my purse, don sunglasses and take deep breath. Will have to pass the bar to leave the complex. Come back with supplies. Two bottles of wine, three bars of chocolate and big tub of ice cream. Don't know what else to do.

Demolish ice cream, eat half a bar of chocolate, finish bottle, start the next one. It has now been about eleven hours since Jack walked out. The longest day of my life.

People are gathering for dinner outside. I watch, wishing Jack and me were amongst them. Have a very good view, if I open the window a bit more can also hear quite well. They all agree dinner is wonderful yet again. It's Little and Large's last night and they don't want to be hungover travelling so are having an early night. Cocoa and books in the chalet. How sweet. I have never even heard them say a cross word to each other, nor exchange a hostile look. They are so well-suited. Like I thought Jack and me were. Getting really worried now. It's dark but I can't turn the light on or they will see that I'm in. And I won't be able to sit discreetly at the window and watch what's going on. Fine. Want to sit in the dark anyway. Matches my mood.

Heart jumps! Shit, Jack is coming in. He stops by the bar to talk to them. Oh, my God, what is he saying? He's swaying, he's drunk. I'm really scared now. Heart is thumping, stomach in knots, feel sick again. Want to run out and hug him, beg his forgiveness. Can't. He's sitting down, joining them for a drink. Oh, for goodness sake, Jack, just come and put me out of my misery. Shows how little he really cares that he casually sits and joins the party while my life is falling apart. All right, I know it's my fault but, bloody hell, he could show a bit more feeling. It would have been better if he'd shouted and yelled this morning instead of walking out. But that's not Jack, he always runs away when there's any hint of an argument between us. Wonder how he's going to tell me it's over? To my face or maybe he'll just send me a note? Or more Jack's style will just ignore me until I take the hint and leave. Well, I've got news for you, Mr Cold Fish, I'm going nowhere without a fight.

Fighting talk goes out the window when I see him coming towards the chalet half an hour later. Now I am really in bits. He comes through the door and looks at me sitting in the window. I don't know what to say, nothing I could say would be good enough or make a difference. End up just saying hi in a strangled kind of voice.

He said nothing for a while, we sat there in silence. Then he said he had thought about going home but didn't think that having a slapper for a girlfriend should cut short his holiday. Words like a slap in the face. Said I could stay or go, whatever. I told him I'd leave first thing in the morning if that's what he wanted. I said I was truly, very sorry.

He went nuts then. I have never known Jack to be so angry, especially at me. I physically recoiled at the sound of his raised, angry voice.

"Sorry is not a damn bit of good, Caitlin!" he said. "You are a lying cheating tart. Going behind my back with that prat, playing footsie in the pool, sneaking out to snog the face off him!" Shit, he had read the lot. He said he had trusted me, I had let him down, ruined everything we had. Ten years down the pan, he said. Hope Mr H was worth it, he said. I tried to say no, he wasn't, but Jack wasn't listening to anything I had to say. He wanted to know how many other men there'd been and wouldn't believe me when I told him there weren't any. Said he couldn't believe another word I said. Yelled that I had been given a chance to be honest which might have helped a bit but just lied my face off. Told him if he'd read all the diary he would know there was no one else and it was nothing with Mr H. He said he didn't know me any more. I just sobbed. He caught hold of my shoulders and shook me, shouting why did you do it? I just kept crying saying sorry over and over. Aren't I good enough for you, he said? Don't you get enough from me? Well, you can't do or you wouldn't fantasise about other men, he yelled. Was he good? he asked. I shook my head, no, no, no. I just kissed him once, I didn't like it, don't know why I did it. Jack wouldn't believe me. Kept shaking me and demanding answers but didn't believe the ones I gave him. Called me a bitch and a whore. I was screaming crying then.

He looked at me really coldly and asked if I thought about Mr H while I was having sex with him. I couldn't speak any more, just kept shaking my head, no, no.

Then his anger passed, and he just looked sad. He told me to go to bed, said I looked exhausted, he was going to stay on the settee. I curled up in bed, grateful he was still there, sad that he wasn't curled up with me. Head racing, heart still thumping, tears still falling down the cheeks. Remembered I said I would leave in the morning, know he still expects me to, will be the hardest thing I ever have to do, leaving him.

Day Twelve

Couldn't sleep, tossed and turned, heard Jack moving about in the kitchen. Was just glad he was still there. A few more hours with him. Eventually dozed off as the sun came up.

Woke a few hours later to the sound of people moving around outside going to breakfast. Jumped out of bed and ran into the living room. No Jack. Heart sank. There was a note on the table. 'No need for you to leave, we can be civilised until the end of the holiday.'

Heart leaps, then sinks again. Leaps because I don't have to leave, sinks because it's just two more days before it ends. Eyes are all red and puffy, if I thought I looked like shit last night, is nothing to the way I look this morning. Jack is outside lying on sunbed, he has taken my towel, it's on the sunbed next to him. Suppose I'm meant to go and join him, keep up the pretence that we're a happy couple. Have a shower, let the water pound my body. Doesn't help. Head outside, sunglasses on, nothing else on of course and I don't have my towel to hide the sticky-out belly. Shouldn't really matter at a time like this, but strangely it still does. Jack asks if I want breakfast and I say I'm not hungry. Don't think I'll ever eat anything but chocolate and ice cream again. That'll really do the fat belly good. He nods towards the empty sunbeds next to us, your boyfriend and his missus have gone then, he says. I don't answer, no point. Mrs Two Bums is making her way towards us, no doubt to ask where we were yesterday. Turn onto my stomach, eyes tight shut, can't face it yet. As predicted, she stops in front of Jack who didn't see her coming. He told her I was feeling ill, too much sun or something and he'd just gone to do some sightseeing. Breathed a sigh of relief, for a moment thought he would tell her. She wobbles off. Didn't say that for your benefit, he tells me, you've made enough of a fool of me without everyone knowing, he says. God, this is not going to be easy.

Little and Large had already left, they said to tell us goodbye. Maria was wandering around the sunbeds selling tickets for the weekly barbecue, I'd forgotten about that. Wonder whether we're going, don't know that it would be a good idea, the mood we're in. Family has decided to stay by the pool today, father is playing with the children in the small pool, mother is reading a magazine. Happy families. Don't suppose I'll ever have that now. Tears start rolling down my cheeks again mixing with the sweat on the towel. Must get a grip.

Jack buys the barbecue tickets. Looks like we're still playing happy campers then.

Mad Irish and Beefy arrive, she asks if I'm feeling better, say fine. Feel like screaming. Jack starts talking sports with Beefy, nice to see he's carrying on as normal. Not. Like he really doesn't give a shit. We have broken up after ten years over one stupid flirtation and a kiss but normal service is resumed within hours for Jack. Starting to feel angry. Good. It's a better feeling than the bloody guilt, the grief and the heartbreak.

Mrs Two Bums really should cover that awful ass, it's an affront to nature. Mr Two Bums needs a good kick up the proverbial to catapult him into taking some sort of interest in life, Call me Mal should stop lusting after other women and appreciate the woman he's got. Mr Piercing should go and beat up the binoculars guy instead of just repeatedly saying he's going to, and Mr Music Man should be sent to an 18-30s hotel where they could throw him into the pool accompanied by loud music. Oh, and dark companion should get together with hunky waiter who is so gorgeous he must be gay. Take deep breath, feel a bit better now. Also feel guilty again, not fair to be spiteful to all of them. Will have to go back to church with Mrs Italy at this rate. She's already paid her daily visit and is settled down next to Mr Italy, happy as a pig in shit. Good for her.

Jack asks if I would like to go the bar for a juice, I say no, thank you and he says why, do you want me out of the way so that you can hit on your next target? Oh, for fuck's sake, I am beginning to think it would be better if I had left this morning.

March behind him to the bar, we sit in silence. This is ridiculous. Can't stand it any more. Say look if it's going to be like this I may as well leave. This is not civilised, this is torture. He says do I really expect him to act normally, I say he seems to be managing fine with everyone else. Call me Mal comes over then to talk about the boat trip tomorrow. I'd forgotten about that too. Our last day, we were going to enjoy another outing on the ocean wave. I have seasick tablets ready to take before we leave, just in case. I expect Jack is still planning to go on that too. Well, I'm not. Stuff it. Decide to spend tomorrow on a day out at the shops and in the pubs on my own. Jack can keep up appearances on his own.

Back on the sunbeds, last few hours lying naked in the sunshine. Started really well, gone tits up now.

Literally. Will be my last naked holiday, all this nudity obviously doesn't suit me, makes me act completely out of character. Try to close my eyes and shut out everything around me. We have more games to look forward to this evening. Oh, fun and joy. I can barely contain my excitement.

Beefy is legless, Mad Irish must really be nagging him today. Did overhear her earlier asking for ice to cool her down. There were rivers running down her boobs, she said, like two giant waterfalls over two little hills. Molehills, Beefy said and anyway did she really think melting more water on her tits was going to help? Apparently she did, so Beefy filled a pint glass with ice at the bar, poured it over the wet boobs then five minutes later she was complaining that it was running all down her stomach and as it was his fault what exactly was he going to do about that?

Jack looks like he's sleeping but I'm not sure. He's probably trying to avoid talking to me, we never did finish the conversation at the bar. Decide I need alcohol if I am going to get through this day. Hunky waiter fetches my wine, I ask if he sells cigarettes and he gets me a packet. OK, I know, very, very stupid, but stuff it. Don't have a light, hunky waiter obliges while smiling and saying they are bad for my health. Heartbreak is also bad for your health, didn't you know? Jack is walking over. Great. Can't even enjoy my first cigarette in six years in peace. Actually, not really enjoying it, feel quite light-headed and bit of a shitty taste in my mouth. Stub it out before he gets to me. The look says it all. Is this something else you haven't been telling me, he says, you're back smoking? Oh, for goodness sake, Jack, give me a break. Then – why didn't you ask me to join you at the bar, are you after the hunky waiter now that your boyfriend has gone? Feel sick again, feel the tears welling up. Can't take any more of this. Gulp the wine, then he says, "Drinking this time in the afternoon, another bad habit I didn't know you had, so far we have adultery, smoking and drinking, anything else I should know?" Can't speak or I will cry, try to focus my eyes on the information tower in the distance, stare really hard to stop the tears falling. Hunky waiter serves Jack a lager, hypocrite. Half an hour at the bar sitting in stony silence is not fun, wine or no wine. Another couple of hours and it'll be barbecue time. This time last week I was excited, planning what jewellery I was going to wear, looking forward to a new experience. This time last week I had Jack. Funny how your life can be so different in a matter of a moment. Don't care about tonight's barbecue, might not even bother with make-up.

Do my last shift on the sunbed, last public nudity hour, never to be done again. Not that I haven't enjoyed the experience, it has been a very liberating feeling, kind of exhilarating at times. Shame about the way it affected me though, made me flirt too much, even have one (very minor) fantasy about another man. Don't even want to think about the kiss, can't imagine, can't think, honestly don't know what I was doing. Just a stupid, stupid woman desperate for attention. How sad is that? And when I finally realise it's just the one man I want the attention from, it's too late. All gone. Dreams, hopes, relationship, future, life. Shit, occurs to me I am also now homeless. Oh, that's just terrific. Where the hell am I supposed to live when we get back home? It'll have to be Aunt Biddy's couch I suppose, Frances is in my old room. Suppose there's always the homeless shelter. Oh, for God's sake, Cate, stop being so bloody dramatic! Jack asks if I'm going to get ready soon for the barbecue, I say it won't take me long to find something to wear, so, no, actually, I'm not. Ooh, wine must be making me bolshy! Good. Jack raises his eyebrows, he wasn't expecting that obviously. Double good.

Hunky waiter is setting up the barbecue, extra strong punch is ready mixed on the bar. Best keep Beefy away from it then. People drift back to their chalets to freshen up. I am being stubborn now, not budging. Jack has to ask again if I'm ready to go back. In a minute, I say. Let him wait.

Can't work out why I'm getting mad at Jack. It's not like he's done anything is it? I'm the guilty one here, the bad person who has ruined everything. Can't help feeling angry though, he could at least have let me explain how I was feeling, could at least have given me a chance. Would I have given him one, I wonder? Don't know is the honest answer to that. Thing is, I know it meant nothing, but if I was Jack I'd find that hard to believe. And even if I did, it would still hurt wouldn't it? It's still a betrayal whichever way you look at it.

Barbecue is hotting up, both the food and the guests. Punch is flowing nicely, Beefy is now seriously drunk. He must be bad because he's completely ignoring Mad Irish's torrent of insults and demands. She even has to get someone else to fetch her punch cup. Whatever is the world coming to?

My bum is still lighter than the rest of me, don't give a stuff any more. Call me Mal makes the mistake of rubbing my shoulder and I jump back and give him an evil glare. Not today, sunshine. Actually not any day, he is rude and invading my space. I may be naked but it is not an invitation for touchy feely. No one else behaves like that, time Call me Mal learnt some manners anyway. There is still a code of behaviour, nude or not.

Maria comes out of the office carrying a microphone, hunky waiter follows bringing a big box. What now? New games tonight? Maria makes an announcement. We will not be playing the standard games this evening. Last week, there were some complaints that they were a little too risqué and even though we are all nude, we are certainly not perverted. Well, not most of us anyway. People look at each other, wondering who complained. Well, it certainly wasn't Call me Mal or Miss B, I think we can safely cross them off the list. The obvious choice is Mr Music Man but he didn't attend last week's barbecue. Just occurred to me Mr and Mrs Haughty were here last week. She might well have done. After all, she didn't mind destroying my life with Jack, what's a little barbecue? All right, I know it was my fault and I'm damn lucky she didn't punch my lights out, but I can't help hating her for what she did. Maria refuses to tell and says it's not the first time people have complained, so the decision has been taken to discontinue the party games. Anyway, she is putting on alternative entertainment for us. Wait for it – it is bingo and karaoke. The day just keeps getting better and better.

Have only played bingo once before in my life, and then under protest. My friends would never believe I am sitting here starkers, pen in hand, preparing to play housey housey. Brings a smile to my face to think of their reaction if I told them. Jack notices and asks if I am thinking about my boyfriend or my next conquest. Cheers lover, you really know how to bring a girl down.

Bingo is actually fun, we play three houses, you get a bottle of wine for winning a line and champers for winning a house. I am getting nicely drunk (yes, again!) and miss a few numbers, so does Mad Irish who is hopeless, it makes us laugh. Jack glares, along with Mrs Two Bums who takes her bingo as seriously as she takes her WI. The elderly woman shouts for the first line. Mad Irish thinks that's the end of the game and crumples her card then hunky waiter informs her of her mistake and she has to unfold it all again. That makes us giggle too. The elderly woman's husband wins the house and everyone shouts "Fix!" Hunky waiter, who is calling the bingo, looks horrified and says he would never cheat. Bless. Second line is won by Mrs Two Bums with the house by one of the new people. Last house, Jack wins the line and very gamely gives the wine to our table for me, Mad Irish and Mrs Italy. Mrs Two Bums decides to join us. She can piss off. She didn't share her wine, we noticed that was spirited away in her bag quick smart. House is won by a newcomer who says she doesn't like champagne, well, not the cheap sort anyway, and offers it as prize to the best karaoke singer. Hunky waiter will be judge, he looks less than delighted at the prospect.

First up on the karaoke is Call me Mal, no surprises there then. Miss Brazilian is rolling her eyes, she has obviously heard it all before. From the look on her face we are in for a real treat. 'Love me Tender' is his first offering and he tries to swing the hips just like Elvis, but looks as though he is suffering from cramps and needs to use the toilet. No one offers to go second, so Mal continues his Elvis impression with 'Hound Dog'. Delightful. Miss Brazilian and new woman get up next with their own unique rendering of 'It's Raining Men'.

Don't know about men, but it's enough to bring down cats and dogs and if I was newbie I would certainly not stand next to Miss Brazilian. Talk about Beauty and the Beast. Beefy fancies himself as a bit of a musician, used to be a bit of a rocker in his younger days Mad Irish says. He's up on his feet next singing 'Every Breath You Take' but looking more like a cross between Meatloaf and Bob Geldof than Sting. Still, he puts his heart and soul into it, screwing up the eyes and everything. At one point, he serenades Mad Irish and she tells him where to stick his microphone. Call me Mal wants to sing another Elvis song and I am thinking by now I would rather pull out my own toenails than listen to any more of this. Thankfully, Mr Italy gets up next and does the 'Chicken Song'. Is actually quite funny. Even more so because he is naked, the big belly, the bum and all the bits are wobbling in tune to the music. Very contagious, everyone starts joining in and soon there are about twenty naked people doing the 'Chicken Song'. Binoculars guy really should have stayed for this.

Haven't seen much of Jack all evening. I've spotted him looking from time to time, no doubt suspicious that I am eyeing up a new mate or misbehaving in some debauched fashion, wanton woman that I am. Should really give him something to look at but can't help just loving him and wanting him. Very hard to be this near to him when I can't get close any more. What's that saying? So near and yet so far away. Karaoke goes on and on in true British fashion.

Getting very drunk, too drunk, Mrs Italy asks if I'm OK and immediately feel weepy. Can't cry here. Say I'm tired, still feeling a bit under the weather, think it's time for bed. Do the right thing and go to inform Jack.

After all, wouldn't want to incur any more of his wrath, would I? Predictably he says he'll stay a while longer, but does give me a peck on the cheek to keep up appearances. Personally, I think we're fooling no one, you don't suddenly become cold and distant overnight, but if he wants to play games, that's fine by me. Don't want to tell anyone anyway, I'd be the bad guy, wouldn't get any sympathy. Course, everyone loves Jack, Mr Bloody Popular. Bet they wouldn't blame him if it was the other way around. Strange how it's always the woman at fault. Mrs H told Jack, put the blame squarely at my door. She just calmly did what she felt she had to do to save her marriage, packed her bags and left for home holding the hand of her cheating husband. If Jack had been the one who had a fling, or a flirtation or a romantic episode or whatever you want to call it, he would still be a good guy. It would be 'Oh, that's men, can't help themselves' or it would be the other woman's fault for throwing herself at him, and of course she'd obviously be a whore, or it would be my fault for not pleasing him, not being enough of a woman or some such crap.

Feeling quite mad now. Look out the window, there's still a large crowd by the bar, Jack in the middle of them all, Mr Fucking Sociable. I am not going to bed, will not give him the satisfaction of being neatly out of the way when he eventually rolls in. Check the fridge, half a bottle of wine, I am turning into an alcoholic. Jack finally saunters back, and is suitably surprised that I am still up. He's not through the door five minutes before I start.

Don't know what came over me really, I have never acted like that before. Well, not with Jack anyway. I think it just got to the point where I couldn't stand any more, my head felt as though it was going to explode, my heart was in such pain I just couldn't have made things any worse. So, I told him exactly how it was. How his lack of commitment, not giving me enough attention, and sorry, yes, I know I'm like a spoiled child sometimes I need so much fuss but then he knew that about me. He has always known that I am needy. Not a very attractive trait, granted, but for one reason or another that's how I am and he knew it, he has known it for ten years but has chosen not to give me the attention I so desperately crave. And ignoring me New Year's Eve, refusing to buy a home, finding it funny when other men gave me attention. He doesn't find it so funny now. I told him we have been together ten years almost to the day and I felt it was going nowhere. Well, nowhere I wanted it to, anyway. Then the way Mr H talked to me, looked at me and wanted me was exciting, made me feel good, important, beautiful, sexy. I don't usually feel that way. It kind of took me by surprise so, even though I always knew in my heart there was no real feeling there for him, and I knew in my head it was wrong even though I told myself it was harmless, I just sort of let things happen. In the end I was just too polite and too nice to back down after leading him on. It was only after I realised what it could do to Jack that I was even remotely honest with Mr H. I really thought no harm had been done and I had honestly made up my mind that Jack's lack of commitment and everything was not half as important as just being with him. I vowed I would never be tempted again, not that I had been seriously tempted with Mr H. I swore nothing like that had ever happened before and never would again. I said sorry for lying, I was scared, terrified of what would happen. Then I told him I loved him so much he was my life, begged his forgiveness and said I was so very, desperately sorry. Pathetic, I know, but I was at breaking point and would have done, said or tried anything just to get him back. Even looking at him was hurting me, I loved every single inch of his body, his gorgeous eyes, that mouth, those hands which used to touch me and hold me, strong arms to cuddle up in. Oh, my God, it took every ounce of self control not to just fling myself at him. I asked him please not to throw away ten years, not to throw me away over a stupid, stupid mistake which I regretted more than anything else I had ever done in my life.

He didn't say anything, just listened, mostly not looking at me. A couple of times he put his head in his hands, at one point he moaned. I finished, I waited, there was nothing else I could say. It was silent, seemed forever before he spoke. Then he said very quietly, but very gently, "Caitlin, nothing alters the fact that you wanted another man, that you met him behind my back, that you kissed him and that you lied to me. And I know what you're saying but I just can't get that image of you and him out of my head. I just can't think of anything else. I'm sorry too, but I really don't see how we can get past this."

I was expecting it, was too exhausted to cry. I just gave up. Told him I'd try to find a flight to go home tomorrow or I'd try to find another hotel for a night, there was really no point in trying to keep up the pretence any longer. He nodded, agreeing, said he'd sleep on the couch again. I took the hint, went to bed alone.

197

Day Thirteen

Slept fitfully, in between crying and agonising over what to do with my life. When I slept had vivid dreams, they woke me up. Soaking with sweat and tears. Never known such pain or despair.

Morning came, as it does. You can't stop the clock, nor turn it back. Everything was quiet, just the sound of the birds singing the morning chorus. Dragged myself out of bed, decided to leave early before everyone was up for breakfast.

No Jack in the living room. Diary was in the middle of the coffee table, wide open. What now? Couldn't believe what I read…

Hey, diary, Jack here. This is the second time I've done this but I'm calmer this time. The first time I opened these pages I was just looking for the incriminating bits, and skimmed over the rest. When Mrs H said what she said, I didn't want to believe it and when I asked Caitlin I wanted to believe her, but somehow I knew Mrs H was the one telling the truth. I read the diary because I know she writes everything in here and I had to know. It was like being hit or something when I realised what she had been thinking and doing. I was so angry. Now I haven't skimmed these pages, I've read them all properly and I understand better how Caitlin was feeling. If I'm honest and I'm trying to be, I can even understand why she did it. I admit I shy away from commitment, that's something she's always known about me, but it wasn't because I didn't love her or didn't want a future with her, I just didn't see the need for a piece of paper, a ring or a mortgage. I thought we were happy as we were and it wasn't until New Year's Eve that I knew Caitlin felt differently. She could have mentioned it before. That took me by surprise and I needed some time to think about it before talking to her. She has never mentioned it since so as the subject hasn't come up again, I thought she was just drunk at the time. I'm not a mind reader, in ten years Caitlin has only once mentioned marriage, she has only hinted occasionally at getting a house, and has certainly never said anything about wanting children. Maybe it should have occurred to me but, like I said, I was perfectly happy with the way things were and I genuinely thought she was too. I'm a bit pissed off at the attention thing, I do try to boost her confidence as much as I can because I do know how insecure she is. (By the way Caitlin, the word is insecure, not needy, and I kind of think it's cute sometimes). Though you've got nothing to feel insecure about. You really are the most beautiful woman here, not just here, everywhere we've ever been, you have an amazing figure, the most gorgeous eyes and hair, and, at the risk of starting another tantrum, there is really nothing wrong with your stomach. Maybe I have neglected you a bit since we've been here, I admit I've been a bit busy making new friends when I know you were expecting a romantic fortnight together. This holiday has been different in more than one respect – there's a camaraderie here that you wouldn't get in an ordinary holiday complex. You've noticed it too. You know what I'm like, man's man and all that, you've noticed I need my daily sports fix. The novelty of this situation did make me neglect you a bit and I'm sorry for that, but you could have just said instead of going after someone else. I have noticed men looking at you, of course I have, and not just here but back at home too. I noticed Mr H looking at you and a few others too, but it never occurred to me that you would look back. That's why I found it amusing. You were my woman and other men were lusting after you, I was kind of proud, macho nonsense I know but there you are, and I had no reason to doubt you. Now I do. Everything has changed, and there's no way it can be the way it was again. Maybe in time I could forgive you but I really don't know if I could forget. I have been sitting here for hours, reading and rereading, thinking and rethinking. I haven't got all the answers, but I know I still love you and you're right we shouldn't just throw away ten happy years. I don't know if it can work, I don't know if we can put this behind us, I don't know if there's any kind of future for us. But I am willing to try, if you still want me. Jack.

My heart is racing, I feel lightheaded. I hadn't realised but I've been crying again, tears blotting the pages. Some sad tears, some happy ones. I love him so much my heart is full and I can't catch my breath. Over and over in my mind all I can think is he still loves me, he is giving us another chance. From being in the depths of despair I am suddenly elevated into euphoria, laughing and crying at the same time. I don't want to think about his doubts, just so pleased to have a chance, so determined to make it up to him, so, so glad to still be with him. Run to the window, he is sitting by the pool, all alone. Now my heart is singing. Dash to the bathroom, quickly wash face, hands, clean teeth, brush hair. Got to put a little eye make-up on, spray a little perfume, go as fast as I can. Can't wait to get near him, can't wait to touch him, God, hope he touches me. Practically run out of the chalet then stop as I reach the terrace, suddenly feel really shy. Also insecure, what if he's changed his mind? Take tiny baby steps towards him, realise I have no towel, don't care. Stand next to his sunbed, heart is thumping, afraid to speak. "You look nice," he says. We laugh nervously, he takes my hand and kisses it. It feels like an electric shock, it feels warm, it feels so good. I melt, I start to cry again.

We are going on the boat trip. Must admit I just wanted to spend the day alone with Jack, but he has paid, he expected us to go and I just wanted to please him. Beamed all through breakfast, actually ate properly for the first time in what seems like ages. There were some very sickly people around that morning, far too many of them had overindulged the night before. There are fourteen of us going on the boat trip again, that's the maximum Captain Handsome will allow. Jack says just as well we booked last week.

The fourteen of us went to wait outside the giant gates for the bus. Another scorcher today, it's going to be really hot out at sea, glad I put my factor fifteen on. Realised I forgot to take my seasick tablets. In all the excitement had completely gone out of my mind, but I'm sure I won't need them, nothing could spoil my happiness today. Clutch Jack's hand, he doesn't squeeze it back but lets me hold it. That'll do for now. He seems very quiet actually. Start thinking he's regretting giving me a chance, stomach starts churning again. Stop it, Caitlin, for goodness sake stop it! Can't just let things be, have to over-analyse everything. Remember what Freud said – sometimes a cigar is just a cigar. Or something like that anyway.

Captain Handsome gave me a nice smile when we boarded the boat. He remembered me, then. Of course, when someone is threatening to chuck up over your clean shiny boat you probably would remember them, wouldn't you? Smile nicely back and get a glare from Jack. Shit, didn't mean it to look flirty or anything, was just being friendly. Make a mental note to be more careful.

This time head for the front of the boat, will be more comfortable and far enough away from Captain Handsome's gaze. Settle on the big yellow cushions, prepare for take-off. Literally. Anchors up and we make our way out of the port. As soon as we are clear of the harbour walls, clothes start being removed. Again, I am in the first three to get them off. Jack isn't so impressed this time. Feel OK so far, fingers crossed there will be no seasickness today. Heart is as light as air, humming quietly to myself, the sun is shining, Jack is at my side, we are out in the middle of the ocean, it is a good day.

Snacks are being served and I decide to risk it and eat one of the delicious croissants, washed down with a bottle of ice cold lager. Very tasty. Call me Mal stops for a chat and asks if we would like him to be our official photographer today. I laugh, I'm in such a good mood and say, of course, we would be honoured. Jack scowls. I ask him if he's OK and he says, "You just can't help yourself, Caitlin, I hadn't noticed before what a bloody flirt you are." Bloody hell, that was a shock. Say sorry, yet again. Make mental note to be really, really careful for a while. Can quite understand Jack being annoyed, after all it's early days, he can't just get over this in a minute. Vow to do everything I can to make sure he doesn't feel threatened again.

It is beautiful out here in the ocean, the land is just a tiny dot in the distance. Captain Handsome asks if we would like music and everyone choruses, "Yes, please!" Whatever would Mr Music Man say? Put more suntan lotion on, making sure I'm well oiled, the sun is really strong out at sea. Ask Jack to do my back and my bum and he says am I sure I want him to do it or should he ask for volunteers? I say it doesn't matter, I was going to lay on my back for a while anyway.

Feel tears threatening again. Don't understand this sudden change of mood. This morning was wonderful, he was so gentle and loving. Now he's barely speaking to me and when he does it's to make barbed remarks. I know I have to be patient but I really didn't think it would be like this.

Mad Irish has sent Beefy to get her a refill. The cool box is just yards away but why move when you have a personal slave? The party is starting early, Call me Mal is on fine form telling funny stories, Mad Irish is louder than ever, one of the new guys is getting stuck in to the lager supply. I mention to Jack that I think he's on his third or fourth already and get a sarcastic comment about me continually looking at other men. OK, will only talk about women for the rest of the day then.

Two German couples are stretched out across the middle of the boat, you have to step around them to get to the toilet or the cool box. Jack says they're bloody arrogant. No one else seems to mind. Settle down to sunbathe, close my eyes. The sun is hot but there's a cool, gentle breeze just caressing my skin. Feels wonderful. Try to doze, haven't had much sleep the last few nights.

Wake up suddenly with the sound of loud laughter. Mad Irish almost fell off the boat. She had to get up to go to the toilet, (it's the one thing Beefy can't do for her), tripped on one of the German guy's feet and went careering towards the rail on the side of the boat. As the rails are only about three foot high, she almost went overboard. Beefy started laughing, she got up and hit him several times across the back and shoulders, calling him all the bastards going. It was apparently his fault, he should have accompanied her to the toilet. Call me Mal and Miss B started laughing, then everyone else joined in. Even Jack had a smile on his face.

Decided to go to the toilet myself and grab another lager. Ask Jack if he wants one. Get another funny look. He says since when did I fetch my own lager, who was I heading off to flirt with this time? This is getting ridiculous. He says he'll fetch them, he can't trust me to move. Well, sorry Jack, but I have to pee. Course he doesn't believe that. Whatever. I really have to go. I am very careful to keep my eyes forward and not talk or smile at anyone along the way. Deliberately avoid Captain Handsome's eyes, I can feel him looking at me. As, no doubt, is Jack.

We are heading towards the shore to dock for lunch, there's the passenger ferry in the distance. Showtime! Feel quite comfortable this week, not bothered at all by dozens of day trippers staring at my naked bits. As expected, lots of waving and hollering, cameras out, binoculars tuned in to maximise the experience. Hear the PA announcement, wonder if anyone does turn and look the other way? Highly bloody unlikely. Call me

Mal and the Germans are waving at the passengers, quite proud of their nakedness. Mad Irish is calling them all idiots who should get a life. Beefy just carries on drinking his lager, will take more than a ferry load of gawkers to put him off his ale. I smile, catch Jack looking at me, wipe it off my face immediately.

Lunch is lovely, deplane guy serves it again, on the neat white trays. He asks if I am feeling OK this week, I seem much better. I tell him I'm fine, thank you, don't know what was wrong with me last week. Catch Jack looking again. Well, what am I supposed to do, ignore him?

Call me Mal doesn't have Mr Music Man for competition this week so decides not to take a dip. I would really like to swim naked in the sea but am not going in on my own. Ask Jack, he says thanks but no thanks. He's not a great swimmer. Nor great company today. One of the German guys jumps in followed by one of the new people so I decide to join them, loudly cheered by the surrounding watching boats. Try to ignore the whoops and lovely remarks like 'nice knockers'. The water feels great, cool against my skin. It is an exhilarating feeling, something everyone should do once. Swim around for a while then float, lying on my back looking towards the sky. More whoops and shouts of 'lovely pussy'. Oh, grow up why don't you? Anyone would think they'd never seen a naked woman before. Well, maybe they don't see them swimming around in the sea often, but there's no need to make such a fuss. Spoils it a bit, decide to get back on board. More whoops and remarks about the ass this time. Wonderful. I suppose at least they didn't mention the belly.

Jack is extremely peed off that I went for a swim. He accuses me of flaunting myself and enjoying the attention I got from the audience on the nearby boat. Nothing I say makes a difference, he's completely paranoid about me and other men. Yes, I know it's my fault but he said he'd give it a go, didn't he? The nasty remarks and foul mood aren't exactly trying hard are they?

The afternoon passes pleasantly enough except I am afraid to talk to anyone or look around too much. Stomach is churning again, I'm on edge, afraid I'll do something else wrong. I have to lie on my stomach for a while, my chest is starting to burn. Ask Jack again to rub the cream on, he obliges without remarks this time. Feels wonderful with his hands on me, and despite the bad mood his touch is gentle. I smile and thank him and he smiles back, then kisses me softly on the forehead. Tears spring to my eyes again, it was so unexpected and so loving. It's amazing I am not dehydrated with all the crying I've done over the past few days. Plus the sweating. Should drink more water to restock supplies.

Really raucous crowd on the boat now. Everyone is in fine spirits, and full of alcohol. Music has been turned up, people are singing along to the songs. 'Chicken Song' comes on the radio, everyone cheers and gets up to do the actions, a boatful of naked people in the middle of the ocean singing and flapping our wings. Surreal. A few records later and the 'Macarena' plays, Mad Irish and Miss B get up to do the actions, I decide to join them. Is really fun, we get a round of applause and loud cheers at the end. Jack is furious, he says I am making a display of myself again.

Suddenly feel very heavy hearted. Can't do this. I'm afraid to talk, move or smile. How long is it going to go on for? This is just day one and already I can't stand it any more. I know he doesn't trust me now, but surely he can't think I am going to do anything right here on the boat in front of him? And with who anyway? They're not exactly prize specimens this lot. What does he think I'm going to do – have a quickie with Call me Mal at the back of the boat or go down on Captain Handsome as he's steering? Bet I'd get another round of applause and some whoops for that!

The boat is heading back towards shore with its cargo of fourteen naked drunken people singing 'You'll never walk alone', conducted by Call me Mal of course. Get dressed, say my goodbyes and thank yous to Captain Handsome. Jack is scowling but I don't care. He is a very nice man and I am a very polite woman. So there.

Back at the complex, most of them go straight to the bar to carry on partying. I'm really not in the mood any more. Besides, would be afraid to talk to anyone.

Jack says he fancies going out tonight. I'm quite pleased about that. We haven't spent that much time alone and it's our last night here so it will be lovely, just the two of us. We both fall asleep for a few hours, too much sun and booze in the afternoon. Feel awful when I wake up. Have a long shower to wake myself up, put lots of conditioner in my hair, the sun is drying it out. Take great care with hair and make-up, wear the white dress which shows off my tan. Have a lovely tan, the girls back home will be so jealous. Maybe I'll tell them it's an all-over one! Jack is still quiet, maybe he'll be better once we're out.

We walked into town, I tried to hold his hand but he moved away from me. Looked around a few shops, he said he was bored and would meet me in the pub. I said I'd join him but he insisted that I carried on shopping. So much for spending time together, he can't wait to get rid of me. My heart's not really in shopping, walk down to the beachfront. Stand and look out at the ocean, the sun is setting in the distance. This time tomorrow we'll be back home and no doubt it will be pouring with rain. This holiday has certainly been an experience. Wish Jack could be back to normal, this is killing me.

Meet him at the bar, a nice young waiter comes to take my order. Jack accuses me of flirting with him. This is getting ridiculous. I ask him how long he is going to punish me for, and when will the accusations stop? He says he doesn't know, he is still angry, takes longer than a day to get over what I did to him. I tell him I understand that, but if we are going to try to make it work, we both have to try. I can't go through the rest of my life afraid to speak to people. Tell him again how sorry I am, he says he knows that but isn't ready to forgive me. I ask how can we go on if he doesn't try? He has no answer for that.

The next couple of hours are awkward. I try to make small talk, he barely speaks at all. In the end I say this is pointless, we may as well go back to the chalet and pack. Then he accuses me of wanting to go back to be with the others and asks which one I have my eye on. He is sorry to have spoiled my evening by taking me away from whoever is meant to be my next conquest. I start to cry then, yes, again, pathetic I know. Tell him I can't do this, can't stand it. He says he needs time to get over it. I say I will give him as much time as he needs and I will wait for as long as it takes, but I won't be with him while he is treating me like this. Don't know where I got the strength from to say it, but I knew in my heart it could never work, it was hurting me more to be with him. Told him I'd move out when we got back home and asked him to contact me when he was ready. I knew I was taking a chance, maybe I would lose him for good, but being with him like this was heart-breaking. So, I would give him all the time he needed and pray that one day he'd wake up and I'd be forgiven and he would still love me, and I'd be waiting. Jack looked stunned, he said there was no need for me to move out, I said I couldn't stay while he was like this, he got mad then and asked what the hell did I expect? Could only repeat that I was sorry, I knew it was my fault, but it was just one stupid kiss and if he couldn't put that behind him then we had no future anyway.

We walked back to the complex in silence, except for my crying of course. Packed our bags, tidied up, and got into bed. Him on his side, me on mine, backs to each other, gap as wide as China between us.

Day Fourteen

Got up early, sat outside on the terrace with a pot of coffee. Everything is packed, all ready to leave. Feel kind of numb this morning, but calm. Couldn't go on as we were. I have to have faith – if Jack really loves me he'll forgive me eventually and come back to me. I understand that what I did was wrong and stupid, I admit I should have talked to Jack about my feelings instead of bottling it up, maybe it wouldn't have happened then. But it's not like I killed anyone, this was not a full blown affair, there was no touching involved, it was something and nothing which was incredibly stupid. And I understand him being hurt and angry, but surely this betrayal is not so big and so terrible that we can't get past it? The more I think about it, the more I think it is really not worth breaking up over. But I know I've made the right decision in leaving him, I can't stay when he's treating me like this. Realise I have always felt lucky that he loved me, always been grateful to have him, and always been afraid that one day something or someone will take him away. I have always lived my life in fear of something and it's time I stopped. If he doesn't come back to me, I won't die. Oh, I know, I've had a taste of how much it'll hurt, and it won't be easy but it won't be life threatening. I need to know once and for all, if he really does love me the way he says he does and if we can have a future together. No more fear. Surely I deserve to live my life without that?

It's been different here, that's for sure. Don't know if I'd do it again though. Can't imagine ever being with anywhere with anyone but Jack. Maybe I'm destined to die a childless old maid? I've always been in search of the dream – the loving husband, perfect marriage, cottage with roses around the door and two wonderful children. Suppose that's the hardest part – giving up the dream.

Coffee pot is almost empty, just like my heart. Hear Jack moving around in the chalet, won't go in just yet. Mad Irish and Beefy are up next door, well, he is anyway, she is shouting for a cup of tea in bed. Hunky waiter comes to open up the bar and prepare for breakfast, pool boy is out doing his thing. Another day in paradise about to begin.

The elderly couple are up and about, settling down at their table, ready for breakfast. Hunky waiter is concerned, they are too early, but they smile and tell him they're perfectly happy to wait. Beefy is on his way to the bar, he is not happy to wait and pesters hunky waiter until he gets a pint. The Dutch foursome are out next putting the towels down on the sunbeds.

Jack comes out onto the terrace, says hi. I say hi back. All that determination is faltering as I look at him. It will be really, really, hard to leave him but I know if I want a real future with him it's the only chance we've got. Yes, I could stay and live on my nerves and be permanently miserable with the sarcastic remarks and constant criticism, but I can't do it. No more fear, Cate, no more fear. I ask him if he slept OK, he says not really, he asks if there's coffee in the pot, I say I'll make a fresh one. Very civilised. We even make small talk over the coffee. Probably best if we stick to small talk, I haven't got the energy for any more rows.

Breakfast is being served, we make our way over to our usual table. Don't feel like eating much today, what a difference from yesterday when my heart was full of hope. People are chattering, good mornings are being bandied about.

After breakfast we gather the cases and check everything is OK in the chalet. Don't know what we're doing this morning, the car takes us to the airport at one o'clock. Two and a half hours left. Would like to stop the clock just to be with him a little while longer. Then again, if I could stop the clock would go back to before the kiss with Mr H and change everything.

We put the cases in the luggage room and sit at the bar for a juice. Jack is still being polite and asks if I would like to lie on the sunbeds for a couple of hours. I say no, not really, would get all sticky and he says there's a courtesy shower so we may as well. I quite fancied a walk along the beach but as usual went along with what he wanted. Don't suppose this is really the moment for a romantic stroll anyway.

Shorts, top, bra and knickers come off. Strangely, feel quite shy about undressing in front of everyone. It's OK being naked, but taking your knickers off in front of an audience is somehow kind of unnerving.

Our usual sunbeds are vacant, no one wants to commandeer them then. The suntan lotion is packed, knowing my luck I will burn in the last two hours. Jack says he will borrow some and asks Mad Irish. Very nice of him. He also offers to rub it on me, don't think I could take that, if I feel his hands on me I will melt and all my reserve will go out the window. Not a good idea, tempting though it is to feel his touch one more time. I say thanks but I'm going to lie on my back so I can do the front myself.

Morning passes too quickly. Go for one last dip in the pool before my shower. Call me Mal joins me, the guy just doesn't give up. I am friendly and polite but keep my distance. He is a big boy and not particularly fit, he can't keep up with my freestyle, leave him panting at the edge. Get out of the pool, Jack is smiling. "You almost gave Mal a heart attack trying to keep up with you," he says. I just nod, surprised. What, no sarcastic comment? Does it mean he's trying to be nice in our last few hours or he has given up on us already and doesn't care anymore? Oh, stop it. Either stop worrying about it or just bloody well ask him. This analysing has to stop.

Go in the courtesy shower, no soap. Terrific. Also packed my deodorant, will probably smell all the way home. Never mind, not like anyone's going to get that close, is it?

We say all our goodbyes, fill in the questionnaire for Maria, put 'would like heated pool' in the comments. Maria says everyone does that. Would like to ask why they don't take any notice then, but don't. Everything else was perfect, we say. And we mean it too. Not the camp's fault we've broken up, is it?

The car comes, driver very discreetly stays near the office, doesn't pass the sign saying 'nudists only beyond this point'. We grab the cases and make our way to the airport. All over.

The airport is incredibly busy, there must be thousands of people here. Wonder where they're all going, what kind of lives they've got? Wonder what they all look like in the nude? Now that would be something wouldn't it? A naturist airport? You'd see some shapes and sizes there. At least plane delays wouldn't be so bad with all those bodies to study.

We check in and get rid of the cases. Jack is still being nice and offers to come around the duty free shops with me. I said I'd take cigarettes back for Maggie, even though being an ex-smoker (one drag doesn't count, I gave away the rest of the packet to Beefy) I never encourage anyone to smoke. Get the carton of Lambert and Butler, buy some mints for the plane, check out the perfume prices, they were cheaper in the shops, I had a much better deal. Jack checks out the sunglasses, he still wants a designer pair but the prices are ridiculous. He'll have a look back home, he says. Good idea, I say. We are still being polite.

Go for lunch, there is a McDonald's here. Wherever you go in the world there is always a McDonald's, at least you know you won't starve whatever the local food is like. So, it's hamburger and fries, not exactly the haute cuisine we had at the camp, but it fills a gap. Jack asks if I would like to go to the bar for a last glass of wine. Very civilised. He drinks a pint in about ten minutes, what's that all about? Thirsty or needs something strong to put up with a few more hours of me? Doing it again, stop it, Caitlin. I sip my wine, he has another pint, just as well he's not driving later, we have a lovely train journey to look forward to after this.

More small talk then he says, "Sorry, Cate, I didn't want it to end like this." Don't know what to say. Then he says, "Look, we need to talk." Then the bloody tannoy announces our plane is boarding, he sinks his pint and gets up. Damn, the timing is terrible, for a moment there I thought he was going to try and sort things out.

We get on the plane, seats 8A and 8B. Good, no one else next to us. Maybe he'll talk some more? I go in the window seat, it's the one thing I'm pushy about, hate aisle seats, all those people back and fore brushing against you. Can't sleep, can't spread your newspaper out, have to keep your legs tucked right in just in case you trip someone up.

We go through all the safety talks, nobody watches, don't know why they bother. For insurance purposes, I suppose. Although if the plane crashes and you're dead you're hardly going to sue because no one showed you the safety procedures, are you? The captain's voice rings out, tells us our flight time will be approximately four hours, he hopes we have a pleasant journey. So do we, what's the alternative? An unpleasant flight where we are thrown about the cabin or something?

The flight attendants come around and serve drinks. Food will be dished up later. There is no film on our flight today. Don't care, although I did enjoy 'Calendar Girls' on the way out. Quite appropriate really.

Jack gets me another wine, I think by now I must be responsible for keeping an entire vineyard going. Will have to dry out back home. No alcohol this week. Will also have to weigh, just know I've gained loads with all that food and drink. Still, I did swim every day and had lots of sex until it all went pear-shaped. No more of that for a while. Might have to get myself one of those rabbit things from Ann Summers that my friend Angie raves on about. Can't imagine ever wanting anyone except Jack, the thought of anyone else touching me is just wrong. Even the moments with Mr H, I knew I would never let him touch me. Not just because that would have been crossing the line, but because I genuinely didn't want him to.

Jack takes hold of my hand. I look at him, surprised. "We need to talk, Cate," he says again. I just nod, my mouth is dry, heart thumping. "Well, I need to talk anyway," he goes on. "I'm sorry I was such a jerk yesterday, I'm still mad at what you did. I understand why you did it, I was a bit of an idiot, didn't give you much attention, was busy with my new mates. You should have told me what a berk I was being, but that's not your style, is it? I wanted to kill him, you know, bastard dared to go after my woman, caveman that I am I wanted to punch his bloody lights out. I'm glad he left when he did or I don't know what I would have done. And I wanted to shake you, make you understand how much I loved you and how stupid you'd been. Anyway, I think I do forgive you because I love you and I know nothing like that has ever happened before. I won't forget but that's not necessarily a bad thing because it'll remind me not to neglect you again. Can you promise me, faithfully, that nothing like this will ever happen again?" I just nod dumbly, I'm in a state of shock. He carries on talking, holding my hand tightly looking intently into my eyes, which are now full with tears yet again. "When you said you were going to leave me to give me time, it was one hell of a shock," he said. "I didn't expect that, I expected you to be around to take your punishment, I suppose. I was a bit pissed off at first, you were the one that had done wrong and you were acting like it was me, but after I calmed down I realised what I was doing to you. You were right, we couldn't have gone on like that, we would both have been bloody miserable." Shit, heart stops. I was right? What does that mean? We are still breaking up? Blink, gulp, don't know if I want to hear any more. Can't speak. "Cate, it made me realise that I couldn't live without you." What? What did he say? "Cate, I love you with all my heart and soul and I don't want to think about a life without you in it. Don't you know that?" No, no, I didn't know that. Heart racing now, did I hear him right or am I just hallucinating? No, I heard him right, he is saying it again. "Can we have another chance?" he says. "I promise not to behave like a jerk, well, I suppose I will make an occasional remark on a bad day but I will try really hard not to. I want to put this behind us and get on with our lives. Can we do that, Cate?" I am just looking at him, still can't speak. He has to ask? Doesn't he know that he is my heart? Feel a tear trickling down my cheek, he wipes it gently with his finger. "Cate?" he says again. I just nod, yes, yes, yes, we can. We can do that. Heart singing now. Realise the air hostess, sorry, cabin crew member, is looking at me. She stops to ask if I'm OK and can she get me anything? People on the other side of the aisle look too. Shit, am making a fool of myself, try to stop crying but fail, the tears keep falling. Jack says thanks, I'm OK. The woman sitting behind leans over and asks if I'm afraid of flying, she says her husband is the same, he looks suitably grateful that she has announced it to the whole plane. Jack says again, no, she's fine, just a bit emotional over something. A bit emotional over something? That's the understatement of the year, my life has been pulled inside out, upside down and backwards over the last few days. Like a rollercoaster ride, one minute plunging the depths, the next up in the clouds.

217

Jack asks if I'm all right, I nod yes. Still can't trust my voice. He says, "We'll be OK, Cate, you do want this too don't you?" I nod vigorously, yes, yes, I do. Then he gets out of his seat and kneels down in the aisle. What is he doing? People all around us are watching. He reaches into his pocket and takes out a box. What is it, what's happening? Then he holds it out in front of me and says, "Please, will you marry me?" What? What? I am aware that everyone is staring but am in shock, can't speak or move. He keeps looking at me, I look at the box, there is a ring, a beautiful diamond solitaire, an old fashioned engagement ring, exactly like I've always wanted. It's shining, the sunlight outside dazzling off the stone.

The woman behind says, "Answer him, dear" and a man down the back says, "Put him out of his misery, love". The flight attendant or whatever they're called is smiling at me encouragingly. People are standing up now looking over their seats, waiting for me to speak.

Try to find my voice. "Yes, please." It comes out squeaky and I start to cry loudly at the same time. People on the plane clap, the air hostess says congratulations, Jack beams and comes forward to kiss me. Oh, I will drown in happiness. He puts the ring on my finger, it fits perfectly, of course it does. We hug, he holds me tight, he kisses my hair, I keep crying all over his clean shirt. He tells me he bought the ring last night while I was shopping on my own and was going to ask me then but the moment was never right. He couldn't help himself snapping at me and then I said I was leaving him. No, that wouldn't be a good moment would it? Am deliriously happy, heart is dancing, singing and doing somersaults. He says it won't be a long engagement, I can plan the wedding when we get back. Mind is racing, I know exactly which dress I want, saw it in Vogue last month, will get Angie's mother to make me an exact replica, she's good at that. Don't know if babies and a house are on the cards, but right now don't care. I look at the ring on my finger and I look at Jack and suddenly feel I am the luckiest and most beautiful woman in the world.

Book Four – Jaclyn

Chapter One

I hated the monthly visits. Hated them with a vengeance. Why the fuck do I put myself through them? Travel back to little old Paxtown, rock up in the care home and pay my monthly dues to my bitch of a mother. She's never pleased to see me, God forbid she could even smile as I arrived. The staff have noticed, they smile and look at me sympathetically. "She's in a lot of pain, dear, it makes her cross," they say. I smile back, but inside I'm thinking fuck off, she's just a grumpy old cow who hates me. And yet I still turn up for my monthly punishment. What's that all about?

So in I go. Sympathetic looks. "She's not too good today, dear," warning me in advance that she's going to be a bitch. When is she not?

"Hello, Mum," I say politely.

"Well, well, look what the cat dragged in," my mother answered. "Didn't think you'd be back after the last time."

"Ah, well, here I am," I said. "How are you feeling?"

"Bleeding awful, not that you care," she snapped at me. "Where have you been the last seventeen years, eh? Didn't care then, so why now?" Oh Lord, here we go again, every single fucking time.

"You know why," I said. "But you don't believe me. Can we please not do this again?"

"We'll do this every time I see you until the day I die or the day you admit you're a lying bitch!" she screamed at me.

"Well, today is not that day, Mother," I said coolly.

She turned away from me. I picked up a magazine and ignored her. That irritated her, I knew it would. "What about your brother and your sister? You haven't even been to see them," she ranted. "You come swanning in here with your fancy clothes, flashing your money about. Who do you think you are? You don't care about me or your family, you walked out on us years ago. Don't give a shit about us. You're obviously doing all right, with that car, the clothes, the bag you're carrying probably cost more than the entire contents of my wardrobe. I'll tell you why you're here, missy, somebody told you I was dying and you've come to gloat. Well, let me tell you, I'm going nowhere, so you can fuck off back where you came from and leave us alone for the next seventeen years too."

"Nice to see you too, Mum," I said. "I won't bother you any longer. But I'll be back next month just to piss you off." I walked out of her room. Damn, it was hard being around her. They said she had weeks left to live, that was four bloody months ago, that woman is going nowhere. She'll live forever just to spite me. Not that I want her dead, of course I don't. Whatever else she is, for better or worse, she is my mother. Don't know what I was thinking coming back here, maybe that dying would make her loving towards me, that maybe she'd finally be pleased to see me? How wrong can you be?

I wandered into the canteen. I needed a bit of a break before driving back to London. I hadn't intended it to be a five minute flying visit but I just didn't have the head for her crap. "JJ, is that you?" a voice called from across the room. Next thing I knew I was being engulfed in Angie's arms. "I can't believe you're here," she said beaming at me. "It's been so long. We always wondered where you went and how you were, me, Caitlin and Maggie."

"How are you all?" I asked.

"We're fine, Maggie is married with three children, little fucking monsters but look like angels just like Maggie. Caitlin is getting married soon, we're planning the wedding now. And I'm good. I'm happily divorced and enjoying my life as a single person again. But how are you? Where did you go? What do you do?"

"I argued with my mum and went to stay with my aunt in London," I said. "I got a job, worked my way up. I'm a marketing consultant now."

"Wow, it must be well paid," Angie said eyes wide. "That jacket is real Chanel right? And the bag – is it Prada?" I was about to say no, you would never mix a Chanel jacket with a Prada bag when I stopped myself.

"Yes," I smiled.

"What are you doing here?" Angie asked.

"Visiting my mother," I said. "She was diagnosed with bone cancer a few months ago. My stepfather isn't very well so can't take care of her, so she's here. My stepsister got a message to me that she was dying so I came to see her. That was four months ago and here we still are," I said.

"You never did get on with your mum did you?" Angie asked.

"She always hated me and I never knew why," I answered. God, it felt great to actually have an honest conversation with someone.

"How's your mum?" I asked. Angie's mum Eliza had been the closest I'd ever had to a mother, she was always so good to me.

"Oh, we call her Eliza Doolittle now, because she does fuck all. Just sits in front of the TV night after night, watching sitcoms and soap operas. Her only conversation is about what such and such character had done. I swear she's losing the plot and thinks they're real people." We talked for ages, Angie was there as a volunteer, she visited residents who had no family. It was typical Angie, always the one with the big heart. Before I left she said they were organising a bridal shower for Caitlin the following weekend and asked me to come. It felt so nice to be real around someone I went against my better judgement and agreed.

On the drive back home I was kicking myself. Why the hell did I agree to go to the bridal shower? How was I going to face everyone? Shit, shit, shit, I said aloud banging the steering wheel. It's not that I didn't want to see them. Angie, Caitlin, Maggie and me had been the four musketeers, best friends since the age of four. They were the ones I missed the most after I left. But also the ones I never wanted to find out what I did.

Back at the flat I looked around and told myself for the millionth time to be grateful for what I had. I say flat, but it was so much more than that. It had two bedrooms, both with en suite bathrooms, a huge open plan living area, state of the art kitchen and huge windows overlooking the Thames. I had two balconies, one from my bedroom and the other in the living area. I sat out there most nights, whatever the weather, reminding myself how lucky I was.

That night I poured myself a glass of wine and wrapped a blanket around my shoulders. Spring was in the air but hadn't yet sprung. After the second glass I decided I would go to the bridal shower, I really wanted to see my friends, have normal conversations with normal people. Then the phone rang. It was him. "I'll be there in twenty minutes," he said. "Be ready."

Chapter Two

I was ready of course when he walked in twenty-three minutes later. Lying on the bed wearing nothing but suspenders, stockings and red, high heeled shoes. He came to me quickly, tearing his clothes off along the way. "I've only got fifteen minutes," he said. "It's the interval at the opera. Open your legs." And he climbed on top of me and I obligingly opened my legs. A few pumps later and he was gathering his clothes from the floor and rushing back to the opera. "Talk soon," he shouted as he left and blew me a kiss. I showered, changed the bed sheets then went back out onto the balcony with another glass of wine. Well, what else would you do when you're a high class call girl?

My current provider was very well to do and paid for my flat plus all bills. I had a credit card which allowed me £1,000 a month for whatever I wanted. A cleaner came in, a valet looked after my car. I had a personal hairdresser and make-up girl. My wardrobe was full of designer clothes and my bank account was busting. But no matter how I tried, no matter how many times I told myself to be grateful, there was still that gnawing in my stomach. I was lonely. That was why I had agreed to go to the bridal shower. I missed my friends. I missed having friends. I missed the gossip, the giggles, the intimacy, the loyalty. I had no one. I had walked out on it all. And here I was with everything. And yet, nothing at all.

When I left Paxtown I arrived at my Aunt Maisie's. She's my mum's sister, but they're not close. She said I could stay a few days but I would have to earn my own living, she couldn't afford to keep me. I looked everywhere for a job and eventually got one waitressing at a greasy spoon café. Pay was shit, but at least it paid and I could give my aunt lodgings for sleeping on her couch. One day, she said one of her friends could get me a really good job with my own place just for being nice to someone. No prizes for guessing what being nice meant.

To be honest, at that time I was desperate. My aunt was almost as much of a bitch as my mother was. She took every penny I earned and looked at me like she hated me. I was used to that from women, except my friends of course. I have always had a pretty face and sexy body. I developed early and I have the kind of hour glass figure that most people crave. Boys at school called me sex on legs. Every single male I ever met wanted me. I am not bragging here, believe me. It is a fucking curse. But it has earned me a lot of money and given me a very comfortable life.

I met the guy Aunt Maisie's friend Joe was talking about and I knew I could do better. So I said to Joe, "Get me someone with money and I'll give you a cut. You are offering a beautiful sixteen year old virgin here, I must be worth more than this dipshit can pay." His eyes lit up and off he went. A week later he returned with a black dress and high heels.

"Put these on," he said, "and come with me. We are going to make some money!"

The first time I set eyes on Steve I thought 'he'll do'. He had an OK body, nice-ish face, and he was a lot younger than the other guy. Steve was a stockbroker. More money than sense. He was twenty-seven, married and looking for excitement. He also had a fetish his wife wouldn't indulge. So, Steve set me up in my first flat in Greenwich and he became my first. My first what? Don't really know how to describe it. Yes, he pays me for sex, but he's not just a client. Yes, he's older than me but he's not a sugar daddy. I called him a provider, because after all that's what he was.

He wasn't my first lover, by the way. I lied about being a virgin. I lost that a year before to my childhood sweetheart Adam. We had plans to move in together when he finished college and got a job. Of course, that didn't work out. Adam was very focused and very organised. He had our future all mapped out. He would finish college, we would get a mortgage and buy a house together. We would spend two years making the house perfect and going on dream holidays and then we would have our first child. Our second would follow two years later. I forgot to say, we would be married first, Adam was very traditional. And very manly, super sexy. I couldn't look at him without wanting him. So I lost my virginity to him on the clifftop the day after my fifteenth birthday, and afterwards we swore we would be together forever.

The day I left I did go and see Adam. I told him I had to leave but I wouldn't tell him why. I pleaded with him to go with me, but of course he wouldn't. Why would he? He had a nice life in Paxtown. He told me to go home and sleep on it, to calm down, it was just another silly argument with my mother. Except it wasn't.

My stepfather Malcolm had gone that step too far. He married my mum when she was nineteen and I was four years old. I still don't know who my father was. Malcolm was mostly good to us, there is no doubt that my mother loved him very much, still does. But, sometimes when she wasn't around, he'd find some excuse or other to give me a slap. I told my mother at first, but she said I must have deserved it, so that was that. Don't get me wrong, he didn't beat me, it was a clip across the ear, a slap across the back of my legs. Worse than the physical punishment was the mental torture of never knowing when his mood would change from being pleasant to yelling at me and hitting me for something I had done. It changed from one day to the next. I remember once when I was about ten I went to get ready for school before putting the breakfast dishes away. I got an earful and a slap for that. So the following day I put the breakfast dishes away first and I got a slap and an earful for not getting ready for school.

As I got older he alternated between being a nasty bastard and a slimy creep. He'd look at me funny and smile nicely, ask me to sit on his lap, stuff like that. My mother said he was trying to be nice and I was a little bitch to try and twist it. So, mostly I kept out of their way. Stayed out with the girls as late as I could, or go to one of their homes after school rather than my own. Caitlin had problems with her parents too, but it was mainly that they were cold fish who didn't care about her. I thought at least they're not hitting her, or hitting on her. I never said it out loud though, no way was I going to tell anyone what fuckwits I lived with, not even my best friends. I have never been one to go for the sympathy vote.

My stepbrother Lawrence was born when I was six, and my stepsister Kate two years after that. My mother was happy, she used to sing as she cleaned our shitty little council house. She reminded me, almost daily, that Malcolm had taken on a fatherless child and that I should be grateful.

The day I left was the day that Malcolm found out I'd been shagging Adam. How he did I'll never know. Maybe he sensed a change in me, maybe he saw or heard something, I don't know. I could see he had been drinking as I went into the house. Nothing unusual in that. But he had a strange glint in his eye. "You've been a bad girl," he said walking towards me, whisky breath on my face. "You're a little whore, you've been shagged, you're busted."

"What are you talking about?" I said backing away.

"You and your little boyfriend, letting him put his dick in you, you dirty girl."

"Stop talking like that!" I yelled at him. "You're disgusting!"

"I'm disgusting?" he said. "I think you are the one that's disgusting, but don't worry your dirty little secret is safe with me. And now that you are a woman it's time you did some womanly duties around here."

"What do you mean?" I asked him, trembling by then, getting really scared about where it was going.

"You know what I mean," he said leering at me. "I've seen the way you look at me. I've watched you parade around this house showing off your body with your boobs straining at a little blouse, swinging those hips. Oh, I won't lie, I was tempted before but I wasn't going to be the one to bust you. Now that you are, we can have a lot of fun." He tried to kiss me and I pushed him away.

"Get off me, you pervert!" I screamed. "You are sick, you are twisted, I'm going to tell Mum about this, even she won't stand for this."

"Come on, don't be like that, I know you want to," he said lurching towards me again. I pushed him really hard, his legs were unsteady due to the drink thank goodness and he fell backwards into his chair. He just sat there grinning at me. "Go on, then," he taunted me. "Go run and tell Mummy. Do you think for one second she'll believe you? Especially when I tell her I found out you were shagging your boyfriend and you had a tantrum when I confronted you, threatening to tell her I'd made a pass at you if I didn't keep my mouth shut. Oh, I can see it now – your mother will be so apologetic about your behaviour and the way you've hurt your doting stepfather I might even get a shag off her tonight."

"You are vile!" I yelled at him and ran out of the house.

I went to the rugby club where my mum was playing bingo. She thought Malcolm was such a fucking saint for babysitting while she went out to get her twice weekly fix. She didn't look best pleased when I ran in and interrupted the session. She was even less pleased when I told her what had happened. She hit me across the head. "You lying, fucking evil bitch!" she screamed. "It was a bad day in hell when you were born! You have been sent to torment me! Stop saying these terrible lies and fuck off out of our lives! You're not wanted, you never were! Get out and never come back!"

Well, that was pretty clear, don't you think? I was the one that got chucked out. So, I went back to the house, grabbed my bag, robbed the rent money out of the biscuit tin and off I went.

Chapter Three

Steve was good to me for two years. I know I was lucky. He could have been a pervert or a psycho or violent or anything. It wasn't as hard as I thought it would be to be a sex slave to a complete stranger. I was completely numb inside, I had gone way past caring and just wanted to get some independence. Steve's thing was that he wanted me to pee on him, which his wife wouldn't do. I had to drink loads of water before he arrived so that I could piss to order. And all the time I was thinking, here you are believing you are the boss of me and I am pissing on you.

After three years, Steve's wife decided she wanted to move back home to the countryside outside London, for them to start a family. He offered to set me up in a place near there, but to be honest I didn't think my kidneys could take any more of the constant drinking and peeing, so I declined his offer. I did, however, ask him if he knew anyone who would like to keep me in the manner to which I had become accustomed. He was really reluctant, didn't want to give me away, but eventually admitted his boss was insanely jealous of him and lusted after me.

So, he was next. Grant. He had more money than Steve and no fetishes, thank fuck. He looked after me for a year or so until I met Brian the banker. Now, he was serious money. It was when I met him that I bought the house in Greenwich. Nothing fancy, two up, two down, but a good location close to the river and somewhere that was mine. Over the next two years I furnished it and made it my own. I stayed there for twenty-four, once a month. Brian wasn't happy that I wasn't available but tough titty. I kept him so happy the rest of the time he didn't complain too much.

By then, I had the reputation in certain circles of being the dream shag, but at a price. I did have the odd bit of trouble with pimps trying to muscle in on me, but thankfully the men I chose as my providers had enough money to buy them off.

I had no illusions about love or happy endings. I had been loved by Adam and my musketeer friends all those years before. I wondered what they would think of me now? I hoped I would never have to find out.

Brian kept me for four years, until on my twenty-fifth birthday I paid off the mortgage on my little house in Greenwich and decided that was enough. Brian was a good, decent guy, but incredibly boring and not in the least bit fanciable. And the sex – don't get me started. He was a firm believer in lots of foreplay. He would tweak my nipples and caress my boobs for ages before moving further down and playing away there for what seemed like an eternity. I had to put gel on before he came so that I was nicely oiled, because despite what he did, or how long he did it for, nothing turned me on. I just wanted him to get it over with so that I could go get a glass of wine and watch the soaps on TV. Of course, Brian never knew he didn't please me, I moaned and screamed and said all the right things, he thought he was a fucking stud. But, oh, it was exhausting.

So, I told him on my birthday that I would be moving out of the flat and out of his life. He was distraught, offered me more money, a better place to live, whatever I wanted. But I just couldn't face one more performance, so I packed my bags and off I went. I loved living in the little house in Greenwich. I had enough money to live on for a year before having to work, so life was good. At least for a few weeks. Just when I was thinking about taking some classes, getting out and making friends, Richard walked into my life. At the gym, actually. I'd noticed him watching me and asking the staff questions about me. I'm not sure whether or not it was a mistake to keep going to the same gym after ending it with Brian. I knew they all knew what I was, Lord knows how. Juicy gossip has a way of getting around, I suppose. But it was because they knew that I felt comfortable there, they never tried to hit on me, they knew they couldn't afford me. Richard, on the other hand, could.

He made me an offer too good to refuse. Moved me into a garden flat in Chelsea, gave me a credit card to furnish the place however I liked, set up a bank account to transfer money to me every month and bought me my first car. Driving around London is not great and public transport is pretty good, so I'd never felt the need before. But once I'd passed my driving test I couldn't wait to get behind the wheel. It was a two-door sporty BMW, silver with fur-lined seats. I loved it!

Naturally, I thanked Richard in the appropriate way. He was the first one to want a bit of variety in bed. He liked anal sex occasionally, can't say I felt the same way but I obliged, with the help of the gel of course. He liked to be tied up sometimes, and very occasionally he wanted to lay stark naked, spreadeagled on the floor, while I walked up and down his body wearing only stiletto heels. I have no idea what his wife thought of the little red marks all over him following those sessions. I assumed he had sex with his wife, I never asked. I stayed with him for four years, then he retired and could no longer afford to keep me in the manner to which I had become accustomed. However, he did have a lot of very rich contacts so I found myself in the very bizarre situation of interviewing four men for the position of my next provider.

Chapter Four

I checked my reflection in the mirror. I was wearing a tightly fitted, but classy, black Chanel dress. I wore red high heels and let my hair down. My hair is dark, almost black, it's long, scooping my waist, it's thick, wavy and glossy. I apply red lipstick and slip a ruby ring onto my finger. There, gorgeous. I am stunningly beautiful, as I've been told on more than one occasion, and I do have the perfect figure. Lucky me, eh? Not really, I would trade it all for a normal life with a husband who loved me, a couple of kids and some friends.

I had my interview questions ready. First, the financial stuff – how much are you offering, what is included in that, I wanted a detailed breakdown. Where would I live and is there a car, a clothing allowance, stuff like that. Other questions were how often would they want to see me, did they have any particular demands, and was there anything outside of normal sex, that they would require in bed.

Number one was another banker. We shall call him banker the wanker because he was. A total prick. He was a sleazeball, when he started describing what he would like to do in bed, it made Steve the pisshead (my name for him due to the fact he liked me to pee in his mouth) and Richard the spotted dick (on account of the heel marks) seem perfectly normal. I thanked banker the wanker for coming and said he would receive my decision in the next twenty-four hours. "It'll be an easy decision, Jordan," he said. "I'm your man!" Well, if I hadn't already decided that no way was he my man, he wouldn't have been after that arrogant exit.

You may be wondering who Jordan is. That's me. When I started in this game I decided not to use my real name, I wanted to hide behind someone else, so I created Jordan. I was also worried that I might bump into someone I knew and they'd call me by my old name which I didn't want anyone to know. So instead of Jaclyn Jordan, I became Jordan Jackson. I figured if anyone from my past turned up they would know me as JJ anyway.

Number two was more promising. He was the CEO of a large company and offered me a really good financial package. He was in his forties, smartly dressed, quite plain but certainly not ugly. His only demand was that I would be available 24/7 as his schedule was so busy he would have to fit me in at odd times. The only sex he wanted was straight, apart from wanting to photograph me in various positions, naked of course. That made me a little nervous, I wasn't sure I wanted photographic evidence of my activities lying around, but he assured me they would be kept in a very safe place, for his eyes only.

Number three was a big boy. At least 6'4" and weighing around twenty stone. The thought of him on top of me made me cringe. His financial offer matched number two, he had no demands. The really weird thing was that he didn't want to have sex with me. He ran a poker night twice a month for himself and a few colleagues and they always hired a call girl to walk around naked serving them drinks. Whoever won the game got to have sex with the girl. He wanted me to be that girl. I pointed out that it would be a lot cheaper to keep hiring a call girl but he also wanted to use the flat he would house me in to hold the games. Well, I may be a hooker but I am not in the business of giving myself to random strangers who win card games, so number three was crossed off.

By the time number four arrived, I had decided to go with number two and take a chance on the photographs. And then in he walked. Lord Augustus Theodore Merrifield the third. Well, with a title like that there's no contest. Unless he was some real sicko he already had my vote. His financial offer was better than the others, he had a flat overlooking the Thames which would be mine, along with a Rolls Royce convertible. His only demand was that I be available at all times and he had no kinky sex fetishes other than requesting I wear nothing but stockings, suspenders and high heels at all times when he was with me. I told him he was the lucky winner there and then and asked how should I address him. He said, "Call me Theo, all my friends do. My secretary will be in touch to make the arrangements. I look forward to seeing you again soon," and then he kissed my hand. Such a gentleman.

Chapter Five

So here we are, four years on, and Theo is still my provider. He's a good guy, I'm more than satisfied with our arrangement. He's in his fifties, he looks like the country gent he is. Not unpleasant, he looks decently dashing when he wears a tux. He has a house in Mayfair where he lives with his wife Lady Mary and youngest son Maxwell. He also has the family pile in the country, of course. His eldest son Augustus is married and has a two-year-old daughter whom Theo dotes on. He likes straight, quick sex which suits me down to the ground. The only problem is he likes a lot of it, and he phones at random times of the day and night. So, if I'm out shopping I can't go further than a fifteen-minute drive away in case he rings. Still, it's a small price to pay for what I get.

At the moment, I have over £100,000 in my bank account, clothes and jewellery worth even more, a Roller and a house in Greenwich which would now sell for around £200,000. So, I'm more than comfortable and, yes, I could stop doing this but what would I do instead? I have no qualifications or experience. What do I put on my CV? High class hooker, earnings in the region of £100k a year, references can be obtained from a number of very wealthy men. I couldn't just sit and do nothing even though I didn't need the money. But who would employ an ex hooker? I could hardly become a schoolteacher, could I? I know I could move away somewhere where no one knew me, but if I was lucky enough to meet a man who loved me I would have to tell him. My conscience just wouldn't let me do otherwise. As for children, I had decided a long time ago that I would never have any. How could I possibly bring a child into my world? And if I left and started a new life somewhere, how could I have a child knowing that one day they could find out their mother was a whore? No, I had long ago decided that I was going to get as much as I could out of this game until I was forty. By that time, I figured my looks would be on the decline so I wouldn't be as much in demand. By that time, I would have enough money in the bank to live on forever. Maybe I would just travel the world. Maybe I would pay a man to accompany me and be *my* sex slave – now, wouldn't that be funny?!

Until then, I hoped Theo would stay around long enough so that I didn't have to find another provider. He was fit and well, with no plans to retire any time soon, and he certainly showed no signs of tiring of me. So, barring a disaster, I figured seven more years with him would set me up nicely for life.

He was very understanding about me visiting my mother. Of course, we had thought it was a matter of weeks. I decided to tell him I needed to visit again the following Saturday and would like to stay overnight with an old friend. I could be back by Sunday lunchtime, less than twenty-four hours of not being on call. The Tuesday before, he called around for a lunchtime quickie. As he was dressing I asked. "What again?" he said. "Didn't you go last Saturday? And what friend? I've never heard you mention a friend before."

"Angie, an old school friend, she's a volunteer visitor at the care home my mother's in. It'll be less than twenty-four hours away."

"As it happens, we're going to the country this weekend, got a shooting party organised, so fine. But I have to tell you I'm a bit suspicious about this whole thing. You know our arrangement means you can't have sex with anyone else."

"Don't worry," I said giving him my sexy smile. "You are the only one I want to have sex with."

So, it was arranged. I agonised over what to wear. Didn't want to look too flashy but needed to be smart. After all, I'm the London career woman, local girl made good. In the end I opted for my grey silk Prada trouser suit and black kitten heels. Let my hair down to soften the effect and kept the make-up to a minimum. When I parked the Rolls outside Angie's house, I almost turned around and drove back. "Come on, Jaclyn," I said aloud. "There's no way they can know what you are unless you tell them, and you're certainly not doing that." Instead of butterflies in my stomach I had giant dragons breathing fire on my insides. I was petrified.

Angie was obviously looking out for me and she opened the door waving. Ah, well, too late to turn back. Caitlin and Maggie ran towards me screaming. "Oh, my gosh, it's really you. Oh, we've missed you so much, we've got such a lot to catch up on." The first hour was easy really, they were so excited that the four of us were back together that they chattered on and on, with no need for me to join in, just smile and nod. I knew the inquisition would come later.

By then, more people had arrived and they were busy handing out glasses of bubbly and offering trays of nibbles. I sat at the window drinking a glass of wine and thinking how strange it felt to be back with them in my home town. But good strange. Adam's sister Kate arrived. Wasn't expecting that. "Hi, how are you?" I asked politely.

"JJ, is that you?" she said. I nodded. "My God, you look amazing! Where have you been?" So, I told her the same story I had told the others, London, worked my way up in a marketing company etc. "You know you broke my brother's heart, don't you?" Kate said. I wondered when he would come into the conversation.

"Sorry, I had to get away," I said. "How is Adam?"

"He's fine, absolutely great," Kate said. "He's got a little boy now, Sam, he's six, lovely child, image of Adam."

"Oh, that's nice," I said. I don't know why but I hadn't expected Adam to have had a child. I wondered who the mother was but I wouldn't ask. "Nice to see you anyway," I said and walked into the kitchen. Maggie was there filling more glasses.

"You OK?" she said looking at me quizzically.

"Yes, fine, I just ran into Kate, you know, Adam's sister. She said he's got a little boy."

"Ah, yes, you and Adam were love's young dream," Maggie said smiling. "He married that girl who was in the year below us in school, she was captain of the netball team, pretty girl, can't remember her name now."

"Maggie," Caitlin called, "People are running dry in here."

"Coming," Maggie shouted back and headed off with the tray of drinks.

Adam, married and with a child. It bothered me. A lot. I know it shouldn't have but it did. "For fuck's sake,

Jaclyn, get a grip," I said to myself. "It was seventeen years ago, did you really think he'd be here still waiting for you? And what would you do if he was – confess all? No, didn't think so." So I got a grip. Went back in, drunk some more, joined in the party games, laughed a lot actually. It felt so great being with my friends again.

After everyone else had left, we opened yet another bottle of wine and took it out into the garden so that Maggie could have a cigarette. As predicted, they wanted to know everything I had been doing. I glossed over the story as quickly as I could. Thankfully Caitlin interrupted. "Why don't we tell each other a big secret that we've never shared before?" she said excitedly. Oh, fuck, maybe not such a good thing she interrupted.

Maggie said, "Secrets? From you lot? Are you kidding me? I have nothing to tell."

"Come on, Maggie," Caitlin said. "There must be something we don't know."

"Did you know I shit myself giving birth to my second child?" Yes, we did, they nodded. "OK, did you know me and Mike had sex in the rugby club toilets last carnival night while you looked after the children?" Yes, they nodded, we did. Caitlin finally accepted there was nothing about Maggie that she and Angie didn't know, so she moved on.

"Angie, your turn."

"Well, actually there is something that I have never told you," she said. "Not because I wanted to keep it from you, but because you'll be disappointed in me, and I'm really ashamed of myself for doing it."

"What is it, Ang?" Maggie said. "There's nothing you can't tell us you know. No judgement here." Angie took a deep breath.

"Remember the day my divorce from Pete came through?" They both nodded. "Remember you took me out to celebrate, and we got really drunk?" They nodded again. "When I got home late that night I phoned Pete and asked him to come around for a goodbye shag." There was a stunned silence at first, then Caitlin and Maggie both started to talk at once. Angie held her head in her hands. "I know, I know, stupid, pathetic, fuckwit, you don't need to tell me."

"Good," Maggie said, "because you are. But you should have told us, yes, we would have given you a well-deserved bollocking, but we would have been there for you, you should know that."

"I do, I do," Angie said. "I'm sorry. It feels so good to get it off my chest though!" she grinned.

"So, did he?" I asked.

"Did he what?" Angie said.

"Did he come around and shag you?"

"Yes, course he did," she replied. "In the morning I couldn't believe what an idiot I'd been. I never did it again, and I never will."

"OK, JJ, your turn," Caitlin said.

"Oh, no, you started this, you next," I replied.

"Fine," Caitlin said. "I'm bursting to tell you all anyway. You know me and Jack went to the Canaries?" Yes, yes, they said, eyes rolling, and it was really romantic and he proposed on the plane. Clearly they'd heard the story many times, I smiled. "Well, what you don't know is where exactly we went – it was a nudist camp!" Caitlin blurted out.

"What?" Maggie gasped. "You were naked all day, with other naked people? Oh, my God, tell all."

Half an hour later they finally stopped questioning Caitlin, and all eyes were on me. My big secret? I wondered. My really big secret was something I was determined never to tell them. But I remembered what they had said, no judgement, nothing you can't tell us, we'll be there for you. So I took a risk and told them my second biggest secret instead. "The night I left home, it was because my stepfather made a pass at me," I said. "My mother didn't believe me, said I was a lying bitch and to fuck off, I'd never been wanted. So, I went."

"Oh, my God, JJ" Angie said, putting her arms around me. "Why didn't you come to one of us? You didn't need to go away."

"I wanted to get as far away as I could," I answered. "And I didn't want any of you to know what a fucking shitty family I had. I mean, why do you think I never invited any of you into my house? You all had such lovely homes, mine was a shit pit. Second hand furniture, crappy old rugs on the floor, one plate each and if you broke it you had to buy another one. Malcolm never worked and my mother spent most of her wages on bingo. I was ashamed."

"But you always wore such smart clothes, you had such nice shoes, lots of make-up and perfume," Caitlin said. "We had no idea your life was like that! You should have told us."

"No, I didn't want anyone to know, not even you lot. I didn't want your pity then and I don't want it now. I just want you to understand why I left so suddenly and why I never got in touch afterwards. And by the way – the clothes, shoes, make-up, even shampoo and bubble bath, it was all stolen. I stole it all." I had no idea why that came out of my mouth. Confessing to my teenage life of sin. Actually, I was younger than a teenager when the stealing started. I was nine years old when a boy at school made fun of the holes in my gym shoes. Straight after school I went and nicked a pair from the sports shop. After that I didn't look back. Whatever I needed, I stole. I told my mother my friends were giving me stuff, don't know whether she believed me or not, don't care.

"You stole it?" Angie said with a look of total shock on her face. "Oh, you poor thing, I really wish you'd told us. We could have helped, you know that." The other two were hugging me too by that point and agreeing that, of course, they could have helped. But I could never have accepted it. I was the poor relation in our group, but I kept up with them by stealing. Truth was, I thought they wouldn't be friends with me if they knew. And yet, there they were, hugging me and saying they were so sorry that they'd never noticed anything wrong, how they would have helped me, how they wish I'd been able to confide in them. All I could say was how much I missed them. And it was true. I did.

Leaving them the following morning and going back to my life in London was hard. They kept hugging me and making me promise to keep in touch. So, before I could stop myself I had invited them to come stay with me for a night out. They all whooped excitedly. I promised to phone Angie to make the arrangements and off I went.

Chapter Six

Theo kept me busy that week, his wife had stayed in the country so he had lots of free time. I mentioned going away the following Saturday, but, no matter what I said, he was convinced I was seeing someone else and refused. It was ridiculous, everyone had days off surely? After all, this was a job. I asked when the next convenient time would be for me to be away for a night and he refused to say. So much for independence I thought to myself. I am trapped. I am a sex slave. I have no control over my life.

The night away, being reunited with my old friends, had affected me far more than I had realised. I wanted to be with them, joining in the girly talk, helping to plan Caitlin's wedding. She had asked me to be a bridesmaid, me and Maggie. Angie was the maid of honour of course. I was thrilled and touched to be asked and readily agreed. But I knew it had been a stupid thing to do. Not only because it was really difficult to get a night away, but because it would mean facing everyone back home, risking someone finding out. And it would mean seeing Adam. He would be there as one of Jack's ushers. I wondered what his netball playing wife would look like. Maggie had said she was pretty. I didn't want her to be pretty, I wanted her to be a troll. Adam was still the only man I had ever loved, the only one who had ever loved me. Oh, some of my providers said they loved me, usually during sex, and maybe they did. But never the kind of love where they wanted to share the rest of their lives with me, or even to share a little of their lives with me. Two of them – Steve, the first one, and Brian the banker – both took me out in public quite regularly. To functions, dances, things like that. They took me because I would look amazing, I would be extremely attentive and have eyes for them only. Their friends, all of whom knew they were married, would eye them up jealously. They both got a kick out of that.

Richard took me out once, but by then word had spread, and everyone knew he was paying me to be there, so he didn't do it again. Theo couldn't if he wanted to. He was always in the society pages of the posh newspapers, being photographed at some event or other. His wife was with him sometimes, and sometimes she was pictured alone at one of her charity good works. When his granddaughter was born, there was a photograph of Theo, his wife, their two sons, his daughter-in-law and the baby. The paper devoted half a page to the birth. I always checked the society pages, not because I was jealous, but because it gave me a kick to know that this very respectable lord was shagging me four or five times a week. And usually with his socks on. A disgusting habit, but then he was always in a rush so I suppose it saved some time. Anyway, there's no way we could appear in public together without being photographed by someone, somewhere. And then everything would go tits up. I shuddered, not a nice thought.

I felt trapped. I just wanted to spend an evening with my friends, for fuck's sake! So I told Theo we needed to renegotiate the terms. I wanted two nights off a month. Every other Saturday, actually. Theo said no. I said I would end the agreement then. He said I was bluffing. I said try me. It finally sunk in that I meant what I said. He offered a compromise of every third Saturday off. I said it would do for starters, and yet again reassured him there was no man involved, I just wanted to spend time with my friends.

I phoned Angie that evening and told her the weekend after next was good for me. I gave her the address of the house in Greenwich, well, I could hardly entertain them in the love nest could I? I paid a cleaner and a gardener to take care of the house for me. I know I could have rented it out and made a lot of money, but I needed it to be there, available for me, just in case. My safe house. I called the cleaner and asked her to put fresh bedding on the day before we were due to stay. I transferred her money to get some shopping in, buy some fresh flowers, make the place look lived in.

I was really excited and really looking forward to seeing them. They were catching a train and I was picking them up at the station. I went to the house first to check everything was in order and wished, not for the first time, that I really did live there. They were suitably impressed with it when they arrived, and they loved Greenwich. We did the tourist thing, saw the Cutty Sark, all of that. Had lunch by the river, then spent the afternoon getting ready for our big night out. I'd hired a limo to take us to Soho. Although I had never been there, I'd done my homework and got the names of the best bars for a good night out.

The bars were as good as recommended, they loved it. "You're so lucky living here," Angie said. I just smiled. "So, are we going to meet this boyfriend of yours?" she asked. I'd told them Theo was my boyfriend, well, he was the closest thing I had to one. I didn't give them his full name obviously, although a mischievous part of me was tempted to!

"No, he's busy," I said. "He works in the city and he's always got to go to some boring function or other."

"Maybe next time?" Maggie said. I smiled.

We had a great time, the day passed too quickly. When they were leaving the following morning I had a strange impulse to go with them. It had really unsettled me, having them back in my life. Theo had noticed the change and became even more convinced I was seeing someone. My first thought was that he was a hypocrite, demanding I stay faithful to him, while he is unfaithful to his wife. But then I realised he has the right to demand it, he is paying for it.

Chapter Seven

I missed the first fitting for the bridesmaids' dresses, it wasn't my Saturday off and Theo wouldn't let me change it. I got to the second one, though, the dresses were beautiful. Peach organza and lace. Caitlin looked absolutely breath-taking in her dress, like a fairy tale princess. The wedding was just weeks away and I needed to change my Saturday off to be there. In fact, we were all supposed to be spending the night before in Angie's house. I had no idea how I was going to do that. I considered faking illness to stop Theo calling around, but I didn't think for one second that he would believe it. And that would put our whole arrangement at risk.

Then there was the hen party of course. Only a night away at a spa hotel, but it was on a Friday. No way I could do that. I would have to come up with an excuse not to go. I didn't want to lie to them but I couldn't bear telling them the truth. Yes, they said no judgement, we will stand by you, no matter what, but I don't think that would apply to being a hooker. If they were scandalised by Caitlin going to a nudist camp, and disappointed in Angie for sleeping with her ex, what chance did I stand? They certainly wouldn't want to remain as my friends, and now that I had them back in my life I couldn't bear to lose them again.

I told Theo the truth, that I was a bridesmaid at a friend's wedding and needed to be away for two nights. Told him he was welcome to check it out, gave him the time and venue of the wedding, the names of the bride and groom. I even said he could send someone with me if he wished, like a kind of chaperone. I think that swung it, he finally agreed. But what he said next concerned me. "I don't think this arrangement is working as well as it used to, Jordan." What did that mean, I wondered? Was he pouting because I had a life outside of him? Was it the inconvenience of not having me on call at all times? I didn't think so. There was something about the way he said it that set alarm bells ringing.

I was especially nice to Theo over the next few weeks, but he seemed a little distant and didn't call as often as he used to. I should have been pleased but I was worried. I only wanted a few more years with him to have enough money to live on for the rest of my life. I really didn't want to have to find another provider.

The night before the wedding we were acting like giggling schoolgirls on a sleepover. I'd called to see my mother earlier that day, the staff said she really did only have weeks left. It didn't stop her being the absolute bitch she always was. So, it was a short, but not so sweet, visit yet again. I tried to put her out of my mind and enjoy the evening. It was so good to be back with my girls. I started to wonder if there was any way I could stay there permanently.

The wedding day was perfect. It was a sunny June day, Caitlin looked amazing and we looked pretty good too. Her Aunt Biddy gave her away, and even she looked lovely. Brightly coloured, but lovely. I had been dreading seeing Adam but he was really sweet. "You look," he hesitated, "beautiful," he said, smiling at me.

"Thank you," I said. "You look pretty good too. I hear you have a son, is he here?"

"No, he's at home with his mother, there are no children invited. I think Maggie insisted on that, because she didn't want to bring her brood!" We laughed. Someone called him. "Catch you later," he said and was gone. So, no wifey with him I thought. And he looked gorgeous, he'd matured very nicely indeed. Broad, muscly shoulders, thick blonde hair curling slightly behind his ears, and those deep blue eyes I used to feel I could drown in. Still could. Oh, stop it, I told myself. Behave, Jaclyn, it was seventeen years ago and he's a married man with a child.

At the reception the bridesmaids and ushers shared a table. I was surprised to find myself sitting next to Adam. Why would Caitlin do that I wondered? Knowing our history and all. Had to admit it was a nice surprise though. We chatted in between courses, nothing too personal, but very pleasant. It was just so nice being that close to him, but it was really tempting not to touch his hand, or rub my leg against his.

As the alcohol flowed, any resolve I had to stay away from Adam melted away like the ice in my glass. Not that he was trying to stay away from me. Every time I turned around he was there looking at me. I went out onto the terrace, to get some air I told myself, but who was I kidding? I was hoping he'd follow. And he did. And we just looked at each other and that was it. Before I knew it we were kissing and I was drowning in those eyes. His touch was electric, his lips soft, yet demanding. Dear Lord, I hadn't wanted anyone so much in years. I had never wanted anyone the way I wanted him.

I was staying in the hotel where the reception was being held that night. I gave him my room number and told him to follow me. Back inside the reception Angie called me over. "Where have you been?" she said. "We're just about to order a bottle of champagne."

"That sounds lovely," I said. "But I've got a bit of a headache so I'm going to lie down for a while."

"You do look flushed," she said sympathetically. Oh, shit, more lies. I would never go to heaven.

Sex was amazing, the night was amazing. I didn't care that he was married, or that he had a child, or that he was cheating on his wife. I just wanted that one night, one night to remember forever when I went back to my sad, miserable, life. A very rich, very comfortable life, I reminded myself. I just wished that I'd never left, if I'd stayed would we still be together? Would I be wrapped in his arms like that every night? Would the child be mine? As for Adam – who knows what he was thinking? Was I unfinished business? Had he always carried a torch for me even though he got married? Or was it just that I am a fucking sex temptress no man can resist? Feel like one of those sirens calling from the rocks, luring the sailors to their death and they are helpless to resist.

We slept for a while, entwined in each other's arms. When we woke, he rolled over and leaned on his elbow, looking into my eyes. "Come home," he said.

"What?" I said thinking I had heard wrong.

"Please. Come home," he repeated. What was he asking me? To move back and be his mistress? I couldn't bear to see him around with his wife and child.

"I can't" I said. "And you shouldn't be asking me to, you're a married man."

"What?" he said, eyes widening. "I'm not married, we divorced five years ago, I thought you knew?" No, I nodded, I didn't. "We got married because Susie was pregnant with Sam, we tried to make a go of it but it didn't work. We divorced when Sam was two, but we've stayed good friends and we're both devoted to Sam." I needed time to process that information. I got out of bed. "God, you're beautiful," Adam said as I walked across the room to make coffee. "You know I broke my heart when you left?" he asked.

"Your sister told me." I said.

"Did she tell you I never stopped loving you?" he said. No, she hadn't. He still loved me? Adam still loved me. My heart was singing, but it was breaking at the same time. I couldn't be with him, not after what I'd done. "I'm sorry I didn't take you seriously that night," he said. "I really thought it was just another row with your mother, I didn't think you'd leave. I tried to find you, you know. After weeks of pestering your family and getting told to fuck off, your sister finally told me the only other family you had was an aunt in London. I phoned her, she told me you had been there but had got a job and a flat and had moved out. Did she ever tell you?" No, the bitch had never thought to tell me. Her boyfriend was making too much commission out of my arrangement with Steve at the time.

I walked back to the bed, coffee forgotten. I got in and snuggled up to him, laying my head on his chest. I couldn't face him, not for what I had to say, I couldn't bear the look that would be in his beautiful blue eyes. "I need to tell you some things, about why I left and what I've been doing since. It's not good, none of it. You're going to hate me, but you have to know why I can't come back, you have to know who I am now. Please don't tell anyone else what I am about to tell you, and please will you not say anything until I'm finished?" He held me tight.

"Jaclyn, there is nothing you could tell me that would stop me loving you," he said. Oh, shit, I thought, just wait until you hear what I have to say and you'll be out that door before I could even say goodbye.

So I talked, with my head on his chest the whole time. And he held me the whole time. I felt him tensing now and then but he didn't let me go. It was such a relief to tell someone everything, every dirty secret. I wished it didn't have to be Adam, he would never look at me again the way he had earlier. When I finished it was silent for a moment. Then he spoke. "Is that all of it?" he asked and I said it was. Then he lifted my face up towards him and kissed me. "See," he said. "Told you nothing would stop me loving you." Oh, Lordy, I cried then. Cried and cried, buckets of tears. I couldn't remember the last time I cried, it might have been when I left Adam all those years ago.

When I finally stopped sobbing, we made love again, and then we talked some more. Adam said he understood, I was just a child with no options. I told him I'd been a grown up for a long time and I'd had money and options but I chose to stay in that lifestyle. He said it was because I had nowhere else to go. Everything I threw at him he had an answer for. Gradually, I believed him. He accepted everything, he still loved me. He had swapped the name tags around to sit next to me. It was like all the Christmases and birthdays I had missed all rolled into one. If I never had any more happiness in my life, this night would be enough to keep me going forever.

He said again. "Come home. I have my own construction business, we're doing OK, I have my own house, you won't need to work, I can take care of you."

"Oh, it's not money, I have that," I said. "I can't risk people finding out what I am. Can you imagine my mother? She would be like, see I knew it, a fucking whore!"

"You're not a whore," Adam said. "It's like you've had a few boyfriends, and not that many. When you said first of all you were a prostitute I imagined there would have been hundreds, but it's not like that."

"Adam, please don't kid yourself," I answered. "A prostitute is paid for sex. That's what I was, what I am. They don't put me up in nice flats and give me money for the pleasure of my company, they are buying my body. I could never come back to a small town like Paxtown and risk people finding out. Every time the girls ask me about my life in London, it gets harder and harder to keep lying to them. Even little things, like when they ask which company I work for, I'm thinking shit what do I say now? My Aunt Maisie knows, if I moved home it would only be a matter of time before the spiteful bitch told my mother. The only reason she hasn't yet is that she calls me from time to time to borrow money which she never pays back. She knows she'd never get another penny if she didn't keep my secret."

"That's like blackmail, what a bitch!" Adam said.

"Welcome to my world," I answered wryly.

"Do you think you could maybe come to London and live with me in the house in Greenwich?" I asked tentatively.

"I'm sorry, that's not an option," Adam said gently. "I can't live that far away from Sam. I have joint custody and I spend a lot of time with him."

"Of course," I said. "I'm sorry, I didn't think."

By the morning, we hadn't slept much and we hadn't found a way to be together. I asked Adam if I could still see him, if I could visit every other Saturday. He said not while I was with Theo. "So, if I move out of the flat, end it with Theo, and move into my house you would come to see me sometimes?" I asked.

"You just try and stop me," he grinned. I promised to come to a decision soon and took his phone number. Leaving him wasn't easy, I wanted to hang onto him forever. I had an awful feeling I wouldn't see him again.

Chapter Eight

Back at the flat, I paced up and down. Couldn't figure out why this decision was hard. Adam was offering me everything I wanted. I could have a normal life, in my little house in Greenwich with Adam a regular visitor. I could even invite the girls to stay sometimes, and I could do what I had planned to do before, take some courses, make some friends. Yet something was stopping me. Suddenly I knew what it was. Money and the security of having lots of it. You see, for someone like me who was brought up with nothing, the best thing about having money is not having to worry about it. To be able to walk into a shop and buy a dress you like instead of stealing it. I was way too scared of running out of money to turn my back on that lifestyle. I couldn't work, let's face it, there is no job I would want that I could do. I am not a waitress or a cleaner, I will not work for a weekly wage which wouldn't even pay my florist's bill. My £100,000 would last a while, but I wouldn't be able to blow it. I couldn't shop for designer labels any longer, I'd have to cut back on so much to make the money last. No more wine club. Oh, I couldn't bear to drink cheap wine.

And then I thought of Adam, I still couldn't believe he loved me despite everything. I wanted him so much. But the fear of losing my security was just too strong. I needed more time, I needed to save more, sell some clothes and jewellery, build my savings up. I worked out that if I stopped spending and sold some stuff, in another six months with Theo I could have another £50,000 in the bank. That would help. A lot. And during that time I would get used to not spending money the way I did. Cut back on the flowers, the manicures, the designer dresses and shoes. Yes, I decided. Six more months. After all, what was another six months to wait after we'd already waited seventeen years?

The next time I visited my mother, I arranged to meet Adam afterwards to give him my decision. When I got to the care home, the nurse called me over. Here we go again, I thought. She's warning me about her shitty mood. But I was wrong. "Your mother is really poorly," the nurse said. "I'm afraid she has days, rather than weeks, left. She's not in a lot of pain, thankfully, but she drifts off to sleep a lot. We thought you should know, you know, just in case you want to visit more often."

"Thanks," I said. I had no intention of visiting more often.

"Hello, Mum," I said as I reached her bed. She really didn't look well, maybe the nurse was right and she really was dying now. She turned her head slowly to look at me.

"Why do you keep coming?" she asked wearily. That took me by surprise, she looked almost vulnerable, and really, really tired. In a moment of clarity I realised why I went.

"I want to ask you two questions," I said.

"I am not telling you who your father is," she said. "What's the other one?" Wow, great, question one down the pan then.

"Why not?" I asked her.

"Look, I'm tired," she said. "What's your other question?"

"Fine," I said. "Why do you hate me?" She looked straight at me and was silent for a moment.

"I don't hate you, I just never wanted you," she said bluntly. Shit, that was a blow to the guts. Don't know why, because Lord knows I've heard it many times before, but you'd think if she was dying she could find it in her heart to say something comforting. How wrong can you be? I kept on, I needed some answers, some information, anything that would help make sense of it all.

"I know you were only fifteen when I was born, is that it? You were too young. Did my father leave you? Is that why you won't tell me who he is?"

"No, he didn't leave me," she said angrily. "And it's fuck all to do with my age. I didn't want you, and I can't look at you without being reminded of him!"

"Why, did you hate him?" I asked. She had never before got this close to being honest with me, I had to keep pressing for answers.

"No, I didn't hate him, I loved him very much," she said. "Now I'm tired, fuck off."

I was even more confused after speaking to her than I had been before. I met Angie in the canteen for coffee and told her about it. She agreed it was very odd. The only answer we could come up with was that my father had died and she loved him so much it hurt to look at me. Pretty feeble, I know, but it's all we could think of. I wondered if Aunt Maisie knew who my dad was? I decided to ask her the next time she came around for money.

I went to Adam's house, it was a lovely detached cottage on the outskirts of town. Strange, I had imagined he would be in some modern apartment or something. As soon as we saw other we kissed and ended up in bed. After a while, he asked me when I was moving out. I told him I needed six more months to be financially secure and that from then on there would be no more arrangements, only him. I didn't expect his reaction. "No, Jaclyn, no. I am not going to wait around for six months while some lord is shagging you. Have you had sex with him since we were together? You have, haven't you! Oh, my God, Jaclyn, how could you?"

"I, I, I don't understand," I stuttered. "You knew I was going back there, and that I wouldn't make any changes until I'd made my decision. I can't leave now, I'm too frightened that I'll lose my security, my money won't last forever. Please Adam, try to understand," I pleaded with him. He got out of bed, dressed, not speaking or looking at me.

Finally he said, "Jaclyn I love you and I always will. But it's clear you don't love me or you never would have gone back to London in the first place, let alone agonised over a decision to be with me, and then decide you want six months more cash out of Lord money bags before you can be with me. Seriously, Jaclyn? Do you seriously expect me to believe that you love me?"

"But I do," I said. "I really do. I always have. But I can't come back here, you know I can't. I need to be somewhere anonymous, where nobody knows me, no questions asked. I want to make a fresh start, I really do, but I can't do it here, and I can't do it anywhere without financial security."

"I'm not sitting around waiting for six months for you to build up your bank account," he said. "Either stay now, or go forever." I cried, I pleaded with him to give me more time. But he was adamant. Stay or go forever. I couldn't stay.

Chapter Nine

By the time I reached the flat I had decided what to do. I would sell the house in Greenwich, and buy something cheaper, closer to Paxtown. That would free up some of the cash I had in the house, and living outside London, I wouldn't need so much money to live on anyway. Can't believe I hadn't thought of it before! I couldn't wait to tell Adam. I rang but he didn't answer. Probably down the pub, I thought. Ah, well, it could wait until the morning. I sung and danced around the flat as I packed up all my personal stuff. I would tell Theo I was moving out the next time he called. Naturally, I couldn't call him. I'd move into the Greenwich house and put it up for sale. Then I'd look for somewhere nice closer to Paxtown. I was so happy and excited!

Of course the bubble burst. At 6 a.m. the following morning the buzzer kept ringing. I thought I was dreaming it, my head was fuzzy from too much celebratory wine the night before. Eventually I got up to answer. "Who is it?" I said sharply into the intercom.

"Miss Jackson, I'm Michael Mansfield, I'm a solicitor representing Lord Merrifield, please let me in immediately, this is a matter of some urgency." Baffled, I pressed the buzzer. What the hell was going on? Was Theo kicking me out? Didn't matter, I was going anyway. I put my dressing gown on and filled the kettle to make a pot of tea, Mr Mansfield sounded posh, I

266

figured he would like a pot of tea with little bone china cups.

He didn't. And I didn't either. I wanted a stiff drink after he told me what he was there for. "Miss Jackson, please forgive the early hour, but I had to come and see you before the press starts camping outside your door," he said.

"The press? Why?" I asked suddenly feeling very sick.

"A journalist from one of the daily rags has found out about your, er, friendship with Lord Merryfield. It is going to be front page news tomorrow. We have tried to stifle it, through the courts as well as through talking to the editor, but to no avail. I'm afraid they have evidence of you and his lordship. Goodness knows how they got it, he's always been so discreet. Anyway, they have. And once that paper prints at midnight tonight, the cat, as they say, will be out of the bag. There is no doubt that all the national press will be interested. They will want photographs of you, they will want your story and they will offer you a lot of money for it. I am here to tell you that whatever offer they make, his lordship will match it in return for your silence. I have a document here for you to sign agreeing to this." My head was spinning, I really couldn't take it in. My only thought was that everyone would know what I was.

"They know he's paying me?" I asked.

Yes, they found an ex client of yours who was willing to give them details in exchange for silence about his arrangement with you."

"Oh, my God, who?" I asked.

"We don't know, but it's immaterial, the press have enough to print the story. Lord Merrifield will give a public apology, of course. At this moment in time, he is begging his wife for forgiveness and praying that she will appear with him in public, a united front."

"I can't believe this," I said, head in my hands, stomach churning.

"My advice to you is to stay low for as long as you can," he continued. "We will appoint a solicitor to represent you, you won't need to worry about legal fees or any other bills."

"A solicitor?" I asked. "Why do I need a solicitor?"

When he told me, I actually did sink to the floor on my knees. Of course, I should have guessed. Not only was Theo a lord, and a well-known one at that, he was also an MP and chair of the defence committee. Shit, shit, shit. They wanted to know if our pillow talk had included any defence secrets. A parliamentary committee was being set up to investigate. Oh, it just got worse and worse. This was a story that was going to run and run. "Of course, you will tell them his lordship never disclosed any such information, either about his work as chair of the defence committee or any other parliamentary business."

"What if he did?" I said, looking scared.

"Miss Jackson, I repeat you will say he didn't. Are we clear? When you are called before the committee to give evidence you will firmly deny that his lordship ever discussed anything like that with you." Called before the committee? In the House of fucking Commons? Oh, my God, it just kept getting worse.

I refused to sign the document, said I would take advice from my solicitor first. Of course, they were paying whoever it would be, and I knew what advice I'd be given, but I was stalling for time. I needed to think.

"Fine, Miss Jackson, your solicitor will be here later today. Do not answer the phone or let anyone else in. Do not go out, the press will be waiting like the bloodhounds they are." Shit, shit, shit.

I didn't know what to do with myself, paced the flat all morning, drinking cup after cup of coffee. This was my worst nightmare. I thought, thank God I had told Adam, so he wouldn't have to read about it in the paper. I wondered if they knew my real name? Hopefully not. If they didn't have that and they didn't know where I came from then maybe, just maybe, the news wouldn't reach Paxtown. I thought of Angie, Caitlin and Maggie. They'd hate me, not just for what I've done, but for lying to them. And my family – oh, crap, Malcolm would be in seventh fucking heaven. I wondered if my mother could maybe die that day instead of finding out? No, the old cow would never do anything that suited me.

My solicitor finally arrived at 2 p.m. His name was Jonathan Thomas. I wondered who would call a child Jon Thomas? Men call their pricks that, don't they? Turns out he was a bit of a prick. He was certainly representing Theo, not me. Sign the document, he urged me. You will be looked after, he said. Tell the committee you know nothing. In the end I just thought fuck this. "Look, Jon Thomas, you little prick," I said. "I am not lying to a fucking parliamentary committee just to save Theo's ass. What about my ass? Who gives a shit about that? I am not signing any documents. If, or when, I get an offer to kiss and tell I will let you know and we will see at that point if I wish to take his fucking lordship's offer or not. You need to know, and you need to tell Theo, I am not lying about anything. I will not offer information, but I will not lie. So, when they ask

I'll be telling them the defence secrets disclosed to me and maybe all the juicy parliamentary gossip too. Now, fuck off!" I held the door open, he had a stunned look, but he didn't argue. Got his papers together and left.

Chapter Ten

It was actually later that afternoon the press arrived. Phoning constantly, pressing the buzzer. I went to the window once to look at them, couldn't believe how many there were. Shit, I really was hot news. Bloody photographers had their lenses trained at my balcony, of course, so I moved back quickly. Had no idea what to do. It was too late to leave the flat. Even in the car I would have to drive out past them, they would probably gather around the car, stop me leaving, that thought frightened me to death. I was trapped in the flat, friendless. Even my own solicitor wasn't on my side.

I must have picked the phone up a hundred times to call someone, but then put it down again. The only one I could call was Adam, he was the only one who knew. But he certainly wouldn't want to talk to me. I hadn't even had the chance to tell him I was leaving. He'd never believe that now. After more pacing, and a good few wines, I dialled his number. I was desperate to talk to someone, even if he didn't want to know.

As soon as I heard his voice I started to cry. Then it all came pouring out. "Are you still there?" I said meekly into the phone. He hadn't said a word after hello.

"I'm here," he answered. "Look, don't worry, I'm on my way. Give me the address, I can be there in about two hours."

"You're coming? You're coming here? You would do that?" And I started crying again. I gave him the address, the code of the underground garage to park his car, and the entry code to the flats.

"Don't answer the phone, don't answer the door, don't look out of the window. I'm on my way."

It was such a relief. Adam was coming. I kept crying. Kept pacing, checking the clock. Two minutes since I last looked. It seemed endless. The phone kept ringing and ringing. I turned it to silent, wondered why I hadn't done that hours before. Finally, a knock on the door. I ran, checked through the peephole that it was Adam, let him in and ran into his arms. I had no idea if he'd want me there but I needed to touch him. He put his arms around me and led me to the settee. "OK, we've got to get you out of here," he said. "Half the world's fucking press is outside the door! Do they know about the house in Greenwich?"

"I don't know," I said. "I don't know what they know."

"We'll take a chance that they don't, if they're there we'll go somewhere else."

"Adam, I'm so sorry," I said.

"We can talk later, let's just concentrate on getting you out of here and somewhere safe first," he said. "Have you got a coat with a hood? And a blanket?" he asked. I nodded and went to fetch them. "Grab anything you need, put the coat on and pull the hood down as far as you can over your face."

He took me down to the garage, every step of the way I was expecting to see a photographer, but we made it. I got in the back of his car and laid down on the floor with the blanket over me. Adam locked the doors just in case, told me not to worry, said he'd run over the bastards if they tried to stop us. Once he was sure no one was following us, Adam pulled over and I climbed into the front. I was praying they didn't know about the house in Greenwich, but as Adam said, they thought I was still in the flat. We reached the house, there was a car outside. "Wait, Adam, wait!" I shouted. "They might be in that car."

"They're not," Adam said. "That's Angie's car."

"Why is Angie here? What the hell is going on?" I screamed.

"I don't know," Adam said, then his face changed. "Oh, shit, I saw Angie at the garage when I was filling up with petrol to come here. She wanted to chat, but I was frantic to get away. I said, got to go, Jaclyn's in trouble."

"Oh, shit Adam!" I said. "She's come to help. Turn the car around, I can't face her."

"Too late, they've seen us," he said.

"They?" I asked, then I saw them getting out of the car to greet us – the three musketeers. Oh, fuck, no turning back.

Chapter Eleven

"For the purposes of the record, please state your name."

"Jaclyn Jordan."

"Miss Jordan, are you known to Lord Augustus Merryfield the third as Jordan Jackson?"

"Yes."

"Did you have an arrangement with Lord Merryfield?"

"Is that relevant? I am here to answer questions regarding national security, not regarding personal matters." His eyes narrowed. He had clearly thought I was going to be a pushover but fuck that. I was fighting back.

"We need to establish the relationship between yourself and Lord Merryfield in order to understand how you may have been party to state secrets."

"What makes you think I was? Have any state secrets been disclosed?"

"Miss Jackson, we are here to establish exactly that. We have reason to believe that Lord Merryfield shared certain information with you, which he was not at liberty to do. In fact, if proven guilty his lordship will have broken a vow, gone against the parliamentary code of conduct and may even face criminal charges. So, you see, Miss Jackson, it is essential that you answer the questions fully and honestly. And then we will establish the truth."

"Fine. I had an arrangement with Theo, sorry, Lord Merryfield, for four years. He paid for my flat and living expenses, plus he gave me a monthly allowance. Before you ask, it was in return for sex."

"So, you were bed partners. How many times do you estimate you saw Lord Merryfield over the period of your relationship?"

"Four or five times a week, over four years. You do the maths."

"So, numerous occasions then. And on any of those occasions did Lord Merryfield discuss his work with you?"

"Yes." He sighed, I was not going to make it easy for him.

"When was the first time Lord Merryfield discussed anything to do with his work with you?"

"I can't remember."

"Please try, Miss Jackson. Was it this year, last year, before that?"

"Probably before that."

"And what information did he give you?"

"Could you be more specific please?"

"Information to do with his work, Miss Jackson, " he said impatiently.

"I'm just trying to establish what kind of information you mean. I thought I was here to answer questions about defence, not general stuff."

"General stuff, as you call it, is information given to you by Lord Merryfield regarding his work in the House of Commons."

"I'm still not clear where to draw the line. For instance, he told me about an MP, supposed to be happily married, who was having an affair with his secretary who is a man. Then there's the woman MP who has three lovers, but butter wouldn't melt when she goes in front of the cameras. Do you think he is the only MP to have an arrangement like ours? I could name you three others right now."

"Thank you, Miss Jackson," the committee chair interrupted. "Mr Devane, please restrict your questions to those matters concerning the defence committee." Mr Devane was not a happy bunny.

I told him some of the information Theo had given me, it was nothing to write home about it. I answered his questions, but volunteered no information. He failed to ask me about the latest defence contract, so I failed to tell him that I knew how much it was worth and who it had been awarded to. Eventually the questions ended, with no real damage done to Theo. I looked across at him as I left the room, he smiled and mouthed 'thank you'.

The committee cleared Theo of any wrongdoing as none of the information I told them about was any threat to national security. He had a rap over the knuckles for being a naughty MP and breaking the code of conduct, but that was it. His wife stood by him, of course, and they were soon back in the society pages showing off their lovely home and family.

You see, the committee chair was the person I was referring to when I told them about the MP having an affair with his male secretary. And I had made it clear I only wanted to answer questions about defence. Thankfully, he was astute enough to read between the lines and stop Mr Devane going down the road no one wanted him to wander down. For Theo had told me something far more damaging than the defence contract or anything else. And the last thing anyone wanted was for that to come out.

Chapter Twelve

I walked out to blinding camera flashes and microphones being shoved at my mouth. Adam was quickly by my side guiding me to the car. He had been such a tower of strength the past few months. The press had found out about the house in Greenwich, so I sold it, for a lovely profit I might add, and bought a penthouse apartment in a small town just outside Reading. I signed the document not to kiss and tell for £200,000. I never would have, anyway. Can't think of anything worse than telling the press all my dirty little secrets for everyone to see. Oh, they hounded me for a while but it finally sunk in that I wasn't talking.

When the hoo hah had died down a bit I went to see my mother. Who, surprise, surprise, had not died in the days following my latest visit, but had in fact continued to live throughout the entire scandal. Needless to say, she was less than pleased to see me. "I always said you were a fucking whore" was the first thing she said.

"Nice to see you too, Mother."

"Dirty, disgusting little bitch, get out of here, I'm ashamed of you."

"*You,* ashamed of *me*?" I said. "You have a fucking nerve. I was dragged up, not brought up, in that shit-pile of a house, with that sicko bastard you married either hitting me or wanting to shag me. And you have never wanted me, and don't even have the fucking decency to tell me why!"

"I see you two are getting on as well as ever," Aunt Maisie said, plonking herself on the chair next to the bed.

I walked out and waited in the canteen until I saw Aunt Maisie leave. "Can I talk to you please?" I asked.

"If you buy me a coffee and a packet of fags," she said, never one to miss an opportunity to get something out of me.

"Do you know who my father is?" I asked her.

"You don't?" she said in surprise.

"No, old bitch won't tell me," I said. Aunt Maisie laughed in a really weird way.

"You're not going to like this, but if you really want to know I'll tell you."

"I really want to know," I said earnestly. "I've waited all my life to know."

"It's your grandfather, our father," Aunt Maisie said. I thought I'd misheard her, asked her to repeat it. She did. I felt sick.

"How? What happened?" I said.

"My father started raping Gracie, your mum, when she was about twelve years old, then me about a year later. We both got pregnant before you came along, but he took us to some backstreet place to have abortions. He was going to do the same with you, but my mother found out Gracie was pregnant. She caught her being sick in the bathroom one morning, took one look at her and she knew. Carted her off to the doctor's where they confirmed she was eight weeks' pregnant. She was beside herself, the shame, the scandal. She told Dad and he, of course, shit himself and said Gracie had to get rid of it. My mother was having none of that, she was a devout Catholic. She nagged your mother for weeks to tell her who the father of the baby was. And Dad threatened her for weeks not to. In the end, I told her." Aunt Maisie took a deep breath. "I need a fag and some air, let's go outside." I followed her to the door, barely trusting my legs to carry me.

She continued, "Dad left your mother alone once he accepted she was having the baby and told me I would be the only one from then on. Wasn't I a lucky girl? I just thought fuck this and told my mother. She didn't want to believe me, but she called Gracie into the room and said 'I know who the father of the baby is'. Gracie burst into tears, she kept saying 'sorry, Mum, sorry, Mum'. Our mother was quite calm at first, sitting us both down and getting all the sordid details from us. When we'd finished she told us to go to our rooms and stay there. We did.

"We heard Dad come in, heard the screaming, the crying, things being thrown. Then she was gone. Off to the convent where she had a breakdown. The police came for Dad after the nuns called them. We were taken into care and had to give statements to the police. Dad pleaded guilty, he had to, blood tests would have shown that you were his. He died in prison a few years later. They said it was an accident, but, of course, it wasn't. Child sex offenders don't get an easy time in prison. Gracie blamed you for all of it. If she hadn't been pregnant with you, it never would have come to light. Dad wouldn't have gone to prison and died, Mum wouldn't have had a breakdown, we wouldn't have been in care. Yes, Gracie has always placed the blame squarely on your shoulders. She was going to put you up for adoption but they said she'd get a council house and money if she had a child, so she kept you. Anyway, she met your stepfather when she was eighteen, and the rest, as they say, is history. I moved as far away from this shitty place as I could. And, yes, I was a working girl like you, until I got too old and ugly. Then I helped my pimp find other girls to work and got a commission. I made a fucking fortune out of you."

Chapter Thirteen

I liked my new place. It was mine with no memories attached, and where no one knew me. I still couldn't believe what had happened, how quickly my life had changed. I didn't go back to Paxtown after talking to Aunt Maisie. I had my answers so I no longer had a reason to visit my mother, who is still not dead, by the way. Malcolm tried to make some money out of the media interest in me, but when they saw him and the shitty little house, they weren't interested. That wasn't how they wanted to portray me, as a poor little kid from a shitty home. No, I was high class hooker only the elite could afford.

Adam kept in touch with me, he was really strong through it all. But he never held me in his arms again, or kissed me. I suppose my national fame was one step too far. The girls had been amazing though. That night at the house in Greenwich, when I confessed all, they were so kind and supportive. Not the reaction I expected at all. They said they knew I was hiding something, my answers were always so vague and I was making way too much money for a marketing consultant. I just wish I had trusted them enough to tell them years ago.

You wouldn't believe how many offers I had after the committee hearing. So many men wanted to be my provider. I had proved that I was loyal and discreet, you can't put too high a price on that in those circles. I had no intention of going back to that lifestyle though, not at any price. I was offered a modelling contract, topless of course, and Penthouse magazine said they would pay me a small fortune for posing naked. I was approached by three publishers for my life story, and invited on national television talk shows. There was serious money to be made, but I turned it all down. I just wanted a quiet life.

Soon though, someone recognised me and my neighbours found out who I was. Their reaction was a mix between avoiding me completely to making all manner of excuses to knock my door and get an eyeful of the high class call girl who had shagged state secrets out of a lord. I knew then, no matter where I went, the past would catch up with me.

So I stopped trying to run. I put the flat up for sale, packed my bags and filled my car, then headed home. Paxtown. It was where my friends were and I needed them. I could put up with stares, the gossip and the jibes as long as I had their support, and I knew I did. I should never have doubted it. I stayed with Angie while I looked for a place of my own. It was really great, sharing a home with someone. Yesterday, I stubbed my toe. Angie called from the kitchen asking what was up, and did I need a plaster or anything. And it occurred to me that was the first time in my adult life that anyone had cared that I'd stubbed my toe.

I will go and talk to Adam soon. He knows I'm back. He doesn't believe I was leaving Theo, he thinks I just want him now because my life went completely tits up. If only he had answered the phone the night before it all happened. Then he would know that I had chosen him. I'd even packed all my stuff up ready to leave. Wait a minute – a thought just occurred to me. Adam went to collect my things from the flat. But they were already packed! So that's proof right? No, maybe not. I had time to do that before he arrived. Damn. Maybe he'll believe me in time. I can wait. As long as it takes.

Book Five – Eliza

Dear Charlie,

It will be a minor miracle if you are reading this letter because no doubt you have been inundated with thousands, even millions of the things, since you let down zillions of people around the world. It is shocking what you did – getting sacked from the best TV show of all time which so many people enjoyed. You have had a very fortunate life, which you appear not to appreciate at all, and don't seem bothered to have upset all the loyal, faithful, people who have supported you. Shame on you, Mr Hanson.

Regards,

Eliza Greene

Dear Eliza,

Call it a minor miracle, call it fate, call it the Gods smiling down on me, or more likely crapping on me, coz your lovely letter popped to the pop of the pile. (And, yes, I do get thousands of the things.) I must thank you for your kind words and support while I am going through this troubled time. And, finally, what business is it of yours or anyone else's what I do with my life. Butt out!!

Charlie

Dear Charlie,

It is the business of all the people who have been so loyal to you. We are the ones who watch the show to increase the numbers to raise the advertising revenue to make it possible for shows like yours to be made and for you to command the ridiculous salary you earned. We are the ones who make you important – if you didn't have us you would be nobody. It is the business of your colleagues on the show – the actors, production crew, writers and all the rest, who have now lost their jobs because of you. Shame on you, again, Mr Hanson.

Eliza

Dear Eliza,

Once again, thanks for your kind words! You need to get your facts straight – I did not walk out on the show and let people down – I was sacked. That is something I had no choice about. Get it right before you attack me.

Charlie

Dear Charlie,

You had a choice. You had a choice whether or not to take drugs, to drink to excess, to spiral out of control, to make a dick of yourself in public. All your choices. And it's rude to write such short letters to people.

Eliza

Dear Eliza,

Who the hell are you? Are you a crazy woman or just someone with a personality problem? Do you get your kicks out of attacking famous stars or what? By the way – don't judge my life – you don't know what I'm about or what I've been through.

Charlie

Dear Charlie,

Boo hoo. I am crying in my soup just thinking about the hard life you have led. It must have been so difficult growing up in London, son of a famous actress, money no object, adoration from every quarter. I can't imagine how much you must have suffered. And, of course, the reason you turned to drink and drugs was because you were too rich – if you hadn't had the money and the lifestyle to be tempted you wouldn't have been would you? So, it's obviously your family's fault for taking care of you so well, and your fans' fault for making you so famous. Good gosh – we practically forced the stuff down your throat.

Eliza

Dear Eliza,

Very funny, ha ha. Again – who are you, crazy woman? And what gives you the right to get so personal with me? For your information – just because I had all the material possessions I wanted didn't mean I had a wonderful life.

Charlie

Dear Charlie,

First of all, please could you write letters in future, not send postcards. I have a very nosy postman and I know he's reading them. I am not a mad woman, unless you count being mad at you. I am an accounts assistant living in Paxtown on the south coast. And I'm not saying you had a wonderful life, just all the opportunities anyone could ever have to do whatever they wanted with their lives. And you chose to do drink and drugs.

Eliza

Dear Eliza,

I am starting to feel quite offended by your tone. Did my TV show ending upset you that much? Is your life that small?

Charlie

Dear Charlie,

My life is not small. I have friends, I go out, I do Zumba. I have a job. Do you?

Eliza

Dear Eliza,

Ah, no mention of a partner there! Do you live alone or are you a spinster with a cat? It would explain your overly zealous interest in my TV show.

Charlie

P.S. What is Zumba?

Dear Charlie,

I do not have a cat. I am divorced but happily so. I have two grown up daughters and lots of friends. And, again, I have a job. I do not get up in the afternoon, do drugs, get drunk and party all night while offending lots of people.

Eliza

P.S. Zumba is a dance fitness class

P.P.S. PLEASE send letters not postcards. The postman is reading them all and telling my neighbour. I am a very private person and would prefer them not to know my business.

Dear Eliza,

Fine, letters it will be. But shame to spoil the postman's fun. What business are they interested in anyway? Our correspondence is hardly newsworthy.

You speak as though you know my life. That is not my daily life. But at least I have a life, I'm not obsessed with someone else's TV show. What happened to hubby? Did he get sick of your nastiness and run away with the cat?

Charlie

Dear Charlie,

The cat was a bitch. A pretty young one, but a bitch nevertheless. By the way, you keep referring to 'your' TV show. As far as I know, it belonged to the network and the producers or somebody big in London, and never to you. You were just a lucky son of a bitch to get the part. Question I am curious about – do you actually live in a penthouse in Mayfair?

Eliza

Dear Eliza,

Why do you want to know where I live? Are you going to start stalking me or abusing me in person and not just via letter? Are you a reporter playing games?

Charlie

Dear Charlie,

If I was a reporter all previous letters would have been front page news by now. The drink and drugs has obviously fuddled your brain and it no longer works properly. That would explain a lot actually. I want to know if you live there because there's a stars' homes tour in London which says that's where you live and if you don't I'm going to complain.

Eliza

Dear Eliza,

What are you barking on about? Are you planning on coming to London and want to see where I live? Please give me notice if you are so that I can try to remain sober and drug free for all of the two minutes of my time I will give you.

Charlie

Dear Charlie,

No, I am not coming to London and, if I was, I wouldn't want to see you. I am very disappointed in you which I thought you would have realised by now. I went to London last year actually and went on a stars' homes tour which was really pretty shitty. We saw lots of back doors of famous people, oh, and Penelope Keith's chimney, whoopy doo. The guide let us stand outside your building for a few seconds before rounding us up again before the doorman saw us. She said you lived there. It was a crappy tour and I am going to send a review in to the papers to stop other people wasting their money. If you don't live there either, it's another thing to add.

Eliza

Dear Eliza,

Get a life! Why do you care where the stars live and whether or not the tour guide tells the truth? She's just trying to make a living! You are a nasty so-and-so. No wonder your husband left with the bitch. Unlike you, I always have plenty of company if you know what I mean.

Charlie

Dear Charlie,

I've read about your company. You have two women on the go and they both pretend to accept it. I think that's shocking and disrespectful. At least my husband had the decency to leave me and not to move his mistress in.

Eliza

P.S. I hear you also pay for company – if you know what *I* mean.

Dear Eliza,

My private life is just that – private. The two women in my life are very happy with the situation, I'll have you know. We are about to go to the Caribbean for a very relaxing two-week break. And, yes, before you say anything, there will no doubt be drinks, drugs and partying. And I will probably also have the damned paparazzi following me so you will read all about it.

Charlie

Dear Charlie,

All right for some. You get sacked, publicly humiliated, shamed and slated. You admit to taking drugs. You get other people sacked. You act like a complete dickhead. You treat women like toys. But you get to go to the Caribbean and the highlight of my week is Zumba. What did I do to the universe?

Eliza

Dear Eliza,

Maybe you pissed it off with your sunny nature. And I was right about your sad life if Zumba is the best you got – ha ha! Tried it by the way, it's good fun and I like the moves but it's bloody exhausting. See I don't spend all my time getting wasted. Also, I told my mum there was a crazy woman writing to me and she told me to get shot of you. Lucky for you I never take her advice or our cosy little chats would be history.

Charlie

Dear Charlie.

You were right – I read about you in the paper. What on earth were you doing stealing a fisherman's boat from the quay while singing 'God Save the Queen' and wearing a Superman costume? They'll never let you back in the Caribbean again. As for your mum – she's a lovely lady and you should listen to her – except for this occasion. I am not a crazy woman, just a pissed-off middle-aged woman who loved to watch your show.

Eliza

Dear Eliza,

How do you know my mum is lovely? Have you met her? She doesn't think the same of you it must be said. What I was doing in the Caribbean was grossly misunderstood by the way. Don't believe everything you read in the papers, even if they do have pix. What are you doing this week – more Zumba? Or getting yourself a cat?

Charlie

Dear Charlie,

Yes, Zumba, Mr Smarty Pants. Also going out for dinner with friends and meeting my daughters on Saturday for shopping and lunch. Talking of daughters, don't you have children? What kind of a role model are you for them?

Eliza

Dear Eliza,

Yes, I have children whom I adore. And I'm sure you're right in that I am not a great role model for them. But I have to be me too. I'll settle down one of these days and be a great dad, you'll see.

So, tell me, how old are your children? What do they do? And what's this talk about friends, you've never mentioned any before.

Charlie

Dear Charlie,

Angie is thirty-two, she's divorced but she's fine. Her ex was putting it about a bit, I'm sure you can relate to that. To tell the truth I never liked him, there was always something a bit sleazy about him. She can do much better. Angie works in the college business department. Kate is thirty, she's a teacher, enjoying her life. She's living with her boyfriend and they're planning on getting married soon. I am looking forward to having grandchildren one day.

I have friends, why would you assume I haven't? I leave the house occasionally and not just to go to work or Zumba.

Now, back to your children – one day is too late, damage is done. Children need you all their lives, not when it suits you. Get a grip you lush.

Eliza

Eliza,

OK, enough is enough. I am not putting up with you insulting me any longer. This is our last communication.

Charlie

Dear Charlie,

Fine you coward. You just don't like hearing the truth do you, you spoilt little boy. I don't care if I never hear from you again.

Eliza

Dear Eliza,

You won't.

Charlie

Dear Eliza,

Are you pouting? Haven't heard from you for a while. How is Zumba? And did shopping with the girls go OK?

Charlie

Dear Charlie,

As said previously, your brain is fuddled from booze and drugs. You said no more communication.

Eliza

Dear Eliza,

Since when did you listen to what I say? I'm just a lush, remember.

Charlie

Dear Charlie,

Zumba is fine, it wears me out but I'm getting my teenage shape back which will be handy for when I start having sex again. Shopping and lunch was lovely, I miss having my girls living at home and don't see them as much as I'd like. Dinner with friends was entertaining – my friend Zoe announced to everyone she was leaving her husband for another woman. Who knew? Complete shock. When you think you know someone inside out they can still surprise you, and never in a nice way.

By the way, forgot to mention in earlier letter, if you are trying to work my age out from my daughters ages you would probably be wrong. I was only eighteen when Angie was born.

Eliza

Dear Eliza,

I wouldn't dream of asking your age or jumping to conclusions about it. Contrary to rumours, I am a gentleman. Now, what's this about someone running off with someone. Are you talking about Zoe or hubby or both? And what's this about sex? Tell me more…

Charlie

Dear Charlie,

Not that it's your business, but I've had no nookie since my husband ran off with the bitch. I am now considering getting back on the horse, so to speak. But I am very nervous due to the fact I only ever slept with hubby. Hence the Zumba. I need to get into shape, try to make myself more attractive to the opposite sex. You, of course, have no such problem, you flit from woman to woman like a butterfly on heat.

Eliza

Dear Eliza,

Shit woman – you haven't lived! Get back on that horse right now. Blokes don't mind a few wobbly bits you know, providing they can bend and shape as required! Not sure if I like being called a butterfly, by the way, but it's better than some of the names you called me previously.

Charlie

Dear Charlie,

I do not have wobbly bits. Just a bit out of shape. And enough talk about my (non) sex life. When I am ready to start riding again I will. In the meantime, life goes on. By the way, I read an article written by some famous psychiatrist who thinks you're a crazy person. I must say having read the stuff you've done lately I tend to agree with him.

By the way, what were you thinking peeing off the top of the Eiffel Tower? Seriously – how old are you?

Eliza

Dear Eliza,

Thanks for that, I can always rely on you to lift my spirits. Maybe I am a crazy person, but goodness knows I've had enough therapy and treatment – you'd think one of those overpaid sons of bitches would have discovered it by now! More likely there is naff all wrong with me, I just enjoy doing everything to excess – because I can.

And I didn't intend to pee off the top of the tower, just was bursting to go and it was a bleeding long way down! It was pee there or piss my pants. And I paid £350 for those trousers, I was not going to piss in them.

Charlie

Dear Charlie,

Shame. It would have been so much nicer for your fans if you were actually ill and not just a dickhead. Maybe you should see a doctor about your bladder problems too, or could it be that you just drunk too much for a change?

Anyway, I am doing my review on the London tours now and you never answered my earlier question.

Eliza

Dear Eliza,

Yes I have a penthouse in Mayfair, so, no, she wasn't lying. I'm curious though – why are you writing a review over a year after the event? You do have a small life, don't you? What did you think of London anyway? Who did you come here with?

Charlie

Dear Charlie,

I went with my husband, it was our last holiday together before he walked out. I had a lovely time, I thought everything was fine, but clearly it wasn't. I feel angry and stupid for not knowing and not noticing and not hitting him and screaming when he left. I am angry at the world and I am not going to put up with it any more. All my life I have been quiet and kind and nice, gone along with what other people wanted and never made a fuss. No more Ms Nice Guy.

Eliza

Dear Eliza,

I can't ever imagine you as a Ms Nice Guy, hope that cheers you up.

Charlie

Dear Charlie,

Read about you in a magazine. Apparently you have ten million followers. Who needs that many? What on earth do you tell them in their monthly newsletter? Got up at noon, smoked a joint, drank a bottle of scotch, shagged a few prostitutes, had dinner with friends, went to bed?

Eliza

Dear Eliza,

Do not mock my fans, they are very intelligent, lovely people. I tell them all sorts of interesting snippets about my daily life, which does not actually go the way you think it does, Ms Smarty Pants. Why don't you join and find out? This month's newsletter is due out next week with lots of wonderful information about me and pictures of course. You can tell me what you think of it. And please be truthful, I know how difficult you find it to be insulting. Ha, ha!

Charlie

Dear Charlie,

Why on earth would I want to be one of your followers? I have better things to do with my life. And before you start – I do. It's my birthday this week and my daughters are throwing me a party, so there. I'm having a makeover which includes a new hairdo for the first time in ages, actually must be all of ten years since I changed my hairstyle, that is shocking, even for me. And I'm buying a new dress with high-heeled shoes. Usually I wear flats because they're comfy and I have this bunion. Anyway, I will suffer for one evening to look glam.

Eliza

Dear Eliza,

Bunions! Ugh – too much information. So, this will be the big five-oh will it? See, if that was me I wouldn't be having a party, I'd be pretending I had a long way to go before reaching fifty. One of the shit things about being famous – everyone knows your age and you can't lie about it. Otherwise I would be thirty-three or thirty-four.

Charlie

Dear Charlie,

You wouldn't get away with thirty-three or thirty-four. Your face is too ravaged after the booze and drugs. I, on the other hand, don't look a day over forty despite the fact I will, in fact be fifty, on Friday. What are you up to these days anyway? Sitting on your bum coz no one will work with you any more?

Eliza

Dear Eliza,

Ouch! Here was I thinking you were mellowing towards me. Yes, doing lots of sitting on bum. In case you hadn't heard, there is a court case going on. I am suing the sons of bitches who sacked me.

And, for your information, I could get work if I wanted to. I am taking some well-earned time out. I worked twelve hours a day on that show for the last six years. I deserve a break. So, please give me a break!

Charlie

Dear Charlie,

Yes, I had heard about the court case. Good publicity stunt. Particularly since you're claiming for all the other cast and crew members too. Did your PR people tell you to do that? Makes you look nice and cuddly and caring and a victim doesn't it?

Truth is you behaved like an asshole and if you were a real man you would admit it, say sorry, go kiss the asses of the producers and beg for your job back. I'm sure your ten million followers will support you.

Eliza

Dear Eliza,

You offend me deeply. I am a victim in all this. And I am trying to do the right thing by everyone through this claim.

Charlie

P.S. They are not called followers, it is not some kind of cult. It is a fan club.

Dear Charlie

You are not a victim. In fact, from what I've read you seem to be a bit of a bully. Hasn't your ex-wife got a restraining order out against you? That's not nice. You should be ashamed of yourself. If my husband had ever raised a hand to me I would have been out of there.

Eliza

Dear Eliza,

Let's get one thing straight – I do not condone violence against women. In fact, I don't condone violence against anyone, I am a pretty peace loving guy. I'm not proud of certain incidents in my past but I never hit a woman. Don't believe everything you read. And as the Bible says – let he without sin cast the first stone.

Charlie

P.S. Happy birthday

Dear Charlie,

I do not pretend to be without sin. But there are sins and then there are sins. By the way, all the flowers you sent for my birthday were really lovely. The only problem is they filled the whole of my sitting room and, unfortunately, I don't live in a large penthouse like you. Now I can't see the TV or out of my front window. My friends asked who they were from and I told them you sent them and they laughed. No one believes me, they think I am a sad cow who spent a month's wages on buying flowers for herself on her birthday. So, thanks but no thanks for any future birthdays.

Eliza

Dear Eliza,

Who said I was planning on sending any more flowers to you, you miserable so-and-so? How was the party by the way, when they finished laughing at you for buying yourself so many flowers?

Charlie

Dear Charlie,

They didn't laugh, they pitied me, it made me mad and spoiled my birthday, so thanks for that. Otherwise party fine, my daughters, my two friends and one of my neighbours enjoyed champagne and cake in my kitchen (due to the fact sitting room was taken over by flowers). That was pretty much it, oh, except my cousin phoned to say happy birthday.

Eliza

Dear Eliza,

Hardly a mega knees-up was it? You need to learn to party London style! If you're not face down in a ditch, in a stranger's bed or a police cell, you haven't had a good night out! By the way, had lunch with my mother and told her what you said about me being mentally ill. She said I must be if I was keeping in contact with you.

Charlie

Dear Charlie,

What does your mother have against me? I really like her. She's a brilliant actress, especially in that film where she won the academy award. You've never had one of them have you?

Don't fancy your kind of night out thanks. But I am going to town this weekend for the first time in a long time. It's a hen do for a woman at work and should be a good night out. Getting yet more new high-heeled shoes to wear. Starting to develop quite a liking for them, although the bunion doesn't agree. What are you up to these days apart from the usual shite?

Eliza

Dear Eliza,

Court case goes on, will take years probably. In the meantime show remains ditched, I remain untouchable and rest of cast are looking for other work. However, I do have millions in the bank, two houses, three cars, numerous women and a never-ending supply of alcohol. So life's not bad.

Charlie

P.S. Please note I never included drugs in the above list. I have officially stopped doing them.

Dear Charlie,

Ditch the court case and drag your sorry ass up to the studio, get down on bended knees and apologise. Or see a shrink, or a doctor, or go into rehab. Get a life.

I am glad to hear about the drugs, but you are definitely overindulging in the alcohol. And you are still acting like a little victim. You are not. You caused this.

Eliza

Dear Eliza,

How was the hen do? Sorry I haven't been in touch for a few days, I did drag my sorry ass to the doctor as it happens because I passed out. And, no, not passed out while under the influence, passed out in the middle of the day, stone cold sober, in my kitchen. He's done some tests, nothing serious you will be sad to hear. Waiting for couple results, but not expecting anything spectacular.

Charlie

Dear Charlie,

Heard you passed out, it was in the papers, didn't you see them? They said you were pissed and on drugs again. Why do they do that? You should sue. I will write to them and complain, tell them you were perfectly sober. People believe what they write, you know. They have a duty to tell the truth not make it up as they go along.

I had a ball on my night out! You'll never believe this but I got back on the horse!

Eliza

Dear Eliza,

Read papers, total bunch of crap, didn't care. Don't waste your time writing to them. Tell me more about horse riding, you wicked woman!

Charlie

Dear Charlie,

It was a total shock. I was quite tipsy but not too drunk (not like you get). We were at a bar and a man half my age took a liking to me. I thought he was taking the proverbial and it took him over an hour to convince me he was serious and did indeed fancy the pants off me. I blame you for the sex.

Eliza

Dear Eliza,

The world blames me for most things at the moment, you having sex is just a teeny molehill on top of a giant mountain. I am confused though – why was it my fault you finally dropped your knickers and ended the drought?

Charlie

Dear Charlie,

Because you kept taunting me about not having a life and getting back on the horse etc. Entirely your fault. You were right about the wobbly bits though – he didn't care. And I'm happy to report all parts bit rusty but still in good working order.

Eliza

Dear Eliza.

Glad to hear it, those kind of spare parts are hard to come by. So, who is he? Are you seeing him again? How many times did you ride the horsey? And even more importantly what was it like?

Charlie

Dear Charlie,

Don't be so personal! But if you must know, he's a sergeant in the army (*very* fit), was here on leave, and says he wants to see me again next time he's around. I don't believe a word of it but it doesn't matter. It was the most amazing night I've had in the last ten years. So, for once, you were right.

Eliza

Dear Eliza,

Shock, horror! Please write that again to be sure I understood properly – you said I was right? To return the favour – you were also right, I am crazy bonkers mentally unstable ill and sick. Doc diagnosed me with bi-polar.

Charlie

Dear Charlie,

I knew it! However, that does not make you crazy bonkers mentally unstable or sick. Just ill. It is an illness which can be treated so don't make a big deal of it. It does also stick two fingers up to your critics. Explains the irrational behaviour, excessive drinking etc etc. Apparently also explains your constant shagging. I went to the library and read up about it. You have all the symptoms. It's not easy to diagnose, you know. You must have got a very good doctor. What am I thinking? Of course you have, the finest in Harley Street, no doubt!

Eliza

Dear Eliza,

Reading a book does not make you an expert, but I am touched that you took the trouble to do so. Anyway, I've got to start treatment, have counselling, and so on and so forth. Real drag to tell the truth. My mum's beating herself up over it coz she thought she should have spotted it when I was a kid, but so should the dozens of docs and shrinks I've seen over the years. Thinking of suing them too. Need an income now I'm unemployable.

Charlie

Dear Charlie,

You do not need an income, you are minted. And you do not need to blame everyone else for your problems. You should have sought help a long time ago. Tell your mum not to worry about it, bi-polar is difficult to diagnose and not very well known, certainly not when you were young all those years ago. I read up about it so I know what I'm talking about.

Eliza

Dear Eliza,

I am sure my mum's mind will be put completely to rest when I tell her your kind words. What it is with you and her? Is she the only person you're nice to? By the way, I am off on vacation with my women this week, going to Mexico for some carnival weekend or other. What are you doing? More horse riding? Or is it back to Zumba?

Charlie

Dear Charlie,

Don't your women have more respect for themselves? They cannot possibly like the situation they are in. Can't you pick one or the other? What are you trying to prove? Hopefully, your medication will kick in soon and the sex drive will lower to normal levels.

Eliza

Dear Eliza,

If sex drive lowers, medication will be stopped.

Charlie

Dear Charlie

How was your fun weekend? Apart from lying on the beach with two stunningly beautiful, obviously cosmetically enhanced and much younger than you women, what else did you get up to? Papers surprisingly quiet about your visit.

Eliza

Dear Eliza,

Sorry to disappoint your opinion of me, but didn't go wild, didn't smash anything or anyone up, didn't make a dick of myself. So there. What did you get up to, oh wild one? Spot of gardening?

Charlie

P.S. Did I detect a touch of jealousy??

Dear Charlie,

Had quiet weekend, it's nice to recharge batteries occasionally. And don't be ridiculous, what on earth would I be jealous of? Sharing you with someone? I wouldn't want you to myself, let alone to compete for your attention with someone else. I wouldn't want giant tits which look like footballs or skin pulled so tight I couldn't smile. I tell you, they are the crazy ones.

Eliza

Dear Eliza,

Can't see the tight skin being a problem, can't imagine you ever smile. And as for giant football tits, who wouldn't want them? You had no one to go out with did you? Why don't you join a singles' club or something? There are plenty people like you in the world, all lonely little souls looking for someone to ride horses with.

Charlie

Dear Charlie,
Piss off.
Eliza

Dear Eliza,

Now, now, no need for that. Go join a class, get a hobby, get out and about more. Are you still doing Zumba?

Charlie

Dear Charlie,

No, stopped a couple of weeks ago. Prefer horse riding, as it happens, so saving myself for that. Can't be arsed to join classes or any of that crap. Work full-time, have loads to do, occasional nights out are fine. I watch lots of TV, hence the interest in your show. My favourite now is Keeping up Appearances – you are off my list. How is treatment going? Are you normal yet?

Eliza

Dear Eliza,

No, not normal by a long way, probably never will be. Treatment is crap. Medication makes me feel like half a person, it's difficult to describe, doc is trying me on different combinations, he says they'll find some that suit eventually. Probably be dead by then.

Charlie

P.S. Either go back to Zumba or resume horse riding on a regular basis.

Dear Charlie,

Horse riding on a regular basis is easier said than done. First you need an available horse, in a reasonable condition, and they are in very short supply around here. Of course, if I had your money and your morals I could buy myself a herd.

Eliza

Dear Eliza,

I'm pretty sure a group of horses is called a stable, you would be buying yourself cows. Don't think they'd be much good for you, although your friend Zoe might appreciate them.

Charlie

Dear Charlie,

Now you're just being a show off, what a surprise. How is treatment going, oh clever one?

Eliza

Dear Eliza,

Treatment going pretty OK now actually. Finally found some drugs I like which are also legal! Counselling not going so well, counsellor is a really hot lady who I keep fantasising about so not helping the sex overdrive much.

Charlie

Dear Charlie,

Don't you get enough sex with the two women you use and abuse?

Eliza

Dear Eliza,

Do not use and abuse. As said before, both very happy with situation. Besides, variety is the spice of life, and also, as you very well know, I have an illness. Urges are officially not my fault – so there!

Charlie

Dear Charlie,

What a load of hooey.

Eliza

Dear Eliza,

Why do you waste a stamp to send me one line? It would be nice if you put some effort into your letters. Producers found out I'm bi-polar. And would you believe – they wanted to talk to me to resolve our current messy court case. I think they may offer me my job back before my illness becomes public knowledge and they look like the shits they really are. I will of course tell them to shove it where the sun don't shine.

Charlie

Dear Charlie,

You seriously mad selfish son of a bitch! If they offer you any opportunity at all to get back on the show you should not even consider telling them to shove it. How could you even think about letting down your millions of followers around the world, heartbroken at the show ending, all the cast and crew who would like their jobs back thank you very much, not to mention the ten million fannies in your club. You should be on bended knees thanking them for even talking to you, and anyway how d'you know they're going to offer you anything, you arrogant asshole? It's far more likely they want to look good for the court case now that you actually have an illness and are only partial, not total, dickhead.

Eliza

Dear Eliza,

I am a seriously unhappy bunny at your tone and total lack of understanding of how things work around here. You never, never, say yes the first time when you are a big star (such as I am, whether you like it or not) because that would be a sign of desperation which would immediately knock a nought off the salary. You go back to your accounts and leave the studio games to me.

Charlie

Dear Charlie,

And how exactly would I know how studio games are played? It's not like I had your privileged lifestyle, is it? When I visited a studio in Manchester ages ago I got off a tour bus and had to queue for an hour just to get in. You get whisked through in your limo (with blacked out windows just in case one of your adoring fans who pays your wages sees you) and go straight through. I bet you never stood in a line in your life did you?

Eliza

P.S. Would you go back to the show?

Dear Eliza,

I stood in line plenty times, there were always queues for lunch at my boarding school. I did tell my mum to sort it out but she never did. And for your information – I do not drive around in a blacked out limo, I actually have a convertible I would have you know, but, due to the wonderful British weather, it is rarely in use. Mostly I have a driver, due to the fact that mostly I indulge in alcohol. I try not to drive around much, anyway, as I do get mobbed a lot which is not what it's cracked up to be you know – it can be quite frightening.

Charlie

Dear Charlie

In words from your own former TV show, I am playing the world's tiniest violin.

Eliza

Dear Eliza,

You really crack me up (not). Had my meeting. Official outcome – we have agreed to keep the lines of communication open. Real meaning – they are watching to see if the meds work and I behave myself.

Charlie

Dear Charlie,

Well, that's progress! So, what's the next move, hotshot? You going to do the whole public apology PR thing to your fannies and followers yet? Still haven't seen anything in the papers about you being officially mad.

Eliza

Dear Eliza,

Publicist wants me to, hot counsellor doesn't. It's out there anyway coz studios know. Matter of time before everyone else does. I'm pretty sure my publicist told the studios.

Charlie

Dear Charlie,

He's right, it's good PR, will help your fans make sense of everything and definitely help with your court case seeing as you are now officially disabled so would be discrimination. Interesting that so far you are siding with hot shrink.

Eliza

Dear Eliza,

You are so wrong! I really must say that again – you are so wrong! Hot shrink, as you call her, is supporting me because I'm not ready to tell the world yet. So, Ms thinks-she-knows-it-all – it appears you don't.

Charlie

Dear Charlie,

Why not? Would have thought you'd have been straight on all the chat shows again telling the world you're sick and getting the sympathy vote. In case you're interested, news from my life is that ex-husband and bitch are getting married.

Eliza

Dear Eliza,

Sorry to hear that, you must feel like crap having such a sad life when he's obviously having a great one. You've got to move on, girl. As for my illness, I don't want the world to know I'm officially bonkers. I'd prefer them to think I'm a wild man, it's better for my image, stuff what my publicist says.

Charlie

Dear Charlie,

Thanks so much for the kind words which made me feel so much worse than I already do. Easy for you to say move on when you have your money and your life. Not so much for me. When the rat left with the bitch I had to sell my home to give them half, I now have to work in a crappy job full-time to pay the mortgage on my tiny one bed flat with even tinier garden. Daughters can no longer stay overnight unless they share a bed with me which they don't enjoy because I am told I snore. After finishing my crappy job, I have to get two buses home on account of the fact that I can't afford to run a car, make my lovely meal for one and watch television. There is no time, money or energy for anything else.

Eliza

Dear Eliza,

Now *I'm* playing the world's tiniest violin. The only person who can change your life is you. And you can do it, if you really want to. And, now that I am an expert on mental illness, I think you are suffering from depression and I think you should see your doc. Also, get something for the snoring at the same time – not an attractive trait in a woman.

Charlie

Dear Charlie,

I am not depressed, I am angry. Not the same thing at all. You are wrong as usual, and are also wrong about not telling people about the bi-polar. I think you're a coward and you think, in some ways, it makes you less of a man, less of a hero to worship. You don't want people saying 'poor Charlie he's got bi-polar' when you wreck a hotel room or something, you want them to say 'wild man Charlie's at it again'.

Eliza

Dear Eliza,

Ageing rock stars wreck hotel rooms, not famous actors. We are more likely to take drink and drugs to excess and make tits of ourselves by very publicly doing something very stupid. Either see your doctor or find a stallion (but sort the snoring first and preferably the bunion too). By the way, more talks arranged with studio.

Charlie

Dear Charlie,

Leave bunion out of this, it is the one thing in my life that refuses to leave me. How did talks go? How is treatment? I saw the front page headlines yesterday. Now world knows you are bi-polar – did you agree to it or did it get out there via your sneaky publicist? How d'you feel about it?

Eliza

Dear Eliza,

I suspect sneaky publicist, although he swears he didn't, of course. I am playing it down, it's just a minor illness, no big deal. Talks were a complete crock of shite, they are playing games to delay court case. When is the rat marrying the bitch? Are the daughters rubbing salt in the wounds by going?

Charlie

Dear Charlie,

Daughters are bridesmaids, it's a big white wedding. They asked if I minded – what could I say? Wedding in three weeks' time. Me and my bunion are planning to hide under the sofa with the curtains drawn. Had a little bit of action this week, you will be surprised to know – Zoe's husband came over for more than tea and sympathy, said he had always liked me. It took me a bit by surprise, I must say. Nothing happened, of course. Not that I wasn't interested, I've always quite liked him. No, it was practical reasons really, I hadn't shaved my legs and looked like hairy footballer, hadn't changed the sheets for a fortnight so they weren't at their freshest and hadn't got around to buying the Stop Snoring spray from the chemist (to keep just in case of a horse riding opportunity).

Eliza

Dear Eliza,

Would you please stop with the personal information! First the bunion, then the snoring, now the hairy legs and dirty sheets – enough already. Also, shows you know nothing about men – he would not have noticed bunion, legs, sheets or snoring if you had shagged him. A missed opportunity for some serious galloping, you silly mare. Would you mind sending me a picture of yourself, by the way? I would like to know who my worst fan looks like, seems only fair as you obviously know me.

Charlie

Dear Charlie,

Sorry have no photographs of me which I like. Why on earth would you want one anyway? To put on the wall and throw darts at? Saw you on that chat show, you were quite good, I thought. At least you weren't off your face. And I have to say that I like that you're not playing the sympathy card coz of your illness, my respect for you has gone from nothing to ten (on a scale of zero to one hundred).

Eliza

Dear Eliza,

Oh, be still my beating heart – praise indeed! How is romance going with hubby of Zoe? Have you shaved your legs yet? If not, tip for you – wax them instead, it's a far better finish and lasts much longer, or so I'm told. Talking of lasting longer, my official sessions with the hot counsellor have ended. Turns out she fancied me as much as I did her and we ended up having amazing sex instead of healing therapy or whatever it is we were supposed to be doing. Upshot is she has now referred me to another counsellor who is male and has wart on his cheek which looks like it is another little person growing out of his face. I can't stop staring at it, keep thinking it's judging me, so sessions with him not going so well either. On the plus side, am still having unofficial sessions with hot counsellor.

Charlie

Dear Charlie,

Why am I not surprised? And why would wart person be judging you? He probably fancies you too. Richard (husband of Zoe) called around this week, actually, and we are going for drink on Saturday. For information – legs will be shaved, have no idea how to wax and far too embarrassed with the length of hairs to go to salon – sheets will be clean and fresh and won't need snoring spray as don't intend to sleep.

Eliza

Dear Eliza,

Again with the personal information! Now when I think of you it is of a hairy monster with giant growth on foot. *Please* send me a photograph so I can at least know what your ugly mug is like and not have that awful image in my head. By the way, talks with studio went better, I think they might want to settle.

Charlie

Dear Charlie,

Have enclosed pic but if you make any shitty remarks will get voodoo doll and prick your parts until they don't work anymore. Date with Richard was lovely but no horse riding. He kissed me on cheek and went home. I am obviously not fanciable. What a waste of a razor.

Eliza

Dear Eliza,

Don't be stupid. Saw pic, hate to admit it, but you are fanciable. Richard is either dickhead, like myself, or has had the confidence knocked out of him on account of his wife turning lesbian and is afraid to try it on. Get another date, get him drunk and find out which it is before you go jumping off any bridges.

Charlie

Dear Charlie,

What the hell have you done? I can't believe you went on international television with that picture of me and said I was the nicest person on earth who some dickwad had ditched to marry an airhead! And on the day of their wedding! It was everywhere – on TV, radio, in the papers, it was the talk of the town and of the wedding, apparently! Had the bloody media camped on doorstep all morning – did you see the footage of Richard smuggling me into his car with a blanket over my head? It was my best blanket, baby blue, freshly washed, looked really good on camera. Richard had his arms around me, all protective like we were an item. I did not, and still do not, appreciate the media circus you forced on me without my permission and against my will, it has been an absolute bloody nightmare. I have even been offered silly money to talk about my friendship with you but what would I tell them – we have been trading insults for months? I can't take money for that. Remain shocked that you said I was the nicest person you know, I know you didn't mean it and I know why you did it, which I appreciate, but it was still a lie. *Please* don't interfere in my life again – it has caused chaos. But rat and bitch were very pissed off, apparently, and said it ruined their wedding day, which was totally amazing!

Thanks,

Eliza

P.S. Also, friends now believe it was you who sent the flowers on my birthday!

Dear Eliza.

Sorry about the media circus, that was always going to be the downside. But glad we pissed off rat and bitch and spoiled their day. Things with Richard going OK then? Any news on the fornication front? Talking of which, I spoke to my two regular women and yet again you were right – turns out they are not both happy with the situation. One of them is in love with me and it's killing her to share me with the other one, plus the hot counsellor and the casuals, while the other one said she doesn't give a damn and is only with me for the money and the lifestyle, plus sex with me which as we all know is pretty amazing. So, it was only fair that I ditched one. Guess which one?

Charlie

Dear Charlie,

Good for you, it's about time you started treating women with some respect. I am hoping you ditched the gold-digger, but have a sneaky suspicion I'm wrong. Are you now ditching hot counsellor too? Things with Richard are nice and friendly, but nothing exciting to report. He calls around regularly and kisses me on the cheek when he leaves. Have tried the getting drunk thing but unlike you he doesn't hold his alcohol well and throws up then leaves.

Eliza

Dear Eliza,

Ditch hot counsellor? Ditch sexy gold-digger? Hell, no! Ditched woman who loved me (which was the kindest thing by the way) – the other one doesn't give a flying whatever who I dip my winky into. Why the hell would I ditch her? What can I say – I'm just a hot blooded male. Unlike Richard who seems to be having trouble doing anything with his winky. You are going to have to make the move lady – giddy up!

Charlie

Dear Charlie,

I do not intend to giddy up. If Richard doesn't want me I am certainly not throwing myself at him. In fact, I really don't think he does want me, he's just lonely. And shame on you for ditching the woman who loved you – have you learned nothing?

I saw on the news the studio has officially killed your show forever and is starting a new show which is a kind of spin-off so they can keep some of the characters. There's lots of speculation about who is going to get the lead role. Personally, I'm hoping they go for Hugh Grant, now he could giddy me up any time!

Eliza

Dear Eliza,

I should get the lead role! They should be offering it to me as a compensation for axing my award winning show! They want to settle out of court now due to my 'illness' but not happening. I am going to sue their asses.

And, by the way, why is it you fancy Hugh Grant but not me? I am far more the English gent type than he is. In fact, I liken myself to a more handsome, young version of Lawrence Olivier.

Charlie

Dear Charlie,

You really think the universe starts and ends with you, don't you? TV shows will go on, life will go on, the world will still turn, you will be surprised to learn that we don't all rely on you. Even your ten million fannies could survive without you, you know. By the way, you now have ten million and one. My daughter Angie has joined, she thinks you're cool for what you did on rat and bitch's wedding day.

Eliza

Dear Eliza,

Would you please stop calling them fannies – they are fans! What happened to the abuse I got months ago for letting down all these people – you seemed to think I was pretty important then. You also thought the show was amazing and dependent on me and it should never have been axed.

I am delighted to hear about my new fan, please thank her for me. Now, I would like to know why you are suddenly telling me my fans don't matter. What changed?

Charlie

Dear Charlie,

I found a lump in my breast. Everything changed.

Eliza

Dear Eliza,

Call the number at the top of this letter, it's for the best consultant in Harley Street, he's waiting for your call. Your travel and treatment are paid for, your daughters too, if they're coming with you. Please don't take offence at your local NHS but this guy's the best there is and you need to do this.

I won't visit while you're there because I would bring the media circus you hate, but if you want to come to the penthouse to recuperate you are more than welcome. It will also prove that I do indeed live here. I will of course still be drinking and shagging but will try to contain it to a maximum of ten hours per day.

Charlie

Dear Charlie,

Thanks for the kind offer. I was going to say no but discussed with my daughters and my doctor and have been persuaded to accept. The waiting lists and treatment here cannot compete with what you are offering apparently. I have to have a mastectomy and radiotherapy so please be assured the bill will be huge. My daughters will not be coming, no offence but I would not wish them within a twenty mile radius of you, they are far too good looking. Penthouse recuperation offer very kind too, but I decline. I don't think arguing with you for a few weeks and watching you in action would be good for recovery.

Kind regards,

Eliza

Dear Eliza,

Understand perfectly about the daughters, probably wise. Also about the penthouse, probably wise. Please take writing pad and envelopes to hospital with you, I would miss your insulting remarks if they didn't continue on a regular basis.

Love Charlie

Dear Charlie,

Op went well I am told, but riding horses will be lopsided in future. Your doctor says he can do cosmetic surgery and I will look good as new but given my previous remarks about footballs would be a hypocrite to accept. On the other hand, could have a decent boob job while I'm at it and lift the other one up a couple of inches too. My decision will make a difference of many thousands of pounds to you so I thought I should keep you informed.

Eliza

Dear Eliza,

Live a little – get the footballs. We can't have you falling off the horse due to being lopsided, could cause serious damage. Did you see the news? My fannies are starting a petition to get me back and get the show back on air. In the first hour almost 50,000 people signed it!!

Charlie

Dear Charlie,

I know. I am now a fannie and started the petition.

Eliza

P.S. Am getting nicely rounded and very pert tennis balls

Dear Eliza,

How's radiotherapy? When are tennis balls being installed? Studio called for talks, your petition got over four million signatures! I am touched and starting to understand your anger when you first contacted me – I didn't appreciate how many people thought so much of me and how much I was letting them down. Been spending more time with my kids lately too, maybe I'm growing up at last. Or maybe not, as last night I got wasted and spent two grand on hookers.

Charlie

Dear Charlie,

You are who you are but you are a man with a good heart. As I am currently recovering from radiotherapy, I will argue I was out of my mind if you ever repeat that. Tennis balls going in on Monday and, all being well, will be home next Friday. Back in three months for a check-up. Read that you are doing radio show and guesting on another show – does that mean you are employable again?

Eliza

Dear Eliza,

Yes, apparently I am creeping back. The big studios are still nervous about hiring me but I'm getting there. Sacked my publicist by the way, he turned out to be a bit of a prick.

Charlie

Dear Charlie,

It's nice to be home, I feel fine and the tennis balls have settled in nicely, got a better shape than I've had for years. Richard called round, I told him he was welcome to call whenever but there would never be anything more than friendship between us, I think he was relieved. I also think you're right in some ways – we should all live life to the full, don't know what's around the corner. By the way, talking of your publicist, he tried to persuade me to do a story saying you'd paid for my treatment, I didn't know you'd sacked him or I wouldn't have spoken to him.

Eliza

Dear Eliza,

It's why I sacked him, don't sweat it. My mum sends her love and is asking if you need anything. Doing a chat show next week – any thoughts?

Charlie

Dear Charlie,

Say you would be willing to do a special episode of Heaven Help Us for free in honour of the millions of people who signed the petition. Say you would be prepared to let bygones be bygones out of respect for them. It would please everyone, (except the producers), make you the nice guy, dropping a lawsuit for your fans etc. It would put the producers in a very awkward position. And it would close the chapter in your life which is unfinished and messy and shite.

Eliza

Dear Eliza,

Do you want a job? You should be my publicist, you have talked more sense than anyone in my life. For you, I will do what you say – but on one condition. You get well enough to come work for me as the angel on my shoulder. The devil on the other one wins far too many arguments and it's time someone gave him a run for his money. You have no life there, there's lots of horse riding in London and stallions who will very much appreciate the tennis balls. Your daughters can come too, whenever they like.

Charlie

Dear Charlie,

That is a very generous and tempting offer but you have never even met me. If you did, you might hate me. I might hate you. After all, you can be a most irritating person. Go do what you know you should and when you get the academy award for the show I will be there and give you my answer.

Eliza

Dear Eliza,

Deal.

Charlie

Dear Charlie,

Good luck with the chat show, I have written a letter to the TV Times urging all your fannies to watch and show their support.

Eliza

Dear Eliza,

You are a genius! Studio has offered to do a one hour special, with the condition that I behave myself impeccably at all times, of course. They will see what the ratings are and then review the situation.

Charlie

Dear Charlie,

Show was excellent, I really enjoyed it. Haven't laughed so much in ages. Tennis balls were bouncing about everywhere.

Eliza

Dear Eliza,

How are tennis balls? Still bouncing about, I hope. Looking forward to seeing you soon. I'm sure you are as pleasant in real life as you are in your letters.

Love Charlie

Dear Charlie,

Thank you so much for everything you did for our mother. And thank you for the invitation to the academy awards, it was really lovely to meet you and we had the most amazing evening. Thanks most of all for the very kind speech you made honouring Mum for your achievements over the past year, your comeback, your award and your good health.

She never told you but you meant an awful lot to her, and you gave her the best chance of fighting the cancer which we all appreciated very much, and will always be grateful for. The treatment she received gave us much more time with her which we will always treasure. Sadly, nothing would have been enough. We miss her every moment of every day and we know you miss her too.

Kind regards,
Angie and Kate Greene.

Book Six – Eleanor

Chapter One

The first inkling I had that my marriage and my life was less than perfect was when a journalist from a national newspaper knocked on my door. He asked to see my husband Steve, who was at work, then he asked if he could come in and wait. "What's this about?" I asked.

"Sorry, love, it's your husband I want, not you. I need to talk to him, and it would be to his advantage to speak to me."

"What about?" I asked again. "My husband and I have no secrets." He laughed then, a sneering nasty kind of laugh. I felt sick, and angry. "You people are disgraceful, turning up at our home, making demands to see my husband," I said. "How dare you! Who do you think you are? You red top rag reporters are worse than pond scum, not happy until you've ruined some poor person's life."

"We don't make it up, love," he said grinning.

"Would you please stop addressing me as love," I said. "My name is Eleanor Fitzroy Thomas, you may call me Mrs Fitzroy Thomas."

"Oh, dear, love, you are not going to be happy when you find out what your husband's been up to," he laughed, and went to sit in his car.

I looked out of the window fifteen minutes later and he was still there, parked at the end of the driveway. I went outside and knocked on his window. "Yes, love?" he said, winding it down.

"You can't park here, it's private property and you are blocking access to our drive."

"Well, that's the plan," he said. "That way your husband can't avoid talking to me when he gets here."

"Talking to you about what?" I asked again in frustration. "Why on earth would my husband want to talk to someone like you?"

"You mean, pond scum?" he said. "OK, fine, I really didn't want to be the one to tell you, but you are asking for it. There's no easy way of saying this so I'll just come out with it. Your husband was keeping a call girl for two years, and that same call girl is now property of an influential MP. We've got an offer for your husband to keep his name out of the papers."

"What? Steve?" I didn't believe it. It was completely ridiculous. "Go away!" I shouted. "And don't come back."

"I'm going to wait for your husband," he said. "And believe me he's going to want to talk to me."

I slammed the door on him and went back inside. My first thought was thank God the children aren't here. Charlotte was at ballet, and William at football practice. Problem was they would be home before Steve arrived, he never got back before eight. They all went for drinks after work apparently and waited for rush hour to pass before getting the tube or train home. I called the only person I could possibly tell. "Cass, something awful's happened, I need your help. Please will you pick the children up and keep them with you tonight?" She said, of course, without even asking what had come up. Cassandra is my oldest and dearest friend and I could rely on her for anything. I told her what the reporter had said, I was shaking as I said it. "I don't believe it, Steve wouldn't do something like that, this is a terrible mistake."

"I'm sure it is," Cassie said comfortingly. "Now calm yourself down, and get yourself a drink. Try not to worry."

"I will," I said, "and, thank you, Cass."

I poured myself a gin and tonic, went to get some ice and fell against the freezer. I had an awful feeling of dread, of bad things to come. By the second G&T I was going frantic and couldn't bear it any longer. I looked out of the window, he was still there, sitting in his car waiting. I opened the door and beckoned him inside. "Nice place you've got here Mrs T," he said.

"Fitzroy Thomas," I corrected him.

"Sorry, love, of course you're from nobility, aren't you? This must be a bit of a shock."

"Please could you just tell me why you are here, and what evidence you have of these ludicrous claims."

So he told me. Steve had been keeping a call girl named Jordan Jackson for two years just after we got married, when we were living in London. Steve had not been discreet, he had taken her to functions and showed her off as his mistress. He apparently handed her over to his boss when we left London. "We've been working on this story a long time," the journalist, Aiden Travis, told me. "We've been watching her and photographing the MP going in and out of the building. We have a shot of them together on the balcony. When we approached him, his solicitor threatened all sorts, said we had no proof she was a call girl, and no proof it was an affair. So we started digging into her background, and finally found someone who recognised her as the girl your husband used to, used to keep, for want of a better word.

We have photographs, we have statements, we have receipts. We have a slam dunk case against your husband that he was with her. What we don't have is a slam dunk case that he was paying for it and that she is indeed a very well paid and highly exclusive prostitute." I couldn't believe what I was hearing. And, yet, somehow it all sounded so true. I remembered all those times in London when Steve would be out all evening. He always said it was work, I was so in love with him I didn't question anything he said.

"What do you want?" I asked Aiden.

"We want your husband to give us a full statement containing detailed information about his arrangement with Jordan. In return he gets anonymity, we don't publish anything about him."

"Why would you do that?" I asked.

"Look, love, your husband is just a junior stockbroker, we're after the MP, he's the real deal. We've no interest in your husband beyond the help he can give us to nail the story we want. But, make no mistake, if he doesn't co-operate we will publish it."

By the time Steve arrived home I'd had six G&Ts, unheard of for me. I hadn't eaten and my stomach was gurgling from the effects of too much alcohol on an empty stomach. When he walked in he looked from Aiden to me and I could see he knew straightaway that something was up. My breeding kicked in, we were not going to have a pantomime in my home. They don't call it stiff upper lip for nothing. "Ah, darling," I greeted him. "Mr Travis here is a journalist with one of the national red top rags. He has uncovered your sordid arrangement with the call girl you had in London when we were first married." Steve's face went ashen, his knees buckled and he collapsed onto the sofa. "Don't worry, darling," I continued. "He's not interested in you, he wants to nail, I think that was the expression he used, yes, nail, someone far more important. I suggest you co-operate with him fully so that the children and I do not have to suffer the indignity of having your sordid affairs revealed on the front page." And off I walked, into the kitchen, back straight, head held high, gin and tonic in hand. I closed the door behind me, and for the second time that night I fell against the freezer. This time I slid down the door, curled in a heap on the floor, and cried.

Chapter Two

After Aiden left, I completely lost my composure. Yelled, screamed, threw things. I behaved the way I had never done in my life before. Having tantrums was just not the done thing where I grew up. Steve said it was my fault, can you believe that? And why, you may wonder. Because I wouldn't pee on him, apparently. And of course, for a price, she would. He actually said he thought I would be pleased that he was getting what he needed somewhere else and not asking me to do that disgusting thing. Don't get me wrong, I'm not a prude, but I draw the line at urinating over my husband. I don't even allow him in the bathroom when I need to pee. Some things should remain private, even between husband and wife.

My mother always told me to make sure I got up at least ten minutes before my husband every morning to make myself presentable before he woke. "No one wants to look at messy hair and an unwashed face when they wake up," she told me. He had never seen me with messy hair and an unwashed face, so did he seriously think I was going to let him see me pee, and all over him? The practicalities of it baffled me. Where would you do it? In bed, the sheets would be soaked and smell of urine, I can't visualise the cleaning lady being too pleased. On the carpet would be even worse, the smell would linger for days. The bathroom is the obvious choice, but the marble floor was so hard I would imagine any pleasure would be seriously dimmed by the discomfort.

I asked him why he didn't just pay a different hooker every time he felt the urge, rather than have just one, which must have cost him a lot more. The flat, the allowance, paying all the bills. Our money, it was our money, it should have gone into a trust fund for our children, not on a whore. He said it was at a time when money was no object, they were all making ridiculous amounts, so much it was difficult to spend it all. He said the convenience of having her there on call was worth the money, plus it was far less risky, health-wise, than going to different women every time. "So, it wasn't just peeing on you then?" I asked. "There was sex too. Was there love? Did you love her? After all, you took her to functions I should have accompanied you to."

"Look, it was a long time ago, I was young and stupid," he said. "Of course I didn't love her, she was a hooker for fuck's sake! I promise you, Ellie, there's been nothing since we left London. Nothing. I gave the reporter what he wanted, nothing about me is going to get printed. Please, can we move past this? We have a marriage, children, a home, a life together. Please don't throw all that away because I made a mistake with a hooker a long time ago."

Of course I wasn't going to throw it all away. Apart from the effect on the children, the heartbreak, the disruption, the practical nightmare of it all, the scandal, the stares and the questions, there would be my mother saying 'I told you so'. Now that I couldn't bear. Her and Daddy never liked Steve. They always thought he was below me, and I was rebelling against my upbringing. What was there to rebel against? I grew up the only child of a very wealthy upper class family, I came to them late in life when they had almost given up hope. They doted on me, they gave me everything, I had my own wing at home, with my own servants. I went to finishing school in Switzerland, I had a coming-out ball and was very much in demand in high society. And then I met Steve, and he took my breath away.

It was at a night club in Soho where I was with my friends at a birthday party. We had all gone down to London for the weekend where we were staying at Cassie's parents' flat in Kensington. They used it occasionally when they were in town for business. Steve made a beeline for me. The attraction was immediate. My friends said he was my bit of rough, and they thought it was highly amusing. But it was so much more than that. He wasn't traditionally handsome, but he looked really fit, and he had a gorgeous smile. I went weak at the knees from the start. He called me Lady Eleanor, even though I told him I didn't actually have a title. Daddy's brother was a viscount but the title died with him.

Daddy died when I was twenty-four. He was sixty-nine and had suffered from a bad heart most of his adult life. He was a sweetheart, Mummy and me still miss him so much fifteen years later. Mummy is as fit as a fiddle. She's eighty-one now and still rides every day. Why she stays at that huge house though I will never know. It's a seven-bedroomed country home with ten acres of land, stables and a grand hall you could easily seat two hundred people in. I know she has the servants and she entertains, but why on earth she chooses to live there instead of somewhere smaller and more comfortable, I do not know. Of course, she has no money worries,

Daddy left her very well cared for. But I'm sure she would be happier if she was closer to us. She loves seeing Charlotte and William, she's a doting grandmother, but she never comes to our home. When I married Steve, my parents wrote me out of their will. They said he was nothing but a gold-digger, he only wanted me for the upper class status and the money I would inherit one day. They were determined he would never get his hands on anything so they wrote me out of the will. I didn't care, I was in love, and, besides, Steve earned a fortune, we didn't need their money.

We bought the house in what is aptly named the stockbroker belt just outside London. Not too far for Steve to travel to work, but far enough away that we could enjoy a country lifestyle. It was a four-bedroomed detached house with large gardens and a double garage. No expense was spared on the furnishings, our home is the epitome of class and money. I had a cleaner, a nanny and a gardener so I had plenty of free time to continue the lunches with my friends and devote time to my charity work.

When William started school, Steve suggested the nanny should leave. A year later, he sacked the gardener because he said I had enough time to do the garden and it would give me a hobby. I know Steve thought I was a spoilt little rich girl, and he was scared I would go running home to Mummy any day, it felt like a test, so I agreed. I would prove that I loved him, and that I could do it. I actually enjoyed gardening, which was a revelation, although I wasn't very good at it. Who knew what satisfaction a person could get from begonias?

So I've gardened, lunched, organised charity events, attended every single school concert, sports match or drama the children have been involved in. I've had manicures, pedicures, massages, hair-dos and spray tans. And, oh, dear Lord, I have been bored. For someone who had led a spoilt, sheltered life, I certainly didn't expect that.

I told Steve that my parents had disinherited me four years ago when William was due to start junior school. I had wanted Charlotte to go to a private school, as I had, but Steve said it would do her far more good to go to an ordinary state school. He said it would be character forming. Charlotte has always been a strong character and she was fine, but William was different. He struggled to fit in, so when it became time for him to go to junior school, I really thought it would be best if he attended Saint Michael's. Steve said no, he needed to learn how to mix with real people. I resisted the temptation to ask him if he thought I was a real person and told him Mummy agreed with me William needed the kind of care and attention he would receive in private school. Steve said if she thought it was so important she could pay. That was when I confessed that I had been written out of the will and that she would not pay for one single thing. I don't know why I hadn't told him before, my parents told me before I got married that they would cut me off and I would never get a penny if I stayed with Steve. I never told him, I was embarrassed to admit my parents had disinherited me. But when I finally told them that Mummy wouldn't pay for schooling or anything, he was so sweet. He said don't worry, we don't need her money, and one day she will see that we are the real deal. The real deal. And all the time he had been paying a hooker to pee on him.

Steve was from a working class background, not poor by any means, except by my standards. He didn't believe in all that upper class nonsense, as he used to call it. So we didn't have a cook or a housemaid, just a cleaner who came in for two hours every morning. Mummy was distraught that I learned to cook, the thought of her daughter in the kitchen making a meal gave her a funny turn. Worse than that, she hated the fact that I washed the dishes. "I never thought I would see the day when my daughter had callouses from washing dishes," she said.

"Don't be silly, Mummy," I told her. "You don't get callouses from dish washing. Remember the advertisement – for hands that do dishes that are soft as your face, use mild green Fairy Liquid." She didn't think that was funny at all.

Chapter Three

So, you can see why I can't turn to my mother. Thank goodness for Cassie. I wouldn't have got through the next few days if it hadn't been for her. I don't think the children noticed anything amiss. Charlotte is a typical teenager, very wrapped up in her own life, and William is so laid back he wouldn't notice if lightning had struck the house. Steve was very loving, very apologetic, then the next minute very angry and saying it was my fault. Cassie said of course it wasn't. "Did he really expect you to pee on him?" she said. "I'm pretty open-minded, but I would draw the line at that. He's making it the excuse for why he did what he did. I think you need to ask yourself Ellie, who pees on him now?"

"Do you really think I haven't asked myself that?" I said. "I'm just afraid to ask him."

A few weeks later, something else happened that took my mind off Steve's indiscretion. I went to get my grandmother's brooch from my jewellery box to wear to a charity luncheon, and it was missing. I emptied the box out and realised that there were a number of other pieces missing too. Bracelets, earrings, a necklace. I rarely went out so didn't wear them often but I knew every single piece of jewellery I had and they were definitely missing.

I was baffled. I told Steve that evening and his face clouded over. "I was afraid of this," he said. "Some of my stuff has gone missing too. Cufflinks, tie pins, and, last week, cash I left on the dresser."

"Why didn't you tell me?" I said.

"With everything that's happened I thought the last thing you needed was a thief in the house, I was hoping I was wrong," he said.

"Wrong about what?" I asked puzzled.

"Maria. I caught her a few weeks ago taking a trinket box out of the house, the one you keep on the hall table. I confronted her and she cried, she swore she would never take anything again."

"Maria? No, she would never, she's been with us for years," I said.

"Who knows why?" Steve said. "Obviously her circumstances have changed and she needs it, but we can't keep a thief in the house. I'll tell her she's no longer needed. I'll be nice about it, after all we have no proof that she's taken anything other than the trinket box. I'll tell her you're doing the cleaning yourself from now on."

"She'll never believe that!" I said. "I don't know one end of a duster from the other."

"Dusters don't have particular ends, actually," Steve said smiling, "they are usually square."

"See!" I said, "I didn't even know that!"

He persuaded me to live without a cleaner for a few weeks, in case Maria got wind of a new appointment and sued for unfair dismissal. I warned him there would be cobwebs, but he said he could live with that. When Cassie called round, I was trying to work out how to empty the vacuum cleaner bag and put a new one in. "For heaven's sake, Ellie, get another cleaner," Cass said laughing.

"Can't, not yet," I said, still frantically pressing buttons trying to get the damned hoover to spill its contents.

"Ellie, this is ridiculous," she said. "You have no nanny, no gardener, your children go to state school and now no cleaner. What on earth is going on?" I stopped banging the buttons and started to cry.

"I think Steve wants us to be normal," I said. "But I don't know how," I wailed.

"Do you want to be normal?" Cass asked gently.

"I don't know," I cried. "I'm trying to do the best I can but I'm rubbish at everything except growing begonias. I want to be a good wife, a good mother, a good person, but I sit in this house every day and keep getting things wrong. I don't know what to do!"

What do you want to do?" Cass asked.

"I don't know!" I cried again.

"Yes, you do," Cass said. "I have known you since you were eleven years old. What do you want to do?"

"Design clothes," I said timidly. "Start my own fashion line, give half the proceeds to the children in Africa who have no food or water."

"What's stopping you, then?" Cass asked.

"I can't even operate a fucking vacuum cleaner!" I cried.

Chapter Four

When I saw the photographs of Jordan, or Jaclyn, whatever her name was, in the paper, my confidence took an even bigger hit. She was gorgeous. I mean, really gorgeous. Why the hell would he stay with me when he could have had her? I am the complete opposite to her. I'm tall, slim and blonde, with a bit of a horsey face, like so many aristocratic families are cursed with. In-breeds, probably. She was dark with the most amazing hair, a curvy figure to die for, and the most beautiful face. I did wonder what on earth she was doing as a hooker, with looks like that she could have had just about anyone. I didn't ask Steve. The subject had been aired, discussed and dismissed. We were not going back there.

When a vase went missing I thought I was losing my mind. What on earth was going on? I even started to wonder if there was a poltergeist in the house. It was there one day, gone the next. I notice these things, now that I am doing the dusting. I told Steve, he said I must have moved it and it would turn up. I was sure I hadn't moved it. We couldn't blame Maria, she was gone. Steve asked who else had been in the house, I told him only Cass. Well then he said you must have moved it, or maybe one of the children broke it. I questioned them, they had no idea what I was talking about, and I believed them. I started to wonder if Maria had been wrongly accused.

A few weeks later, the gold napkin rings had gone. We only ever get them out for special occasions but as it happens I had gone in that cupboard just days before to get the lace tablecloth for a charity tea, and I had put them back in their place. When I opened the cupboard to put the tablecloth back, they were gone. What the hell was going on? I really started to think I needed to call a priest in. Steve agreed it was strange. Who was in the house today, he asked. Only Cass, I said. Oh, he said. "Oh no, Cass would never… " I said.

"I didn't say anything," Steve said. "I'm sure she wouldn't."

I would trust Cass with my life, I would. It was inconceivable that she would steal from me, and to let Maria take the blame. I dismissed the thought, and decided that my poltergeist theory was more likely. Until my watch went. It was a gift from my father the year before he died and it was engraved 'To Eleanor, my special beautiful girl, love Daddy'. I never wore it, I was too afraid to lose it, but it was gone. Cass knew how much it meant to me. But again, she was the only one there that day. My head was whirling I just couldn't believe it. I decided I had to ask her, maybe she was having money problems I didn't know about. But she only had to ask, I would have given it to her.

I went to her home the following morning after dropping the children off at school. "Well, hello, what are you doing here so early in the morning?" she greeted me. Cassie's house was a lot grander than mine, set back from the road by a sweeping driveway, with turrets and balconies, it looked like a fairy tale castle. She couldn't need the money, I decided I wouldn't mention it. We had coffee in the morning room. Cass knew me well, she knew something was on my mind.

"Things are still going missing," I said eventually.

"Are you sure? What things?" she asked. I told her. "Look Ellie, you've been under a lot of stress, are you absolutely certain that they have been stolen?"

"Of course I'm certain!" I said. "Do you think I'm going crazy or something? Is that what you want me to think?"

"What the hell do you mean?" she asked coldly.

"What do you think I mean?" I screamed. I felt like I was falling apart, my whole world was unravelling and I had no idea who to trust any more.

"Get out," Cassie said, in a cold, dead voice. "Get out and never come back."

Steve held me that night as I sobbed and then we made love for the first time since the journalist had landed on our doorstep. Him and the children, they were all I had. I vowed to be the perfect wife and mother, learn how to clean properly, grow something other than begonias, and take cookery lessons too. Steve said that was lovely, but maybe what I needed was a job, to get me out of the house, make new friends. First of all, I thought he was crazy, when would I have the time? And I wondered why he had changed his mind about me working after always saying he didn't want me to. But he knew me well, and he knew I needed something more in my life. So I said yes, I would look for a job.

Chapter Five

That was how I ended up in the high street of the next town five days later. There was a job available in the florist's, and seeing as I was getting to grips with gardening, I thought I should be able to do it, and also learn something from it. As I was walking toward the florist's shop I passed a jeweller's and happened to glance in the window. And there it was – my watch!

I went inside and asked about it. They said it was second hand, but a very good piece, priced at £700. I asked where they got it from. They said they were not at liberty to disclose. I told them it was mine and it had been stolen. I told them what the inscription on it said. The manager came out of his office and nodded to the sales assistant who went to the window, retrieved the watch and took it to the manager. He looked at the inscription. "Madam, we bought this watch in good faith," he said. "And I mean no disrespect, but how do we know this was stolen from you?"

"Sir," I said. "I mean no disrespect either, but this watch was stolen from me. I am prepared to give you whatever you paid for it, in return for the name of the person who sold it to you. I presume you keep records? If you fail to do this I will call the police and you will have to explain why your shop sells stolen goods." I could see his mind ticking over trying to decide if I was bluffing or not. Then he nodded again to the assistant and she fetched a book from the office. He opened it then looked up at me.

"£350 please, Madam," he said. I wrote him a cheque for cash, he sent the assistant to the bank to get the money. When she returned he gave me the watch and showed me the entry in the book.

Chapter Six

It took all my strength to walk out of the shop with my head held high, my legs felt as though they would buckle beneath me at any moment. I felt nauseous, I wanted to scream. I couldn't believe what I'd seen. But the book entry was very clear – the watch was sold to them by a Mr Steve Thomas.

I went straight to the bank after the jeweller's. The nice lady at the counter looked pitifully at me as she showed me our accounts. The current account, which Steve's wages went in and the bills came out of, was £12,000 overdrawn. The savings account was empty. Although I wasn't surprised that we were in a financial mess, I hadn't expected it to be quite so bad. After all, if Steve was stealing from me, there had to be money troubles.

Next I called at Maria's to apologise for sacking her and accusing her of theft. She had no idea what I was talking about. "Mr Thomas told me you wanted to do the cleaning yourself," she said. "He gave me a really good reference, I can show you." And she did. There it was, a glowing reference, not only praising her work but also her impeccable character. Bastard, I thought. You evil bastard.

I went to see Cass, but she wasn't there. I would have gone down on my bended knee and begged her forgiveness. How could I ever have doubted my best friend? How could I have been so stupid, so gullible.

Risking a lifelong friendship rather than doubt my loving husband.

Then I went to the only place I had left. Home to Mummy. I didn't tell her everything, just enough so that she would understand I had to leave him. "Please can me and the children come her, just for a while, until I can sort something out?" I asked.

"Eleanor," she said. "Your father and I told you, we begged you, we pleaded with you, we threatened you, but you still went and married that man. And now you stand in front of me saying it was all a mistake. Well, I'm very much afraid it is your mistake and I will certainly not be digging you out of this mess you have got yourself into. What about the talk? The scandal? People already feel sorry for me because you married well beneath your class. You live in a modern house for goodness sake's. In a cul-de-sac. A child of mine living in a cul-de-sac!"

"Well, we won't be living there for much longer," I said. "The bank is on the verge of repossessing the house. Steve re-mortgaged it a few years ago, I had no idea, he forged my signature on the documents. We now have no equity in it and the payments are thousands of pounds in arrears. Mummy please, what about Charlotte and William? Surely you can't see them thrown out of their home?"

"I'm sorry, Eleanor," she said coldly. "When you went against our wishes to marry that man, you broke your father's heart. You are the reason he went to an early grave and broke my heart too."

"Mummy, don't say that!" I said. "Daddy had a bad heart for a long time before I even met Steve. Please don't say you blame me for his death. You can't mean it."

"Oh, but I do," she said. "You weren't here to see your father, a broken man after what you did. We doted on you, we gave you everything. You should have trusted us, believed in us, we knew he was no good."

"I thought you were just being snobs, I didn't know that you had seen something in his character that I obviously missed! I can't believe you are blaming me for Daddy's death. I'll never ask you for anything again," I said, and I left.

This was the worst day of my entire life by far. How much worse could it get? I wondered. My next call was to our solicitor where I demanded he see me immediately. After an hour in his office, he promised to have the divorce papers drawn up and sent out that week. The grounds were unreasonable behaviour. I know I could have gone for adultery but I really didn't want to name a prostitute on my divorce papers. Besides, there was enough unreasonable behaviour with the theft, the lies, forging my signature.

When I got home, there was more. I went through Steve's desk where he kept all the bills and correspondence. There were dozens of letters demanding payment. Credit card statements with thousands and thousands of pounds owing. Some were in my name, although of course I had absolutely no idea they existed. I kept those, I would get in touch with the companies and tell them I had not signed for them. If they wanted to take Steve to court, or get him arrested, so be it.

Even the electricity bill was overdue and they were threatening to cut us off. I couldn't believe what I was seeing. How did this happen? Steve earned good money. Is this why he wanted me to get a job all of a sudden? I suddenly remembered what that journalist had said – he's a junior stockbroker. Except he was a team leader, he had a promotion about ten years ago. I checked the bank statements, the wages being paid in were not those of a team leader. When had he been demoted? Yet another fucking secret!

Then I noticed the cash withdrawals. Every week, a few hundred pounds. We didn't carry much cash, we always paid by cheque. I knew what it was for. Oh, yes, I knew exactly what it was for. We were practically bankrupt, about to lose our home, but he was still withdrawing hundreds of pounds every week. Who is peeing on you now, Steve?

Chapter Seven

I called Cass six times. Each time, the housekeeper took a message. She never returned my calls. I wasn't going to ask her for help, only forgiveness. I had no other real friends. The ones in our set, I went to school and grew up with, had married well as they say, and I wasn't really good enough for them anymore. The people I met through my charity work, and our neighbours, thought I was a snob and too good for them. I don't know where I would need to be to fit in. It didn't matter as long as I had Steve, the children and Cass. Now I only had the children and I could really have done with a friend.

In desperation I visited Aunt Margaret. She's an aunt by marriage, her husband, the viscount, was my father's elder brother. They had one adopted daughter, my cousin Abigail. We had never been close, I hadn't seen Aunt Margaret or Abigail for years. My father had died just before his brother, so the title died too with no male heirs to pass it on to. Sexist, I know. But that's British aristocracy for you.

My hands were trembling as I drove towards the house. It's not as grand as my parents', nor do they have as much money. But Aunt Margaret retained the title of 'Lady' so she still commands greater respect wherever she goes. Her and Mummy have a not-so-friendly rivalry thing going on. A maid answered the door and showed me into the drawing room. She appeared a few minutes later with a tea tray, and told me to make myself comfortable while Lady Margaret finished her phone calls.

She was making me wait. She knew I wanted something. I hadn't just appeared out of the blue to see how she was. It was about twenty minutes before she made an entrance. She came towards me feigning a smile, we did the usual air kissing in greeting. "Eleanor! What brings you here?" she asked. "It's been such a long time. How long has it been? Is it ten years? Do you know, I really think it may be that long."

"I'm sorry, Aunt Margaret, I should have kept in touch. I won't waste your time with platitudes, I am desperate for help and I have nowhere else to turn."

When she heard my mother had turned me out, her attitude changed. "Eleanor, you and the children can stay in the gate house temporarily," she said.

"Oh, thank you so much!" I cried in relief.

"Oh, it's not because I'm being kind," she said. "I just can't wait to see the look on your mother's face when I tell her in front of everyone at bridge next week." Much as I hated to see my mother humiliated in public, I had no choice. My children needed a roof over their heads. My grandfather had set up a trust fund which paid me a monthly allowance, it was the only money I had. It would be enough to feed and clothe us, but I would need to get a job if we were ever going to have a decent life or a place of our own again.

Over the next few days, I started moving things over to the gate house. It had two bedrooms, one each for the children, there was a put up bed I placed in the corner of the lounge for me. I took clothing, books, personal things. Then I started moving pictures, ornaments and anything of value which I knew Steve would sell. He didn't notice at first, when he saw a picture had been taken down, he asked where it was. I had replaced it with a cheap one from a charity shop but I told him I was refurnishing the house, and swapping items for others of the same value. It was a good way to change things around without spending money, I said. It was a swap shop for well -do people. He was pleased that I wasn't spending money. He didn't question it again. It was the first time I had lied to him.

When the divorce papers arrived, I put them with all the other documents in the briefcase which was hidden at the back of my wardrobe underneath a pile of shoe boxes. The boxes were empty of course, the shoes had been removed to my new home. I carried on as normal in the meantime, cooking and cleaning as best I could. Ferrying the children around to various activities, helping them with their homework. I even had sex with Steve. I could do it, I could carry on as normal while the cold, hard rage inside and my desire for revenge was stronger than my heartbreak.

Chapter Eight

Leaving day finally came. I had taken the last of the boxes to the gate house, and even with the cheap replacements the house looked bare. I picked the children up from school and took them to our new home, where I told them that we were going to live there and Daddy was going to move nearer his work. They asked questions, of course, Charlotte wanted to know if we were getting divorced as so many of her classmates' parents were. I answered honestly and said yes. I told them Mummy and Daddy were friends but we didn't want to live together any longer. I told them we loved them both, it was nothing to do with them, just that we had grown apart. I said we had to sell our house because we no longer had money to pay for it, so we were living in the hate House for a while and Daddy was looking for somewhere. They needed to know that money was going to be tight from now on.

Charlotte was quite nonchalant about it. All she asked was why we didn't go to Grandma's big house instead. I told her Grandma liked peace and quiet at her age. Charlotte said in a house that size we could have gone without seeing her for days. I just smiled. William cried, I think more because it was a huge disruption to his life that he didn't quite understand, than for any kind of pain at living away from his father. Steve got home late and left early, they hadn't had a lot to do with him, to be frank. They wouldn't miss his physical presence, that's for sure. But I didn't kid myself into thinking they would be fine, I knew there would be issues at some time or other, but the first hurdle was over with.

Next was telling Steve. When he got home from work that evening I was sitting at the kitchen table, briefcase on the floor under my chair. He looked at me and knew immediately something was up. "What's wrong, Ellie? Why are you sitting here like this? Where are the children?" They were at Aunt Margaret's, I said. "What, the same Aunt Margaret you haven't spoken to for years? The one that shuns you in public because you married a commoner!"

"One and the same," I answered, "She wants to piss my mother off, but that's another story. I need to talk to you. I know about the money," I said. I had decided to go for one thing at a time and get as much information out of him as I could. His face went white.

"What do you mean?" he asked in a strangled voice.

"That we haven't got any," I said matter-of-factly. "The savings account is empty and the current account is £12,000 overdrawn." I could see his mind ticking over.

"Oh, Ellie, I'm sorry, I should have told you. There were a few investment opportunities I just couldn't afford to pass over so I used the savings for that. I'm expecting them to start paying out dividends in the next few months so it'll all be put back."

'Oh, dear Lord,' I thought. 'He's still lying.'

"OK, so how do you explain the fact that the mortgage is in arrears?" I asked.

"Ellie, why have you been snooping around? What's all this about? You know I handle the finances, I always have. We've been fine, haven't we? You've got a nice house here and a pretty good life. Look, don't worry about it, I'll sort it out."

"How will you sort it out, Steve? Your wages aren't even enough to cover all the bills. When were you going to tell me you'd been demoted?"

"What do you mean, demoted?!" he shouted. "Now I don't know what's going on, but this is too much. I'm going to the pub."

As he stood up I said coldly, "I'm not finished. It would be advisable if you sat and listened to the rest of what I have to say. And it would be so refreshing if you actually told the truth for once." I reached down and pulled some documents out of the suitcase. "Exhibit one," I said. "Bank statements which show clearly that you have been dipping into our funds for quite some time now, not taking a lump sum a few months ago. So, can we please stop the crap about investments and at least admit we're penniless? Exhibit two," I continued. "Here is a letter signed by your team leader, that's right, to say that you are employed by the company as a junior stockbroker, earning far less money than you ever have. Would you like to explain that?"

"How did you get that?" he gasped.

"Quite easily, really," I said. I phoned your boss's PA to ask for confirmation of employment, said I needed it for some paperwork. And, hey presto, here it is."

"Shit, Ellie," he said, with his head in his hands. And then he started to cry. I had never seen him cry before, but strangely I didn't want to comfort him, the ice cold rage was still there, I felt nothing but that.

He blubbered, said three years ago he'd made a few bad decisions which lost his clients and the company a lot of money, he'd been demoted and overlooked for promotion ever since. His salary was cut by more than half overnight, but he was too ashamed to tell me. "I couldn't," he said. "You gave up everything to be with me, I am meant to take care of you and the children. I kept hoping something would come up, but it never did. So, bit by bit, the savings went on paying bills, and then I had the overdraft, and now there's nothing. I'm so sorry Ellie, please forgive me," he pleaded.

"You know I would have," I said. "If you'd been honest with me from the beginning, I would have. I would have cut back, got a job, we could have bought a smaller house. But you preferred to keep it all from me, and go behind my back. For instance, you remortgaged the house three years ago, but you didn't tell me, let alone ask me. As it's in joint names I should have signed and consented."

"I only did it because I was desperate," he said. "It didn't need your signature, I was trying to keep us afloat until I could get back on my feet."

"Oh, dear," I sighed. "Are we still doing this? Lying, I mean." I reached down into the briefcase again. "Exhibit three," I said. "A copy of the remortgage document where you have quite clearly forged my signature. Now, please think carefully before answering the next question." I looked at him intently. He banged on the table.

"What the fuck are you doing, Ellie? What is this all about? I am not staying here listening to this!"

"Sit down," I said coolly. "Unless you want me to call the police for forging my signature to obtain £30,000."

"You wouldn't!" he said.

"Oh, yes, Steve, I would," I answered looking him straight in the eyes. He sat back down.

"Fine, I forged your fucking signature, big deal. We needed the money and I didn't want to worry you."

"What about taking out credit cards in my name, and then not paying them?" He was silent. I went back into the briefcase. "Exhibit four, here are three statements from credit card companies saying I owe them a total of £73,000. Two are threatening court action if the debt is not paid in full by the end of the month." He just looked at me, still silent. "So, when you ran out of places to get money you started to steal," I said.

"No!" he shouted. "I did not steal anything, how dare you accuse me of being a thief just because you don't want to believe your precious friend did it. Did she put you up to this?"

"My precious friend, as you call her, my dearest oldest friend, is no longer in my life thanks to you. She didn't take kindly to being accused of stealing either. And what about Maria? You accused her too."

"She did steal the trinket box, I caught her," he said. "So, I assumed she had stolen the other stuff too, until it continued after she left." I reached down again, sighing.

"Exhibit five, a copy of the reference you gave Maria when you told her that I wanted to clean the house myself. Steve, please do us both a favour and start telling the truth so that neither of us have to be here longer than is necessary."

"OK, fine, it was never Maria, I suspected Cassie all along but she was your best friend and I knew it would upset you. I thought you would tell her Maria had been sacked for stealing and that would act as a warning for her to stop."

"Seriously?" I said. "My God, how do you manage to think up these lies so quickly? You are really good at it. But then again, you have had years of practice. Are you going to continue denying you are the thief?"

"Ellie, no matter what money troubles I've had I've never stolen anything, I swear on your life. I'll sort the finances out and I won't hide anything from you again."

"Oh, dear," I sighed again. "Exhibit six, the watch my father gave me and a copy of the receipt for the measly £350 you received for it. I believe that is your name and signature right there, and your passport number which you showed them to prove your identity. Now, please don't be thinking up any more ridiculous lies. I will not believe them. I know you are the thief."

He stood up, holding his head in his hands. "What the fuck are you doing Ellie? I was desperate, I tell you! My world was crashing down around me. I was trying to sort it out without involving you or worrying you."

"Ah, if only that were true," I said. "But you see, there is just one more thing. You are spending hundreds of pounds a week on prostitutes who pee on you. So, you see, you're only desperate to keep your dirty little addiction fed, while your wife and children are about to lose the roof over their heads. Your wife, in fact, has bankrolled quite a few of your sessions, to the tune of some £103,000 I believe. You did not use the savings, your wages, the remortgage money or the credit cards to pay our bills, you used it to pay your whores. The private detective I hired took all of an hour to get proof of that. I believe you have a favourite called Amber. Quite appropriate really, you know amber nectar pouring all over you. Don't get the joke? Well, I thought it was funny."

He face hardened. "All right you fucking bitch, what do you want from me?" he shouted.

"Ah, that," I said reaching into the briefcase for the final time. "A divorce please. You just sign here and here." He knocked the chair over then, his face was contorted, and he came towards me. I didn't move. "I must warn you," I said calmly. "If you hurt me physically in any way, I will report you to the police and it will be added to the list of grounds I have to divorce you. Which I would gladly show to your children, your colleagues or any poor woman who ever enters your life in the future." He stopped in his tracks, clenching his fists. I knew he wanted to hit me, but he knew I meant what I said.

He sat back down. "You can have your divorce," he said and signed the papers. "I never loved you anyway. I married you for the status, the social circles I would be welcomed into, and, of course, one day the family home and all that money. What a fucking mistake that turned out to be! Instead of welcoming me into your social set, they kicked you out. And then I find out years after our wedding that we are never getting your parents' money. If it wasn't so fucking tragic it would be laughable."

"You never loved me?" I said. "I gave up everything for you, but you never loved me?"

"Seriously, Ellie, look at you!" he said nastily. "You're tall, fair and skinny and you look like a fucking horse! What is it with you all rich folk that you all look like fucking horses? Maybe that's it! Maybe you are all fucking horses, God knows some of you, like your saintly mother, spend more time with horses than people."

"I'm not your type?" I said. I don't know why I kept punishing myself by asking more questions, but I just had to know.

"You've seen the photographs of Jordan," he sneered at me. "Now, she's my type! The exact opposite of you." That was enough. I gathered all my papers together and replaced them in the briefcase. Then I left, ignoring the torrent of abuse he was shouting at me the whole time.

Chapter Nine

We settled into the gate house. It was smaller than anywhere I'd ever lived before, but I was grateful to have it. The children were fine. Aunt Margaret let them roam the grounds, ride the horses and take tea with her in the drawing room. I was never invited, I didn't expect to be, I hadn't visited her in years, she owed me nothing. I finally found a job after weeks of searching. I had been to university and finishing school but I wasn't qualified for anything. I tried getting cleaning jobs, I was much improved at that, but once I opened my mouth I could see they were thinking no way could this posh cow clean a house. A local restaurant needed a silver service waitress, well, I was perfect for that, I knew exactly where the cutlery should go and how the table should be laid. The fact that some of my former, so called friends, visited regularly, was unfortunate. They made a point of asking how I was, and saying how sorry they were to hear of my circumstances. Bitches. My mother complained she could no longer go there due to the shame. Her daughter waiting on her own family and friends. Oh, the disgrace of it all. Well, I told her I had to make a living, and if she wasn't prepared to help then I didn't have a choice. She said she would dine out elsewhere.

Steve called around about six weeks after I had left him. He had made no effort to contact the children, I assumed he finally wanted to talk about visitation arrangements. But no, he wasn't there for that. "Ellie, I've been arrested and charged with fraud," he said frantically. "I've got to go to court. I'll lose my job and everything. How could you do this?"

"Me?" I said. "I thought you were the one who forged my signature and spent it on prostitutes. I have no intention of being saddled with over £100,000 worth of debt that is nothing whatsoever to do with me. I have to provide for two children, which reminds me we need to make an arrangement for maintenance. I would really rather us come to an amicable agreement than go through the courts."

"Ellie, please," he pleaded, "I could go to gaol. I will lose my job, I am already in one almighty fucking mess. Please withdraw your statement. You loved me once, please, for the sake of our children, they won't want to see their father go to prison, please Ellie."

"Unlikely you'll go to prison, it's a first offence so stop being so dramatic. I can't withdraw my statement or I could be prosecuted for wasting police time. Besides which, I have no intention of saying those debts are mine. And, yes, I did love you, right up until the day I discovered you had stolen the watch. But you never loved me. So, I owe you nothing. If you want to see the children please let me know, I will not stop you. But I will require maintenance payments so I would be grateful if that could be arranged as soon as possible. Now I really have to go, bye." And I shut the door. I saw him standing outside in the driveway, he looked broken. And all I could think was 'good enough for the bastard'.

Mummy got flu, it was going around everywhere, and then she developed a chest infection. I had told her to get the flu jab, but no, she said she was as strong as a horse and didn't need one. So I used it as an excuse to visit, and tried to make peace with her. We went through the pleasantries, how are you, how are the children, isn't the weather cold for the time of the year, all that nonsense. Then I reached for her hand. "I'm so sorry, Mummy," I said.

"Don't be silly, Eleanor, it's just flu," she said.

"No, I mean I'm sorry I hurt you and Daddy. I don't regret marrying Steve because I wouldn't have Charlotte and William if I hadn't, but I am so very sorry for hurting you. I wish I had realised how right you were years ago, after William's birth. I'm sorry it's taken me so long to see it."

"Well, I'm sorry too, Eleanor," she said, and my heart lifted. Then fell as she continued. "But if you're asking for forgiveness I can't give it to you. You were everything to your father, his two eyes, his wonderful girl, he loved you more than anyone, even me. And I watched as he broke his heart, as the pain and the stress took a toll on his health, and finally how he gave into it, a broken man. There is no doubt in my mind that if you hadn't gone against our wishes and married that man, your father would have lived for many more years, dicky heart or no dicky heart. So, I'm afraid your apology is too late, and I cannot forgive you. I am sorry that I can't find it in my heart to do so. But I can't."

"Mummy, please, I just want us to be friends again, like we used to be," I said, "I understand how much I have hurt you, but I want to try to make it up to you in any way I can. Mummy, please, I really need someone on my side at the moment."

"I see what you're doing," she said. "You think you can worm your way back into my house, my money!"

"No, no," I said. "I just want us to be friendly, I want to make peace, I want to be able to come here and talk to you about my day, that's all."

"Rubbish!" she said sternly. "You think I am weakened by this flu and you are seizing the opportunity to come back here and live the life of luxury. Well, it isn't happening! Shame on you, Eleanor. Your father would be turning in his grave if he saw this." I just looked at her, coldly. This woman I had loved my entire life. This woman I would have trusted with my life. And suddenly I saw her as she was.

"If Daddy could see this, it would be you making him turn in his grave," I said. "You are jealous of me, you always were. Daddy loved me more than you. I bet you were delighted when I married Steve so that I would be in Daddy's bad books. And you are delighted to be able to punish me now. Now that I am penniless, friendless and homeless. Let me tell you something, Mother, I will have the last laugh. You just wait and see."

"I'll be waiting a long time, then," she shouted after me as I left.

Chapter Ten

Life went on. One dreary day after another. My desire for revenge kept me going. To get the bitches who mocked me while I served them their meals, when I had come from the richest family of them all, and, as such, used to command the most respect. Oh, yes, money speaks volumes. The only thing that trumps it is nobility. A title. A bloodline that connects you to the throne, no matter how far removed. So completely fake. So empty. Those same girls who went to school with me, who skied with me, who holidayed in the south of France at our villa, they were the same ones treating me like shit now. 'Oh, waitress could we have more bread please?' or 'Oh, waitress, I do believe this lobster is slightly undercooked. And I asked for French dressing on my salad, not vinaigrette'. Oh, I would get them back. One day. I would live for that day.

The divorce went to the court and we were granted a decree nisi. I had to wait six weeks for it to be absolute. Steve arranged to see the children every other Friday. I resisted the temptation to say that was very big of him because actually I was quite pleased he didn't want to feature in their lives very much. They were better off without a lying, cheating, thieving bastard of a father who used our money on pissing whores. The judge gave an order for maintenance, but it wasn't much due to the fact that Steve was so much in debt. He had moved into a flat in south Croydon, bit of a come down for someone who could have once bought the flat with a month's wages.

The only bright light in my life was the children. It was remarkable how well they adapted, and how supportive they were. I worked three lunchtimes and two evenings a week. When I was at work, Charlotte took care of William and helped him with his homework. It was alien to me, leaving a fourteen-year-old take care of herself and an eleven-year-old. I had a nanny until I was twelve and after that there was always the housekeeper and the servants to watch over me. What a spoilt, sheltered, absolutely fake life I had led. Believing myself to be loved, protected, cared for, always. Believing myself to be popular with many friends. Believing that I was actually attractive and a good catch. Well, I suppose I was a good catch with all that family money. It was one of the things I had loved about Steve. I believed he didn't care about the family money, he wanted me for me. Well that's another theory out the window. I am actually unattractive, unloveable, unwanted. It was only ever the money, not me.

If it hadn't been for the children and the burning desire for revenge, I would have driven the car off a cliff. If I'd thought for one second that my mother would have taken in my children, cared for them and given them everything they could ever want I would have done it. But I couldn't be sure. And I couldn't leave them with no one, I certainly couldn't leave them with 'every other Friday' Steve. So, I carried on, with absolutely no plan for this revenge I wanted. Just trying to make ends meet and get through the day.

And then one day was brighter. The sun shone through the clouds and my shitty world became just that little bit better. Cass knocked on my door. I couldn't believe it when I saw her. "Hey, you," she said. "I heard you'd moved back into the neighbourhood,"

"Oh, Cass, I'm so, so, sorry," I said. "I never meant to accuse you, but I admit I was going to ask you about the thefts, it was Steve, he put it in my head, but it was my fault, I never should have doubted you, not even a little, not even for a second." I started to cry, it was the first time I'd cried since finding the watch. Cass led me back inside, with her arms around me, and let me cry.

"It's OK," she said. "I'm not going to pretend that I wasn't hurt, and I'm not going to say I understand why you doubted me. But you are my friend, you are going through hell, and I am here for you."

"Oh, Cass, I'm so sorry," I said again.

"Tell me all about it," she said. So I did.

Much later, Cass agreed with me, I needed to get revenge, I needed closure. Steve was due to appear in court, but no one expected he would get anything other than a slap on the wrist. He was paying a pittance towards the children and still had his job, which paid enough for the flat and the pissing hookers. He was quite content to see the children every other Friday and not have to worry about how they were living the rest of the time. Like who was feeding them, clothing them, taking them to drama class or soccer practice. Who was juggling a life to give them the best possible in the circumstances.

It was so amazing to have Cass back in my life. I had a friend I could talk to, trust, someone I knew was there for me. She offered me money but I refused. We were managing. I went to the local shop once and was 49p short for groceries, the owner told me not to worry about it, pay it back when I could. That was a really humbling experience. To be 49p short to pay for food when I had thought nothing of paying £490 for shopping previously. But mostly for the kindness of the shop owner who could see I was buying food for my family and just didn't have enough money to pay. I tell you, I will never take things for granted again.

The decree absolute came through. Steve turned up on the doorstep the following day for his visit with the children. "Still living here then, Ellie?" he said taunting. "Mummy still not allowing you to come home?" He laughed. "Poor little rich girl has to work as a waitress and rely on the charity of her aunt. Bet you never saw that coming!" I wanted to kill him. I have never even wanted to hurt anyone before, let alone kill them and end their life. But my hatred for him, the way I detested him was something I had never felt before. I really wanted to kill him. The only thing that stopped me was that my children would be taken into care with a dead father and a mother in prison.

"Charlotte's not coming," I said. "She's out with friends. William! Get your coat, your father's here. Have him back by nine, please," I said and walked away.

Chapter Eleven

Twelve weeks later, Steve called at the gate house to pick up the children. One of Aunt Margaret's gardeners told him we were up at Mummy's house. So he drove up, not happy that I hadn't informed him about the change of plans. I had actually left a message on his phone at the flat but he clearly hadn't been there to pick it up.

The housekeeper showed him into the drawing room and served him tea while he waited. After twenty minutes or so, I walked in. "What are you playing at Ellie?" he said. "Where are the children?"

"Oh, they're out riding," I said. "Sorry, Steve, I did leave a message on your phone to say they wouldn't be coming today."

"Why the hell not?" Steve said.

"Well, you cancelled the previous two visits so we weren't sure you'd be here for this one, and they wanted to go riding, so I said yes," I answered.

"This is such a waste of my fucking time," Steve said. "Why are you here anyway, made friends with Mummy have you?"

"Oh, no," I said. "Mummy passed away five weeks ago. Her chest infection turned to pneumonia, the doctors tried everything but she was just too old and weak to fight it. Don't worry, you don't have to be polite and give me your condolences," I said.

"Why are you here if your mother died?" he asked. "You were written out of the will."

"Yes," I said, "about that. It turns out there was a clause in the will that if I divorced you and got you out of my life I would inherit everything after all. I tell you it was a nice surprise for me. So, now this is my house, we live here so you will need to collect the children from here from now on. They are in private school now, of course, so if you ever need to pick them up from there you will need to liaise with me first. Oh, and we are going to spend the summer in our house in the Hamptons, so unless you are visiting New York you won't be able to see the children during the summer break. I almost forgot, we're spending Easter at the villa in the south of France. Yes, Steve, I have everything, everything. Millions, and I do mean millions, in the bank, plus all the property in my parents' portfolio. Oh, one thing I meant to mention – your case comes to court in a few weeks' time, doesn't it? I know the judge who is going to sentence you. Turns out I was wrong about you not going to prison for a first offence. You need to be prepared that it's likely you will spend some time in gaol."

He did swing for me then, but I had already pressed the bell for the butler who stood between us and very politely asked sir to leave. I danced my way to the lounge and poured myself a large G&T. I would have paid a fortune to have seen that look on his face, it was priceless!

Steve got two years' imprisonment. He never contacted the children and they didn't ask about him. I will always feel guilty that I didn't choose a better father for them. I made it clear that the bitches who had cut me out of their lives and looked down on me in the restaurant were persona non grata. They were never invited anywhere again. For someone in our social set that is a punishment worse than death. I paid back the shop owner the 49p, I sent her a cheque for £50,000 which was enough for her to retire on. For the restaurant, which had given me a job when I was unemployable, I gave them patronage. I dined there at least once a week and let it be known it was *the* place to be. Their takings doubled within two weeks. Aunt Margaret is welcome at my home, my charity functions and balls. I know she only helped me to score points over my mother, but it doesn't matter, she helped me, and more importantly she was good to my children.

I have set up a fund to help disadvantaged women and children in the area. It will pay for a variety of thing including education, training, days out and activities. I know first-hand how difficult it is to make a life for yourself and your children, with no suitable qualifications and no support.

Yes, money matters and money talks. But some of the most important lessons I learned in life were when I was without it. You know what's important, you know who your friends are, and you know who you can turn to when you're in trouble. Now I can afford to give my children everything, but I will make absolutely sure they grow up appreciating it, and that they know the difference between the hangers-on and the fair weather friends, and those who are the real deal. Like my oldest, dearest friend Cass. I don't think I will ever want or trust another man, but that's fine. I have my children, I have my best friend, I have security, and I have an absolutely kick-ass lifestyle. I can live with that.

Book Seven – Carol-Ann

Chapter One

"It was just a dream!" I repeated. "A strange one, yes, but a dream nevertheless."

"No, no, it's like a prophesy or fate or something, you have to find him." I looked at my best friend Robbie and shook my head.

"You are crazy, are all gay men crazy?" Chris walked into the room with drinks.

"No, just him," he said smiling. "Now what is this dream Carol-Ann?" I sighed and repeated what I had told Robbie.

"OK, I was at the gate to Heaven waiting to go in, but, instead of Saint Peter, my ex-boyfriend was there. Bradley Walters. And he told me that I couldn't go in yet because I had to return to earth to save his soul. I told him not to be silly, that I hadn't seen him for years, then I asked what he was doing there, and where was Saint Peter? He said he wasn't really there he was dreaming it, but that he would forget the dream and I would remember it. He pleaded with me to save his soul, he said I was the only one who could do it. Then I woke up."

Robbie said, "See, Chris, she has to find him, it's a sign!"

Chris said, "Hmm, maybe." Robbie was already looking for the telephone directory to try to track down Bradley.

He'd left Paxtown to go to university and never came back, despite swearing undying love to me. I regularly asked his parents for news and they always said he was fine but wouldn't give me any other information. Finally, the penny dropped and I realised I had been well and truly dumped. He had been my first love, I was absolutely besotted with him. I was only sixteen when we met, he was a year older. We had one blissful year and then he went to uni. For the first few months he phoned constantly and visited when he could, then the visits stopped and gradually so did the phone calls. It broke my heart, I have never felt so much pain. I wanted to die. I cried constantly, I was a mess. It was Robbie who helped get me through it.

We had been best friends since junior school. I had always known he was gay, but no one else did. We were inseparable. As we got older I was his beard. Everyone thought we were an item, so we let them think it. When I started seeing Bradley, people were consoling Robbie, despite his protestations that he was fine and we were still good friends. Not long after it ended with Bradley, Robbie left too. I knew why, but I never would have told anyone, even though I knew his parents were going through agony trying to find him.

It was such a relief when it all came out, thanks to that article in the paper. Robbie got in touch almost immediately and it was as if we'd never been apart. I visit them once a month and we speak on the phone every day. It's great to see him so happy. My love life, on the other hand, was a bit of a disaster. There was no one for a while after Bradley, my broken heart needed time to mend. When I met Alex, it took a while for me to trust him. He persisted, he was patient, he was kind and loving. We got married on my twenty-first birthday and divorced not long after my twenty-sixth. Turns out he was kind and loving to a lot of people, not just me. Since then, I have had a few relationships, none of which have lasted more than a few months. At the grand old age of thirty-four, I am thinking of getting a cat. Or maybe I could move in with my gay best friend and his boyfriend.

"This is hopeless, there's a bloody load of B Walters in the phone book," Robbie said. "The only thing I can think of is to contact someone who was in uni with him, maybe they know where he moved to. Can you think of anyone?"

"We're really doing this?" I said laughing. "It was just a dream!" I shouted. Robbie would not give in, so I went through all the people I remembered who had been at uni with him. Most were just first names, no chance of tracking them down. Then I remembered Mitchell Matheson, he was really friendly with Bradley and he now had his own law firm in London.

Robbie was on the case and found his office number. It was the weekend so we couldn't ring, but I said I would first thing Monday morning. On the train on the way home, I was smiling to myself. Robbie was so dramatic! How his family never knew he was gay, I had no idea. I got home to my pokey little bedsit, which is all I could afford on my hairdressing salary. So much for my dream of owning my own salon. I am so bad with money, it just runs through my fingers. My parents are always on to me to sort out my finances. Then I get the 'why aren't you more like your sisters?' lecture. I am the middle of three girls. My eldest sister Rowena is intelligent, confident and a shining star. My little sister

Babs is the cute, loveable baby of the family, who can do no wrong. I'm just the one in the middle who can rarely get anything right. I'm not looking for a pity party here, just stating facts. But I really would like to feel special, instead of the spare part. I had felt special to Bradley, I remembered. I wondered where he was and what he was doing. I didn't intend to hunt him down though, it was just a dream.

Then that night it happened again. There I was at the Pearly Gates and there was Bradley, pleading with me to help him. "It's not just a dream, Carol-Ann, please, I need your help," he said. I woke in a sweat. It had felt so real.

"Well, what else have you got to do with your boring little life?" I asked myself.

Chapter Two

I rang the law firm. Mr Matheson was far too busy to talk to me. I asked if he could ring me back and gave the salon number. The bored girl on the other end of the phone said she would certainly pass on the message but without any information regarding the matter I needed to speak to him about, it was highly unlikely he would in fact return my call. I wondered what I could say to get him to ring me. I was chatting to a client, giving her hair a trim, and wondered out loud how I could get the attention of a big London lawyer. "Give me the phone", she said. I looked at her in surprise, but I fetched it. I dialled the number, the same snooty cow answered. "Good morning, this is Jaclyn Jordan speaking, you may know me as Jordan Jackson. My friend Carol-Ann here is trying to speak to Mr Matheson but I understand you have been quite dismissive. Please tell Mr Matheson to ring her back asap if he ever expects to get my business. I believe you have the number. Good day," And she put the phone down.

"Wow!" I said. "Are you really going to do business with him?"

"Good lord, no, but he doesn't know that," she laughed. "He's been chasing me to publish my memoirs, along with the law firm, he runs a small publishing house. He is probably wetting himself right now." And then the phone rang. Jaclyn smiled and handed it to me.

Mitchell Matheson was not pleased to hear it was me, or what I wanted. He asked about Jaclyn, I said you mean my good friend Jaclyn, she is right here waiting to see how helpful you are. Turns out he could be very helpful when he tried. Bradley had dropped out of university before the end of the first year, he had stayed in the city where he got a job at a pub called the Red Bear. That was all he knew. I said thank you, he asked when Jaclyn would be in touch, I said whenever it suited her.

I called Robbie. "Bristol is a big city," I said. "He could be anywhere, he could have moved on."

"I'll find the number of the Red Bear," he said. "You see if you can get any more information out of his family." They were surprised to see me after all this time, but were no more helpful than they had been before.

"He's fine," they said. "He doesn't want to keep in touch with anyone, thank you." Robbie said the landlord at the Red Bear had only been there five years, and had never heard of Bradley, but there was an old guy who was a regular back them who remembered him.

"Got into trouble with the police over drugs," he said. "So they sacked him."

We started ringing all the B Walters in the Bristol area, but none of them were him and it would have taken ages to get through them all. Eventually, Chris came up with a brainwave. "Do you remember when they found that body in the quarry? The reporter, Annie, she did research to find information on all the missing people. Maybe she could help?" It was worth a try. I rang the Globe but they said she no longer worked there. One of our clients said she worked at the new housing development. So I went there the following lunchtime and visited the marketing suite. Annie was very nice, and very helpful. I was lucky to catch her, she was finishing at the marketing suite that week, after being offered a contract to write features for a national women's magazine, which paid a lot more. She told me to start in the library, look through the Bristol papers at the time he was arrested and see if there was a report on it. She also said she knew a reporter on one of the Bristol weeklies, someone she had been to uni with, she said she'd give her a call to see if the paper had any information on him, or whether they had any other suggestions.

I thanked her, gave her the salon number and headed for the library. It had become a mission and was really quite exciting. I had no idea what I would do if I found Bradley, but I was really having fun looking. I didn't find anything in the library, it was painstaking looking through all those old papers, for what would probably be a tiny piece on a barman being prosecuted for doing drugs. I went back to work where Tina, my boss, gave me a bollocking for taking such a long lunch hour. It was fine, she knew I worked harder than anyone else there.

Annie came up trumps. Her friend in Bristol had recognised the name from a story they had covered the previous year. She told Annie the details, and the date and page of the report in the paper. I was stunned. Bradley wasn't just taking drugs, he was dealing drugs. And on top of that he was found guilty of assault with a deadly weapon. He was given eighteen months' imprisonment as it was his third offence, and is currently an inmate at HMP Bristol, due for release in three months' time.

Chapter Three

I wrote him a letter. A nice one. I didn't explain why I looked for him or how I found him, just said that I would like to catch up with him one of these days. It was chatty, breezy. "Breezy, my ass!" Robbie said. "You are fawning, it would be sooo lovely to catch up with you, you old drug-dealer you!"

"Robbie, behave" I said. He'd been so excited since we had tracked down Bradley and found out that he was in prison.

"So romantic," he gushed, "it's meant to be." Even Chris told him to calm down.

I got a reply. My hands were shaking as I opened the letter with the HMP Bristol stamp on it. It was such a nice letter. He was really pleased to hear from me, he hoped I was well. He's sorry he hadn't kept in touch, but, as I knew, his circumstances were less than desirable. I wrote straight back, just chit chat really, stuff about the salon, my friends, nothing very interesting. But I did say I would be happy to visit him if he wanted. I held my breath before I posted the letter. Should I have said that? Yes, I decided and in it went.

The visiting order arrived the following week, at the same time as another letter from Bradley. He was delighted that I wanted to visit and looked forward to seeing me, but wanted to warn me that he looked very different from the way he had when I'd last seen him.

Well, so did I. I had a waist in those days and boobs that stayed up when I took my bra off. How things change.

I was nervous about the visit though. I had no idea what to expect. I mean, visiting a prison is hardly something you want to put on your bucket list, is it? It was quite intimidating actually. We, the visitors, were herded in like cattle, into a room with no windows, prison guards watching our every move. We had to go through a scanner, like the ones at the airport, I panicked in case my new bellybutton bar would make it go off, but, thank goodness, it didn't. I had never seen such a mix of people in my entire life. Most of them scared me more than the guards. I kept my back to the wall and waited until it was my turn to go in.

It was exactly as it's portrayed on television. You are shown to a table and then the prisoners come in. All wearing the same jumpsuits, all dignity and individuality taken away. Well, it was their fault, they did the crime, now they had to do the time, as they say. When Bradley said he looked different, he wasn't kidding. I didn't recognise him at first, even after he sat down opposite me. I was about to say, ever so politely, excuse me I am waiting for someone, when I looked into his eyes and saw that it was him, after all.

"You don't look like you did in the dream," I said. He looked at me, confused. Shit, why had I said that? Couldn't just say, hello, how are you, what's the weather like in here, like a normal person. "Sorry," I said. "I'm rambling. How are you?" He looked terrible, thin, drawn, black rings under his eyes. He had a tooth missing and his hair was long and greasy, tied back in an elastic band. He placed his hands on the table and told me to do the same.

"It's the rule," he said. "They watch in case you pass anything to me." Pass what? I wondered. Did I look like a drug mule? "It's good to see you," Bradley said. At least the voice and the eyes were the same. I looked at his hands, the ones that were the first to caress and touch me. They were thin, bony, with tattoos over the knuckles and scars. There was a scar on his neck too. I wondered where else he had them.

"What happened?" I asked. I have never been one for tact or small talk. He laughed.

"I've missed you," he said. "But you have found me and come to visit me, so I will tell you the not so wonderful story about how I got from being a promising law student to a prison inmate." He smiled, "It's OK, I don't mind telling you, it's so good to see a friendly face, and it's so good to just to tell the truth. I got into drugs at uni but I couldn't afford to buy them on my grant. I got a part time job at a pub but it still wasn't enough to feed my habit. So I started dealing to get my supply for free. I got caught, of course. Got a suspended sentence, lost my job and got kicked out of uni. I was too ashamed to go home. I had very few options, so I started working full time for the guy who was supplying me. I made a decent living, enough to keep me in a flat and pay for what I wanted. But it's a dangerous business. I got beaten up, I got knifed, I had kickings. So, I started carrying protection. A knife of my own. I got caught carrying the knife during a routine stop and search, luckily I only had a small supply on me, which I said was mine. They did me for carrying a weapon and drugs, I got three months in nick. That's pretty much my story until last year when another dealer tried to muscle in on my patch. We had a bit of showdown and I knifed him.

He survived, it was just a nick. But the bastard CCTV cameras had caught it all. So here I am."

"Oh, my gosh, Bradley, that's so awful," I said. "Do your parents know?"

"Fuck, no," he answered. "I phoned them a few years back and said I wasn't ever coming home and that I didn't want any more contact. I thanked them for everything they had done for me and I said I was really sorry. My mother was sobbing, my father was pleading, he kept saying there was nothing I had done we couldn't fix, please come home. I put the phone down. How could I ever tell them how their precious son had turned out? Do you know what they gave up for me? They worked day and night to provide me with everything, they wanted me to have the opportunities they never had. They were so proud when I got my A levels and went to university. The thought of letting them down is worse than anything else I have gone through."

"Bradley, they love you, they would understand, they are good people," I said. "You can turn your life around, it's not too late." He laughed but it didn't reach his eyes.

"Oh, dear sweet, Carol-Ann, you always saw the best in everyone, always so positive. I can't face them, no way, not like this. And how can I turn my life around? If I stay here in Bristol when I get out, I have no other option other than to go back to my old ways. It's the only way I can make a living. With my record, no one else is going to employ me. And where else can I go? I've got no money and no friends. There's no hope."

It was at that moment I actually started to believe in the dream. He really did have no hope. And, unless I could offer him some, he would go back out and do exactly the same things, and worse. Until either he was killed, or he killed. I understood why I had to save his soul. So I said: "You have me. I am your friend. And I will help you if you let me." He looked at me intently.

"Why?" he asked.

"For old time's sake," I said.

Chapter Four

I visited Bradley every two weeks for the next three months until his release date. After four visits, I had finally persuaded him to come and stay with me when he got out. He took a lot of persuading. He wouldn't be able to get a job, so he couldn't help to buy food or pay the bills. He was scared of bumping into his parents if he moved back to his home town. So, I told him it would be temporary while we worked out something long term. But the important thing was that he didn't go back to his old life. He had to move far away from it to ever stand a chance of turning his life around.

When his release date came, Bradley had changed his mind again, and it took a lot of cajoling to get him into the car. As we got closer to Paxtown, I could see he was getting more and more nervous. He ran out of the car and into my bedsit. He looked around. "Well, this is cosy," he said.

"At least it's bigger than your cell, Buster!" I said. He laughed.

"Seriously, Carol-Ann, we can't both live in here. There's no room to swing a cat."

"Why do people say that?" I wondered. "Who would want to swing a cat? It's cruel. Anyway, we'll manage for now."

And we did, he cleaned and made meals when I was in the salon. His probation officer visited, he said Bradley had definitely done the right thing by not moving back to his old place. He sorted out dole money and booked Bradley in for driving lessons. He said taxi firms were always looking for drivers, and they wouldn't be too bothered about his criminal record, providing it wasn't sex offending. I persuaded him to let me cut his hair, and he made an appointment with a dentist to get his teeth fixed.

It was three weeks before Bradley ventured out of the bedsit to go anywhere other than the probation office, the dole office, or for driving lessons. I eventually persuaded him to come for a walk along the clifftops. He was worried in case we saw anyone who recognised him. I said his parents would have to find out eventually. He wasn't ready, he said. He held my hand as we walked along, it was the first physical contact we had had, and it felt nice.

As the weeks went by, Bradley got healthier and happier, and we became closer and closer. It felt almost like the old days, except for his scars, both mental and physical. His probation officer arranged for him to visit a drugs rehabilitation centre as a volunteer to help others trying to get clean. I was worried that being so close to so many addicts he would be tempted to go back to his old ways. But he didn't, he said he had no desire to let drugs control his life again, and he felt sorry for those poor bastards in the centre who were trying to break free.

Turns out he was very good at helping them, so his probation officer arranged a counselling course for him, so that he could take it a step further. Bradley passed his driving test, but contrary to what the probation officer had told him, no one would give him a job. I thought it was so unfair when he was turning his life around, he deserved a chance. But Bradley said he really hadn't expected any of them to employ him, after all who wants an ex-con and former drug addict to work for them?

I finally persuaded him to go and see his parents. He looked well, he'd gained weight and the grey, drawn look had gone. His hair, of course, was immaculate, seeing as I was his personal hairdresser, and his teeth had finally been fixed so that he didn't look like a pirate or something when he smiled.

To say they were overjoyed to see him would be a gross understatement. I have never seen so much happiness shining out of people. He was welcomed as the long lost son, which he was, they didn't care what he had been doing, or where he had been, only that he was back safe and sound. They all cried, I did too, it was so emotional. He said sorry over and over, they said it didn't matter, it was fine, everything was fine. I left them to talk, and Bradley filled them in on everything that had happened. It didn't matter what he told them, their joy and delight at having him there never wavered. I wondered whether my parents loved me so unconditionally. Maybe, they were used to me disappointing them but they still greeted me with open arms when I went there.

Chapter Five

Later that day, we made love for the first time since we were teenagers. He was so sweet and loving, it was so nice to be held in someone's arms. He asked me why I had tracked down. "I was just curious about what happened to you," I said. I didn't tell him about the dreams, it sounded so patronising to say that I was saving his soul. "You broke my heart, you know," I told him.

"I know, and I'm sorry," he said. "I was having such a good time at uni, not just the partying, everything about it was amazing. And I just couldn't be tied to you, I needed to be free. We were too young, the time wasn't right – maybe it is now?"

"Yes," I agreed happily. "Maybe it is now."

Bradley came with me to visit Chris and Robbie, I had worried that they would have nothing in common, but they all got on really well. They had a neighbour, Jessica, who was always in their flat. I admit I was a little jealous that she was their new best friend, but I really liked her. She told Bradley about a local drug and alcohol rehabilitation centre which was looking for counsellors. She knew because she had attended there as an alcoholic. How she stayed friends with Chris and Robbie and avoided drinking I will never know, they were very partial to their martinis and cocktails. Bradley didn't drink either, he knew that as an addict he couldn't risk being under the effects of alcohol. So, when Jessica called around I was delighted, she could keep Bradley sober company while I could let my hair down and enjoy with Chris and Robbie.

When we got back from the last visit, Bradley said he was seriously thinking of applying for the job Jessica had told him about. "But it's in London!" I said.

"I know, and the more I think about it, the more I realise that I can't ever have a normal life here in Paxtown. Everyone now knows what I did, what I was. People who used to be friends cross the road rather than speak to me. My parents have suffered too, they are being shunned by neighbours due to their criminal druggie of a son. It's as if they are tainted by being associated with me, everyone's afraid it's contagious or something."

"It'll pass," I said. "In time, people will forget and accept you again."

"I don't think so, Carol-Ann," he said smiling gently at me. "And even if they eventually did, what do I do in the meantime? I can't get a job anywhere, no one wants to know me, I have no life here." I understood, I did, but I panicked.

"Are you saying you are leaving me again?" I asked.

"Hell, no!" he said. "I want you to come with me." I was so relieved I ran and hugged him. Then I panicked again.

I thought about nothing else for the next few days. I wanted to be with Bradley so much, he had come so far and I was really proud of him. But the thought of leaving Paxtown, my family, my friends, my job. It was really scary. Then I thought I could still visit them, Bradley would be visiting his parents regularly, it's not like we were leaving never to return. But still I couldn't quiet that niggling doubt. Bradley said, "You're scared it's not going to work, aren't you? You're afraid that you'll leave everything behind and then I'll leave you?"

I nodded. "I suppose I am," I said.

"How can I prove that everything is different now?" he asked. I shrugged, I had no idea.

Five minutes later, he said he had the answer. "I can prove to you that I will never let you down again. Marry me," he said. "Please."

"Oh, my God, yes!" I answered. "Please."

Chapter Six

So Bradley applied for the job, and went to stay with Chris and Robbie for a few days when they called him for an interview. While he was there he looked around for a flat for us but didn't have much luck. He got the job, we were thrilled, we went for an Indian meal with Chris, Robbie and Jessica to celebrate. They wanted him to start immediately, so Chris and Robbie offered him their spare room to stay in until he found somewhere for us. They would all keep an eye out for a job for me too. I would stay in Paxtown in the meantime, and go up to London at the weekends. Although I missed Bradley it was nice to have the bedsit back to myself. It really was tiny, we were falling over each constantly. And the weekends were really romantic, when we made up for lost time.

After six weeks, with no sign of anywhere for us to live, I said I would take a week off work to flat hunt. Bradley said there was no need, he was on the case and he was sure something would come up soon. But I was getting impatient to start my new life and marry Bradley, so I decide to surprise him and went to London the following Wednesday. They were all at work, so I let myself in with the spare key they'd given me, and waited. I heard Bradley's voice in the corridor first, he was talking to Jessica. I went to the spyhole, I couldn't wait to surprise him. They were kissing. I couldn't believe what I was seeing. Bradley and Jessica were kissing!

I ran back to the sofa and waited for him to come in. But he didn't. I heard the door of Jessica's flat open and shut. He was in there, with her, and I could guess what they were doing. I was so angry. I had saved his soul, I had helped him turn his life around, he was supposed to marry me. How could he do this?

I will still sitting there fuming when Robbie came home. "Hey, you, this is a nice surprise," he said, hugging me. Then he saw my face. "What's wrong?" he asked.

"You may well ask what's wrong," I barked at him. "Bradley and Jessica are shagging. Did you know? Did you know what was going on?"

"Oh, shit, Carol-Ann," he said, putting his arm around me and kissing my head. "We had our suspicions, Chris and me, but when we talked to them about it, they said they were friends, ex-addicts supporting each other. Bradley swore there was nothing more than that, he said he owed you everything and would never let you down. We've never seen any kind of physical affection between them, so we believed him. I'm so sorry, babe. What happened? How did you find out? Is that why you're here?" I told him the sad story. He gave me tea and sympathy. Chris came in and we went through it all again. Chris was furious.

"We gave him hospitality and this is the thanks we get! I'm going over there now." Off he went.

"Heaven help him now," Robbie said eyes rolling.

"He deserves it, slimy double-crossing, cheating bastard," I said.

When Chris returned, Bradley was following him. Chris signalled to Robbie to leave the room and they left us to it. I just looked at him, wondering how he was going to explain this. So much for undying love and devotion, I thought. "I'm so, so, sorry, Carol-Ann," he said kneeling in front of me. "The last thing I wanted to do was hurt you, you have done so much for me. You saved me from my shitty life, I wouldn't have done it without you. I really did mean to marry you, but Jess and me, we just couldn't help ourselves. I'm sorry, but we are madly, deeply in love, we tried to resist but just couldn't. We both feel terrible about it." So, worse than I thought. Not just shagging. Love.

"I thought you loved me?" I said.

"I do, I always will, and I will always be grateful for what you did for me, but I'm not in love with you, I never was."

"So, you were marrying me out of duty, gratitude?" I asked. He nodded his head.

"I'm so sorry."

"Yes, you've said that but it doesn't help," I said. "It doesn't give me back the six months of my life I have lost, does it? It doesn't help to console me with the fact that yet another relationship has failed and I am back on my lonesome. And it certainly does not compensate for the shitty way I feel, like a fucking idiot to believe in you. Go back to your girlfriend, I never want to see you or talk to you again." He left, saying more sorries. Which made me want to thump him.

Chris, Robbie and me got nicely drunk. I resisted the temptation to bang on Jessica's door and call her a lying whore. Chris and Robbie agreed I was the much better catch. They tried to mend my ego, bless them, but it was too badly bruised. It was late when we went to bed, I needed to be pissed and exhausted before I could get to sleep.

I woke suddenly, or thought I did, then realised I was dreaming again. I was back at the Gates, but this time Bradley wasn't there, only a guy who looked like an angel. "Hello, Carol-Ann, I'm the gatekeeper," he said.

"Are you letting me in this time?" I said. "I've made a right mess of my life, I'm quite ready to come here." The Gatekeeper laughed.

"Oh, dear, no, it's not your time, there's more work to be done. Souls to be saved."

"Like Bradley, you mean?" I asked. "I saved his soul and what thanks did I get? He breaks my heart for the second time." He laughed again. "It's not funny!" I said indignantly.

"Your heart isn't broken," he answered. "It's not even dented. It's your pride that was hurt, that's all. You didn't love Bradley, not the way you did when you were younger. A marriage with him never would have worked."

"Why send me to save him then? Why play with my feelings and my life?" The Gatekeeper sighed.

"Carol-Ann, it was never intended that you had a love affair with Bradley, you were simply sent to save his soul. And you did. If he had gone back to his old life he would have knifed someone to death and his soul would have been lost forever."

Wow, that was mind blowing! "So, I'm like a guardian angel then?" I said. He sighed.

"You are nothing like a guardian angel, they have far more important work to do."

"More important than saving souls?" I asked.

"Much more important," he said. "They stop wars and acts of terrorism, they help hundreds of families faced with disease or famine. Yes, these things still happen, but it would be so much worse if it wasn't for them."

"Oh," I said, suitably chastened.

"Saving souls is important too," the Gatekeeper said. "Which brings us back to business."

"Business?" I said. "What business?" He sighed again.

"Oh, for goodness sake, have you not been paying attention? The business of saving souls. It's why you were chosen. You are one of our special helpers."

"Special, me?" I said smiling. "I have never been special. That's so cool! But can I be called a soul saver instead of a special helper? It's got a nicer ring to it. And why was I chosen?" Another sigh.

"Fine, you can be a soul saver. You were chosen because you have a good heart and a generous soul. You are empathetic and you care about people. You are also very friendly and chatty, which I am now thinking may have been a mistake. There is only one rule – you cannot tell anyone."

"I've already told Chris and Robbie," I said. "And this is so exciting, please can I just tell them about it?"

"Absolutely not," he said. "Chris never believed the dream and Robbie thinks it was a one-off fate thing. One rule, Carol-Ann, stick to it, or no more soul saving. Now can we please get back to actually saving souls instead of chit-chatting? I warn you, our future conversations will be much briefer than this, I am a very busy person."

"Future conversations! Oh, how exciting!" I said. "Please can I ask you just one more thing before we get back to business?" He sighed again. Goodness, this guy likes to sigh, I thought.

"One more question."

"OK, you said I wasn't meant to be with Bradley? Am I meant to be with someone? Is there like a soulmate out there for me?" The Gatekeeper looked stern.

"As this is our first conversation and you are new to this, I will answer. But, please remember in future, this is not about you, this is about saving souls. Yes, there is someone out there for you. Now..."

I interrupted, "There is?" I said excitedly. "Who is it? When will I meet him?" He took a deep breath.

"No more questions!" he said crossly. "For the last time, this is not about you. It is about Alice, she is only eighteen years old, she goes to the same coffee shop every lunchtime and nurses the same mug of coffee for an hour, then she leaves. She is going to kill herself unless she gets help, and if she does that her soul will be lost."

"Oh, no, that's terrible," I said. "Why, what's wrong with her?"

"She was raped and she hasn't been able to tell anyone, so she hasn't had any help. She can't cope much longer."

"Oh, the poor girl, which coffee shop?"

"Marky's in the High Street," he said. And then I woke up.

Chapter Seven

I caught the early train home in the morning. Left a note for Chris and Robbie. 'Got to go important stuff to do. Talk later. C-A'. I was back in time for lunch and headed straight to Marky's. I spotted her straightaway, sitting in the corner alone nursing her coffee mug, staring into space. So young and so pretty. So tragic. I bought a tea and went straight to her table. "Mind if I join you?" I said. "I hate drinking tea alone." She looked at me blankly, then looked around at the empty tables. She shrugged her shoulders. I sat down. There was no time to waste.

By the fourth day, she smiled as I entered the coffee shop. It didn't reach her eyes but it was a start. I sat there every day with her for an hour and I talked. I am very chatty, as the Gatekeeper said. Sometimes she actually listened and thought about something other than her own pain. Poor girl. I just wanted to hug her and tell her I knew what had happened, and I wanted to help. But I had to wait for her to tell me.

The second week, she wasn't there. I asked the girl behind the counter if she'd seen her. "Not today," she said. "It's unusual for her." She worked at the estate agents just along the road. I ran there and asked for her.

"She hasn't come in today, it's not like her," the receptionist told me. I asked for her address, said it was a matter of life and death, and finally persuaded her to give it to me. Great, it was on the other side of town. I drove like a maniac and parked on the pavement outside. A middle-aged woman answered the door.

"Hi," I said breathlessly. "Is Alice here please?" The woman looked at me oddly, clearly Alice didn't have many people calling.

"She's not well, dear," the woman, I assumed to be her mother, answered. "She's gone back to bed. I'm just on my way out to the shops so I'll be a few hours but you're welcome to call back later if you like."

"Thanks, would it be OK just for me to pop up and say hello?" I asked. "I can let myself out." That strange look again, but she smiled and said of course.

I ran up the stairs, calling her name. I was dreading what I might find. But, thankfully, she was still alive. Startled, shocked to see me bursting into her bedroom, but very much alive. And then I saw the pills, dozens of them set out into neat little rows. The bottle of water next to them, and the glass filled ready. She saw me look and tried to hide them. "It's OK, Alice," I said. "I could see you were depressed about something, but I can help, please trust me."

"Nobody can help," Alice said sadly.

"I can I promise you," I said.

"I only met you last week," she said. "Why are you here, and how did you find out where I lived?"

"I had a bad feeling when you weren't at the coffee shop," I said. "And it looks like I was right. And you know sometimes it's easier to tell a virtual stranger something rather than someone you know. Please, Alice, just tell me, and I can help."

She broke down, she cried and screamed and she told me. When her mother came home, I told her. We took Alice to the hospital where they had a rape crisis centre.

She spoke to a counsellor. They gave her medication to help temporarily and admitted her for a few days, to give it time to work, and for her to have the counselling she so desperately needed. I promised to visit the following day.

Her doctor was a dish! I tried to focus on Alice but I couldn't take my eyes off him. He was quite tall, with dark hair and deep brown eyes. His hands made me go weak. They looked so strong, yet so gentle. I wondered what they would feel like touching me. Alice saw me looking. "Sorry," I said. "I am here to give you my full attention, honestly."

"It's OK," she smiled. "Just because I'm off men doesn't mean you have to be."

"That was almost a joke!" I said. "You must be feeling better."

"I am," she said. "So much better. I know there's a long way to go, but for the first time I have hope that I can live a normal life. I have people helping me and I feel so much stronger just knowing that. I wish I'd told someone before, but I was so ashamed. I know now it was nothing I should feel ashamed about. It will be a very long time before the memory of what happened isn't in my mind most of every day. But I do believe the day will come when it won't be ever present in my thoughts. I have you to thank for that, if you hadn't come to my home that day, I would be dead now. Thank you so much, if ever I can do anything for you just ask."

"Nothing to thank me for," I said. "But if you can get me that dishy doctor's number I would be ever so grateful!" She laughed, it was the first time I had seen her laugh. It lit her whole face up. Then it clouded over again. But that's fine, one step at a time.

The second day I went to visit, dishy doc was actually waiting for me. "Your friend says you asked for my number," he said smiling. I smiled up at him and I swear there was a spark. It was like an electric current between us. "Would you like to go for coffee after visiting?" he asked. Would I? Would I!

"That would be nice," I said.

"I'll come find you after visiting," he said.

"You do that," I answered smiling.

Chapter Eight

Doctor Dylan Norris and I were practically inseparable after that first coffee. We talked and laughed for hours about everything and nothing. When he kissed me for the first time, I swear my heart stopped. You could almost touch the electricity between us. He came with me to visit Chris and Robbie, who took to him immediately. I even introduced him to Bradley and Jessica when we bumped into them in the hallway.

Sex with him was so much more than sex. It was like our bodies fused together to become one. We instinctively knew what the other was thinking and feeling. If I thought I had loved before I was wrong. It was nothing compared to the way I felt about Dylan. I wondered if he was my soulmate and whether I could ask the Gatekeeper next time I saw him.

Come to think of it, I must have been overdue for a visit. Alice was doing well, she had gone home, she was taking her medication to help with the depression and to help her sleep. She was receiving regular counselling and was in regular contact with a volunteer at the centre, a former rape victim herself, who was available for Alice twenty-four hours a day. I still called every week to check on her but she didn't need me any more so I wondered why I hadn't been summoned by the Gatekeeper. It had been nice to be a soul saver, to be special, to be useful, to be able to help people. I hoped my short career wasn't over.

It wasn't. A few weeks later I ended up at the Gates again, and there he was the Gatekeeper. "Hi," I said breezily. "I was wondering when I'd be called again, I thought you might not need me anymore." He sighed. Of course.

"This is a job for life, you will always be called back," he said. "But you do usually get to have a break in between soul saving. Alice was a special case. You did well there, she is out of danger now." Wow, praise from the Gatekeeper.

"Your next job is Joseph, he's sixty, his wife is dying of cancer, and he is going to steal money to take her on one last holiday. But he will get caught and imprisoned and she will die alone."

"But his soul won't be lost, will it?" I asked.

"Oh, yes, it will. He will become so angry that he will commit many evil acts before he dies. You do not need to know the details." I shivered. That sounded ominous, bit scary really. But as a soul saver I would, of course, do my best to help prevent the evil.

"Before you tell me where to find him, can I ask you something? Is Dylan the one? It feels like he is, you know." More sighing.

"I told you last time I would not be answering any more questions about your personal life. This is not about you. You will find Joseph in the park, he walks his dog at 6 a.m. every morning."

"6 a.m!" I said. "That's the middle of the night." Too late, I was back in bed. Ah well, I sighed, best set the alarm for 5.30 a.m.

Chapter Nine

Dylan asked me why I was so tired. I wanted to say because I am getting up at 5.30 a.m. every bloody morning to join Joseph on his dog walking. It had been four weeks, I was making progress but it was slow. I didn't want to go to bed at nine and miss spending time with Dylan, so I tried to get by on six hours sleep a night. It wasn't working very well. I am strictly an eight hours a night girl. I fell asleep in the salon more than once, one time in the middle of dying someone's hair. I just hoped this job with Joseph would finish before I lost my regular job.

I said I wasn't sleeping well, that's all. Dylan asked me very kindly if there was anything I would like to share with him. Oh, I so wished I could. If only I could share my special secret with him. I was bursting to talk about it, but I couldn't. Rules are rules, as the Gatekeeper would say. I had no doubt that I would lose my soul saver job if I broke it. So I said no, there was nothing, everything was fine. "You know you can tell me anything," he said, looking straight into my eyes.

"I know," I said. I made a mental note to ask the Gatekeeper if I could just tell Dylan, the next time I saw him. Which would be a bloody long way off the way things were going.

I moved into Dylan's house after we had been together for six months. It felt so right, he had to be the one, I thought. That same week I finally had a breakthrough with Joseph and convinced him not to turn to a life of crime. I wondered what evil deeds he would have committed? He was such a sweet old guy. It was a timely breakthrough, that first week I had to pretend I couldn't sleep and I was getting up at 5.30 a.m. to go jogging. Jogging, me! Bless him, Dylan didn't question me although I don't think for one second he believed I was jogging. I never even ran up the stairs, unless he was chasing me.

It was six weeks later, I found myself at the Pearly Gates again. There he was, the happy, smiley Gatekeeper. And there too was Dylan! I looked at him, and he looked at me, then we both looked at the Gatekeeper. "Why is Dylan here?" I asked. "Please don't tell me I have to save his soul. He's perfect." Dylan laughed. "Why are you laughing?" I said.

"I was going to ask the same thing about you," he said, and reached for my hand. The Gatekeeper sighed.

"Yes, you are both soul savers, except Dylan has been doing this for a lot longer and he knows not to talk too much, unlike you, Carol-Ann. Somehow, I don't think you will ever learn that. The reason you are both here is because this is a two-person job."

"Does this mean we can talk about it?" I asked, interrupting him again. There was the sigh.

"Yes, it does. You may chat your head off to him about it. Good luck," he said turning to Dylan, who just smiled and looked into my eyes lovingly. "Back to business please," the Gatekeeper said, "there will be plenty of time for you to fawn over each other when you get back."

"So, is he the one?" I had to ask. "He is, isn't he? It feels like he is." More sighing.